THEATRE
A View of Life

THEATRE

A View of Life

Marshall Cassady
San Diego State University

Pat Cassady

Holt, Rinehart and Winston
New York   Chicago   San Francisco   Philadelphia
Montreal   Toronto   London   Sydney   Tokyo
Mexico City   Rio de Janeiro   Madrid

To Howard and Ruth Mizer
and Hazel Cassady,
and in memory of Clarence Cassady

Cover photograph from the Broadway production of *Amadeus*—Zoe Dominic-Franz Furst.

Excerpts on pages 43, 66, 72, 80, 129, and 167 from pages 41, 204–5, 66–7, 205, 19, 28–9, and 95–6 in *Showcase* by Roy Newquist. Copyright © 1966 by Roy Newquist. By permission of William Morrow & Company.

Excerpts on pages 39–40, 69, 80, and 218 from *Early Days: My Life and the Theatre*, by Phillip Burton (New York: The Dial Press). Copyright © 1967 by Phillip Burton. Used by permission of The Dial Press.

Excerpts on pages 66, 76, and 94 from *The Actor's Ways and Means* by Michael Redgrave. Copyright Michael Redgrave Productions, Ltd., 1953, 1979. Reprinted by permission of the publishers, Theatre Arts Books, New York, and Heinemann Educational Books Ltd.

Color plates 15–18 courtesy of Herman Buchman.

Library of Congress Cataloging in Publication Data

Cassady, Marshall.
    Theatre, a view of life.

    Includes bibliographies and index.
    1. Theater.   I. Cassady, Pat.   II. Title.
PN2037.C29   792'.02   81-6332

ISBN 0-03-050551-8   AACR2

CBS COLLEGE PUBLISHING
Holt, Rinehart and Winston
The Dryden Press
Saunders College Publishing

Preface

The purpose of this book is to explore the many areas of theatre. Exploration can lead to understanding, and understanding to appreciation. Each of the chapters deals with the artists or the other people and elements that come together in the creation of any theatre production.

The emphasis is on the individual contribution of each theatre artist and the final collaboration of many people. The book is simply written for the student with a limited background in theatre; yet it presents a comprehensive view of a unique form of art. The material is designed to appeal to students who want to experience theatre as an art form, in much the same way they learn to appreciate other forms of art. Two features of the book make it especially helpful to such students. The running glossary familiarizes them with new terms, and the scenarios provide a set of plays related to the descriptive text.

The book begins by defining the unique aspects of theatre. Succeeding chapters lead students step by step through the various areas, so that they learn not only to appreciate but to judge theatre as art. They learn that as audience members they are an important facet of the overall production. They lose their individuality to a certain extent and become collaborators, with special responsibilities and goals.

The book is organized to show how each theatre artist adds something unique, yet something fitting, to each production. In its most elemental form, theatre requires an audience and an actor/playwright. Chapters 2, 3, and 5 explain the responsibilities and goals of each of these persons. The actor/playwright (or actor and playwright) must have something to present and a place for the presentation. These matters are discussed in Chapters 4 and 7, "Dramatic Structure and Style" and "Theatrical Space." Theatre cannot exist without the work of the various designers, nor without the director. Even if a production is staged in an open field with everyday clothing and natural lighting, the production has been "designed" in this way and conveys a different atmosphere and feeling than does a play that is presented with an elaborate set, magnificent costumes, and a myriad of special effects. Even the actor who doubles as director has to plan, even if it is on the spur of the moment, moves, pauses, and reactions. We explore designing and directing in Chapters 8 and 9. Each play is of a certain genre, discussed in Chapter 6. The genre, with the style, ties all the elements together and often determines the purpose for writing and performing the play. Chapter 10 further defines purpose and goals in discussing the three types

v

of theatre: educational, community, and professional. Chapter 11 discusses the final collaborators, the people on the business end of producing a play.

The approach is different from other introductory theatre texts in a number of ways. First, we emphasize that theatre is a total and collaborative art, requiring the contribution of many artists, the audience, and business-people. Secondly, it leads the student in a simple, easy style through each step in bringing a production to life. We want students to appreciate theatre: its extensity, the aspects that set it apart from other art forms, its ever-changing state, and its value to each of us. With this approach, the student should become an honest and knowledgeable critic whose interest will grow throughout life.

An important aspect of *Theatre: A View of Life* is the Instructor's Manual, which includes various aids for further study and exploration. For each chapter there are suggestions for discussion, activities, and individual projects to share with the class. The Manual refers to the supplementary reading lists at the end of each chapter and suggests how to use them to supplement the text. For the student interested in any particular aspect of the text, the Manual lists additional readings. To obtain a copy of the Instructor's Manual, write to your local sales representative or to the Theatre Editor, Holt, Rinehart and Winston, 383 Madison Avenue, New York, N.Y. 10017.

We are grateful to the following, who read the manuscript and made valuable suggestions: Vincent Angotti, Auburn University; Joseph Arnold, California State University, Fullerton; Michael A. Berkson, Illinois State University; Clarence P. Blanchette, Martin H. Brody, Montgomery College; Wayne H. Claeren, Jacksonville State University; Walter S. Dewey, Northern Illinois University; Geoffrey D. Fishburn, Miami University, Ohio; Roy S. Fluhrer, University of Idaho; Saundra M. Hall, West Chester State College; Diane Hostetler, North Seattle Community College; Charles A. Jones, Washington State University; Joseph Karioth, Florida State University; Gerard A. Larson, California State University, Sacramento; Richard J. Oman, Muskegon Community College; James W. Rodgers, University of Kentucky; Richard A. Weaver, Texas Tech University; Richard A. Welsbacher, Wichita State University; and Ronald C. Worsley, Henry Ford Community College.

Our thanks go also to Bill Douds, Isabelle Kopp, Jeff McIntosh, Kathi Cassady, and James D. Kitchen for assistance with the photographs and to Harold E. Kauffman and James D. Kitchen for editing and proofreading the manuscript.

M.C.
P.C.

Contents

3 The Actor   64

4 Dramatic Structure and Style   101

5 The Playwright   127

6 Dramatic Genre   147

7 Theatrical Space   171

8   The Designers   187

9   The Director   211

CHAPTER 1
Theatre as Art

Theatre is imagination. It is emotion and intellect. It is art. It has form, but that form moves and changes as constantly as clouds in a stormy sky. Through theatre we gain enlightenment and bring order and change to our environment. Theatre embraces all the world's cultures and perspectives, answers questions, predicts our tomorrow, and mirrors our today. It enhances individuality, yet brings us closer to one another. It enriches our lives and frees our creativity. Like all art forms, it expands our awareness and appreciation of life.

Perhaps the oldest of the arts, theatre closely approximates life. In many plays the characters "act" as real people do. They seem to experience emotions we all experience. They become entangled in uncomfortable situations, and they react in much the same way we do. Even the setting for a production often looks at least somewhat like real life.

Modern and Primitive Theatre

Although theatre is one of the oldest art forms, primitive theatre apparently bore little resemblance to modern theatre or to what most of us think of as theatrical entertainment. For instance, we think that theatre began simply with people nonverbally reenacting stuggles with their environment. Out of this probably grew stylized patterns portraying varied activities such as the hunt for daily sustenance.

As cultures become more refined, theatre became more elaborate. Language developed, and plays began to be recorded. The first of which we have knowledge dates back to around 3000 B.C. in Egypt, although we do not know whether such "drama" ever was performed. Egyptian culture was greatly admired by the ancient Greeks. Greek theatre, from which most of our present theatre practices evolved, may have been based on the theatre practices of Egypt.

Despite advances, the theatre of Greece had inauspicious beginnings. Religious in nature, the earliest "plays" consisted of little more than men in robes standing in a semicircle around an altar and chanting hymns of praise to Dionysus. He was worshipped to ensure the fertility of both crops and human beings. Later on the Greeks gave religious festivals at which they presented a variety of plays. Slowly theatre moved away from its religious base.

Different as they are, primitive and modern theatre serve similar purposes. Both, for instance, relieve a sense of "otherness." This term means that each person is isolated and can never fully know or understand others. At first babies perceive their surroundings and different people as a part of themselves. As they develop, they realize that they are isolated and that others are different entities.

Primitive people felt this strangeness or alienation because each tribe or settlement outside their own was, in effect, a different country. There

All the essentials for theatre are present in this performance by the Theatre of Youth Company. A gym floor provides playing space for the two actors who are performing for a group of elementary school children. *(Photo courtesy of Theatre of Youth Company of Buffalo, N.Y.)*

probably was little mingling with other tribes, so it was natural to fear them. In theatre, people attempted to deal with the "otherness" of their gods and neighboring tribes. They confirmed their own tribe's identity and power.

The modern theatregoer attempts to cope with "otherness" by seeking to understand it. At the theatre an audience can watch the "others" on stage. We witness their struggles and conflicts at a safe distance. There is no need to be active or afraid, because these "others" cannot affect us directly.

Besides the concept of otherness, primitive theatre and the theatre of today have other things in common. They have the same basic elements: actors, a dramatic performance, a space, and an audience. For any form of art to fulfill its purpose, it has to communicate something to somebody. Whether this communication in theatre involves a single actor performing before passersby in the park or an elaborate staged musical, the same essentials are present.

Theatre Compared with Other Art Forms

Any art form has to communicate. To a greater degree than many other arts, theatre is specific in its communication. A symphony communicates feelings and beauty through the intricate arrangement of sound, but the-

Dialogue the conversation between or among characters in a play; the lines or speeches of the characters in a play.

atre uses more than sound. Even its sound or **dialogue,** the lines or language of the characters, conveys more exact content than can music alone. A musical phrase is less specific than a spoken one. Music can stir us to excitement, but spoken lines can define a specific reason for excitement.

For instance, in James Goldman's *The Lion in Winter*, Henry II's sons plan to attack and kill him in the dungeon of the castle. Each of them is hoping to become king. Queen Eleanor, however, reveals the plot, after which we have the following dialogue:

Henry Brave boys; that's what I have. Three warriors. Who had the first crack? How was I divided up? Christ—
Richard You drove us to it.
Henry Why stop now? You're killers, aren't you? I am. I can do it. *(To Geoffrey.)* Take a knife. *(To Richard.)* Come on. What is it? Come for me.

Henry II confronts his son Richard in this scene from Heidelberg College's production of *The Lion in Winter.* Director and scene designer, Mary Sesak. *(Photo by Jeff McIntosh.)*

When we hear these lines, we can understand Henry's shock, disbelief, and scorn, as well as his decision to goad the boys into action or to call their bluff. The lines transmit mood and emotional intensity, as well as information.

Theatre is not only more specific than nonverbal art: it is more encompassing than a novel, a poem, or a painting. It combines so many elements. It is one of the most unlimited forms of art. Despite a certain framework—the three-act structure, for instance—theatre is limitless in what it can convey.

Finally, theatre is more personally involving than other art forms. Live theatre arouses a direct aesthetic response in audience and artist. Both are affected by the work.

> The living experience of a play . . . is a river of feeling within us which flows, now fast, now slow, now placidly between broad banks, now in a torrent between narrow ones, now down a slope, now over rapids, now cascading in a waterfall, now halted by a dam, now debouching into an ocean.[1]

Let us look at some aspects that make this "living experience" unique.

Theatre Is Temporal

Theatre can also be distinguished from many of the other arts in that it exists only for a period of time. A particular production can never be witnessed again once the final line has been delivered or the final action performed. In this respect theatre differs from painting, sculpture, literature, and architecture. Works in these arts can be enjoyed again and again in exactly the same state.

The same play can be presented time and time again, but each performance will differ from any other. The director, the designers, and the actors of one production have a different interpretation of the play than do any other artists. One actor's appearance, movement, and voice differ from those of any other actor who takes the same role. Stages differ in size. **Properties** and costumes differ from production to production. The third night of a production's run will be different from the first night and the second. The actors continue to grow in their roles. They experiment; they attempt to find out what will work best; they are affected by the audience.

Theatre Imitates

A play, like our own lives, takes place in time. Moreover, theatre directly imitates human experiences by allowing the spectators to identify with characters who are represented as real. Members of the audience can put themselves in the characters' places and feel as the characters do. Theatre satisfies our **mimetic instinct;** it resembles life as it actually is lived or could be lived.

Properties articles that can be moved or carried in the course of a play. Set properties include such objects as curtains and paintings; hand props include anything that the actors use or carry.

Mimetic instinct the human need or desire to imitate; through the mimetic instinct we acquire much of our learning.

[1]Eric Bentley, *The Life of the Drama* (New York: Atheneum, 1964), p. 3.

Although we can read about the performances given by the great actress Eleanora Duse, who lived from 1859 to 1924, we can never actually know what her acting was like because we cannot witness her live presence on a stage. *(Photo courtesy of the Billy Rose Theatre Collection; The New York Public Library at Lincoln Center; Astor, Lenox and Tilden Foundations.)*

Theatre Interprets

Theatre comes to imitate life through the efforts of many people. The playwright, the actors, the director, and the designers all add their own backgrounds and experiences to a production. They judge; they overlook; they point out specific traits to the exclusion of others. They select, and through this choice, add their own personalities or their perceptions of the world. They interpret events and actions in the play from differing viewpoints. All art is subjective, but in theatre a number of viewpoints combine to make the form totally distinctive. Each of the individuals involved contributes something personal to the total production, which then presents life in a many-faceted manner.

Theatre Combines Art Forms

Theatre encompasses not only various viewpoints, but many forms of art. It includes architecture in the setting, sculpture in three-dimensional

The characters in a play often are represented as real people. This is a scene from *Toys in the Attic*, produced by the Old Globe Theatre. The play was directed by Craig Noel, with set design by Nick Reid and costumes by Susan Muick. *(Photo by Bill Reid and courtesy of the Old Globe Theatre.)*

forms and the use of lights and shadow, dance in the planned movement **(blocking)**, painting in the setting and makeup, literature in the words, and music in songs and the flow of the language. Artists of diverse talents work together to bring about a unified production. Theatre involves much artistry and planning before the ultimate communication between artists and audience occurs.

Blocking the planned movement or business in a play; the stage directions for the actor.

Theatre is a combination of art forms, as illustrated by this scene from *No Strings*, presented at Kent State University, under the direction of Earl E. Curtis. *(Photo by C. James Gleason and courtesy of Kent State University Theatre.)*

Theatre as Imitation and Ritual

How did such a complex art form arise? Generally, we believe that theatre had its beginnings in two basic human traits. One is the mimetic instinct; the other is the need for **ritual**.

The Mimetic Instinct

Ritual a repeated pattern of behavior, which may have its basis in religion, pageantry, or individual behavior. It originally meant a controlled sequence of action to achieve a supernatural goal. Now it also refers to a type of play structure in which a pattern of action is repeated.

Just as primitive people portrayed what was important in their lives, modern theatre artists most often begin by communicating what they have learned from the world around them. In other words, they imitate. Usually the imitation is only a starting point, and the playwright, actors, and designers allow their imaginations free rein. The perceptions of theatre artists or other individuals are colored by background and experience.

Psychologists state that each of our new experiences is built upon something we already know. We relate a new situation to our past awareness and thus build our memories and experiences. We have certain expectations, which are only slightly altered by new surroundings or new people. Occasionally, we encounter something outside our realm of experience or meet a person to whom we cannot relate, but we use our past as a point of departure in learning or in creativity.

Essentially, theatre artists use the same technique, but they need not be bound by what is, only by what could be. They explore and, through the art of theatre, present a whole range of thoughts and feelings. Thus theatre can be a vehicle of learning for both artist and audience. It can broaden our cultural and humanistic horizons. It can give us confidence by showing us we are like others, and it can help us explore our individual selves.

The actor often has little more than imagination and creativity to convey a message or to create a mood. *(Photo by Gary Anderson of* The Coshocton Tribune *and courtesy of Footlight Players of Coshocton, Ohio.)*

Ritual

As people began to understand that forces outside their control, such as weather, dominated certain aspects of their lives, they began to believe in the power of supernatural beings. Consequently, they tried to please the gods through dance and movement. They believed that if they performed a certain ritual, a pattern of events often highly stylized and invariable, the weather would become warmer or there would be rain to grow crops. As time went on, the rituals became more formal. The people added costumes, specific movements, and music. At first the entire tribe might participate, and the supernatural forces were the audience. Later, only certain members of the tribe participated. Now the rest of the community, as well as the gods, was the audience.

Primitive people used ritual for other reasons too. A portrayal of the hunt with the successful killing of game was a kind of magic to assure that the hunt would be successful. Then a dance could be performed after the hunt to show how it went. This dance probably was more for communication and entertainment than for pleasing the gods; but in such behavior primitive people still combined ritual and imitation.

Theatre in Everyday Life

The tribal organization is the origin of society. The articulation of its needs is the origin of theatre. Song and music and dance in which purpose and poetry were one and in which the entire community participated were devised as school and language and the source of common strength. The subsequent history of the theatre is an effort to recapture this initial unity at a complex level of civilization. In this sense, the history of the theatre is the history of man, for the stage deals with man's conflict with himself and the external world.[2]

Through thousands of years theatre and "tribal organization" or government have continued to change, just as styles of painting, architecture, and sculpture change. However, basic human nature has not changed. In our own lives we join in *rituals*, *pretend*, *imitate*, and *play roles*.

Everyday Ritual

Just as primitive people dressed up and gave rituals for entertainment and to please the gods, so do we. We participate in parades, for example. We dress up to attend church services, which follow a pattern or ritual. We belong to organizations that have badges and uniforms and observe handshakes, passwords, and patterns of progression for advancement. At football games, fans wear the team's colors. There is the singing of the national anthem, the introduction of the players on each side, and a band show at halftime. These rituals are loosely structured, but they usually follow a set pattern.

[2]Allan Lewis, *The Contemporary Theatre* (New York: Crown Publishers, Inc., 1962), p. 1.

Ritual enters into many areas of our lives, for example, the introduction of the players before a football game. *(Photo of the Cincinnati Bengals, courtesy of Nicholas A. Kitt.)*

When we stop to consider it, this type of behavior is closely allied to theatre. A theatre performance is rehearsed and presented more than once. Organized ritual is rehearsed too, although many times not so formally, and performed over and over. Often the "audience" participates in the ritual, whereas in theatre the audience will usually participate less directly. For example, one ritual in the Christian church is communion. The drinking of wine and the eating of unleavened bread involves both "actors" and "audience"—the clergy and the congregation. The ritual is not rehearsed by the congregation but learned through repeated imitation of others.

Pretending

Children play a game in which those on one side try to find and "shoot dead" those on the other side before they themselves are "killed." The children assume roles (as actors), follow certain loosely drawn rules (the format of the play), and treat themselves or the members of the other side as the audience. When one side has "eliminated" the other, the game ends. Like the portrayal of the hunt in primitive times, this game is close to theatre. It contains all the basic ingredients: performers, a play, a space, and an audience. Like many children's games of "pretend," it involves imitation, communication, and entertainment.

Children dressing up for "make believe" can be considered a basic or elementary form of theatre. *(Photo by James D. Kitchen.)*

We also are forced to pretend or "make believe" in social situations. We "enjoy" a party because we don't want to hurt the host's feelings. We "like" somebody's new outfit for the same reason. We often pretend to be interested in subjects that have little or no interest for us. The reason, of course, is that beyond the present situation the pretense may help us reach some goal or receive a later reward. If we are "interested" in a professor's particular theories about World War II, then maybe the instructor will look upon us more favorably when grades are due.

Imitation

Like pretending, imitation helps us achieve certain goals. A baby cries, and the mother rushes to the crib to change its position or to feed it. Later the child imitates the first cry, and the mother comes once more. The baby has learned that a certain action elicits a certain response.

Most important, as children we learn to imitate others. In this way we gain much of our knowledge. We learn to speak by imitating our parents. We see how others behave in social situations and imitate them.

The basic instinct for imitation carries through our lives. We watch someone seated near us at a formal dinner to see which piece of silverware to use; we observe how to operate a car or play a game. We want to be correct in any situation, so we do what we think is expected of us, based on what we did or saw others do in similar situations. We are using the same instinct in everyday living the actor and the playwright use in creating characters for a play.

Role Playing

Imitation often takes the form of **role playing.** We all assume roles to gain a certain response. In everyday situations there usually are no memorized lines or formally rehearsed parts. Each time we play a certain role, we gain practice for the next time. We use a certain vocabulary in a particular situation, and under similar circumstances we refine and improve this vocabulary. In playing the role of job applicant, we even may rehearse answers to expected questions. Role playing in everyday life and acting in a stage production both are forms of theatre, although the latter usually is much more polished.

Role playing changing one's way of behaving in different situations; modifying behavior to fit the situation.

An actress waits to make her initial entrance on stage. At the moment she is playing the role of actress but soon will be playing a role or portraying a character in a theatre production. *(Photo by Bill Douds.)*

We assume roles for every occasion. You may now be playing the role of conscientious student, which implies several possibilities. Maybe you really have a desire to learn. On the other hand, you may only be pretending to be a conscientious student to impress your professors. At various times or in different sets of circumstances we allow different aspects of our personalities to surface. We follow different, relatively established patterns of behavior from situation to situation.

Because the image of ourselves that we want to project to others varies, we are not always the "same" person. You speak differently to the dean of your school than you speak to your best friend. At school, one of your professors may play the role of an English instructor. That person also may be a parent and spouse, a co-worker and friend, a shopper, and a competitor on a bowling team. Different actions and conversational styles go with the changes in role.

Even the clothing we wear contributes to the parts we play. Think of a time you wore a gym suit as opposed to a time you had on dress clothes. Now think what would happen if you were to wear a gym suit to your history class. You dress for one role, and the costume is inappropriate for the other.

Each of us plays emotional roles also. Maybe you play at being the outraged student when you think you deserve a higher grade than you received. At another time you may play the hurt friend at some imagined or real slight. Excellent examples of these games appear in Edward Albee's *Who's Afraid of Virginia Woolf?* Fortunately, most people do not play

---

Who's Afraid of Virginia Woolf?
Edward Albee, 1962

Act I, "Fun and Games," introduces to the audience a middle-aged history professor and his wife. George and Martha have asked another couple, Nick and Honey, to their home after a faculty party. Nick, an assistant professor of biology, apparently is doing a series of experiments that are destined to alter humanity. While the young couple is present, George and Martha carry on what obviously is a continuing quarrel. They cause their guests embarrassment, but the young couple remains, influenced no doubt by the fact that Martha is the daughter of the college president. Martha belittles George for various failures, and the couple mysteriously refers to a son. Act II, "Walpurgisnacht," brings up some painful incidents from George's past. Maybe the incidents occurred and maybe they did not. It also is established that Nick and Honey were married because they thought Honey's hysterical pregnancy was real. Honey becomes drunk, and Nick and Martha leave to make love. In Act III, "The Exorcism," Nick and Martha return, having failed to make love satisfactorily. George then announces the death of his and Martha's son. The son is imaginary but both accepted the myth of his existence. George now has exorcised the son to get even with Martha for going off with Nick. The play ends as a new phase in the relationship between George and Martha begins.

such vicious games as George and Martha do, but everyone does play games.

At the theatre, we play roles as designers, technicians, performers, or audience members. In the latter role we may play the "superior sophisticate" who has a broad cultural background, whether or not we have.

We find the theatrical all around us. Children "show off" to gain attention. We tend to dramatize certain situations to gain sympathy. For instance, we tell a long tale about the minor traffic accident in which we were involved. We are theatrical in creating caricatures of people with whom we have had an argument. Our voices become unpleasant and exaggerated, maybe with a hint of truth, when we relate what the other person said and how we were wronged.

Theatre in Evolution

Life and theatre do have much in common. One of their strongest similarities is that neither one stands still. In surface styles and in the values that underlie them, both change all the time.

> In every area of the modern theater—language, setting, dramatic style, acting technique, theme, stage decor—we seem to find diversity, heterogeneity, and open conflict. Instead of a smoothly developing tradition, a continuing exploitation of a limited number of theatrical resources, and an ever narrowing and finer focus on a few key ethical and metaphysical questions—all the marks of the great theatrical traditions of the past—the theater of the modern age seems to jump nervously and without progression from extreme to extreme, from one bizarre experiment to its opposite, and from one explanation of human nature to its reverse.[3]

Many historians and critics have stated that our present theatre is in a state of revolt. It *is* changing, but theatre has always changed. Romanticism was a revolt against the rigid rules of earlier neoclassicism. Realism and naturalism were revolts against the artificial sentimentalism that romanticism became. (These movements will be discussed in Chapter 4.) Of course, the theatre is in revolt. It always has been a changing art, and change is one of its most exciting aspects.

For instance, during the sixties there was a move in theatre, as in life, toward freedom of expression and dress. Forbidden topics now became the subjects for plays. Nudity, often for its own sake, became the

[3]Alvin B. Kernan, ed., *The Modern American Theatre* (Englewood Cliffs, New Jersey: Prentice Hall, Inc., 1967), p. 17, reprinted from *Classics of the Modern Theatre*, Alvin B. Kernan, ed., (New York: Harcourt, Brace & World, Inc., 1965), by permission of Harcourt, Brace, Jovanovich, Inc.

A scene from San Diego State University's production of *A Moon for the Misbegotten*, directed by Ken Harris. *(Photo courtesy of San Diego State University—Dramatic Arts Department.)*

usual rather than the exceptional. We began to see such productions as *Hair* by Gerome Ragni, James Radi, and Galt MacDermot, and *Oh! Calcutta!* by Kenneth Tynan. The former, billed as ''The American Tribal-Love-Rock Musical,'' tries to explore young people's relationships with the older generation. It shows them questioning such ideas as loyalty to their country, dress codes, ''proper'' behavior, and facing up to responsibility. It received notoriety for its brief use of nudity and its freedom of verbal expression. *Oh! Calcutta!*, revived in the late seventies, reinforced the trend toward permissiveness through its use of nudity and highly suggestive scenes. Off-Broadway theatres presented both heterosexual and homosexual sequences. All such presentations protrayed changes in the attitudes of the times.

Many such productions depended on shock value to attract patrons. When the shock value faded and these productions were not widely attended, the theatre again experienced change. Part of this change was the nostalgia movement of the early seventies, with the revivals of the musicals *Irene* by Montgomery, Tierney, and McCarthy, and *No, No, Nannette* by Harbach, Mandel, Youmans, and Caesar, and O'Neill's *A Moon for the Misbegotten*. Nostalgia was strong in *Grease,* (Jim Jacobs and Warren Casey), which tried to recapture the fifties, as did *Happy Days* and *Laverne and Shirley* on television. Theatre was rebelling against current plays but as yet had developed no widely accepted ideas that were entirely new. Meanwhile, since many taboos had been broken, playwrights had freedom to explore previously unapproachable themes.

Each change in theatre is important. It not only mirrors the times but leads the way to emerging attitudes. The total abandonment of inhibitions in some of the plays in the sixties and seventies opened the way; now such plays as *The Changing Room* can be played partially in the nude, not for the sake of nudity but to present realistically the environment of a locker room. The three-act play by David Storey takes place in the locker room before, at halftime, and after a rugby game. The members of the team change from street clothes to uniforms and later from uniforms to street clothes. The play emphasizes the refusal of human beings to accept a defeated attitude toward life, symbolized by the sport of rugby. Freedom of expression also allowed the presentation of *That Championship Season*, which contains a great deal of swearing and sexual references, not for their shock value but to represent the reunion of a high school basketball team.

Universality

Just as many plays from earlier periods have little meaning for us now, many plays of the present probably will mean little to future generations. For a play to have lasting value, except as a museum piece or as a reflec-

Our Town
Thornton Wilder, 1938

Set in Grover's Corner, New Hampshire, the play deals with life, love, death, and the hereafter, as experienced by the people of a small town around the turn of the century. The drama concentrates on George, son of the town's physician, and Emily, daughter of the newspaper editor. The Stage Manager acts as narrator.

The two young people are seen going to high school together, falling in love over ice cream sodas at the drugstore, getting married, and suffering as Emily dies in childbirth. In a touching third act, the two young people are reunited briefly after Emily has found out how painful a return to life can be, because the living take all of life for granted.

Universality
the trait of having meaning for everyone in all places and times.

Empathy emotionally relating to or identifying with a character, a theme, or a situation in a play.

tion of the time and place in which it was written, it must possess **universality;** it must be relevant for all people at all times. Obviously, this description is an overstatement; nothing will have meaning for every individual. If someone were to present a Shakespearean drama to one of the aboriginal tribes of Australia, the production would not convey much. Nevertheless some plays have themes that move audiences many years after the playwright has written them.

A play with universality deals with common feelings and beliefs. It enables us to **empathize** (identify) with a character in a play or with the circumstances of the characters. In Thornton Wilder's *Our Town* we have little trouble identifying with the characters, because their experiences growing up, living together as families, and dealing with death are similar to our own experiences. Wilder reinforces the universal belief that each of us should learn to appreciate and notice others.

> Every action which has ever taken place—every thought, every emotion—has taken place only once, at one moment in time and place. "I love you," "I rejoice," "I suffer," have been said and felt many billions of times, and never twice the same. Every person who has ever lived has lived an unbroken succession of unique occasions. Yet the more one is aware of this individuality in experience (innumerable! innumerable!) the more one becomes attentive to what these disparate moments have in common, to repetitive patterns. As an artist (or listener or beholder) which "Truth" do you prefer—that of the isolated occasion, or that which includes and resumes the innumerable? Which truth is more worth telling? Every age differs in this. Is the Venus de Milo "one woman"? Is the play *Macbeth* the story of "one destiny"? The theatre is admirably fitted to tell both truths.[4]

[4]Thornton Wilder, *Three Plays by Thornton Wilder* (New York: Harper and Row, 1957; reprinted by Bantam, 1958), pp. ix–x

Death of a Salesman
Arthur Miller, 1949

Willy Loman, a traveling salesman, has always felt that social success or "being well-liked" is the key to financial success. When the play opens, Willy is sixty-three and no longer able to sell. He is at the point of hallucinating and talking to himself; for him the past and the present intermingle. Through flashbacks (scenes from the past) we learn how Willy's world has fallen apart. He always viewed himself as the ideal father and husband. His image shatters when Biff, the older of his two sons, finds him in a hotel room with a woman. Willy had led Biff to believe that social popularity and success on the football field were more important than education, and he pampered both sons. The younger son, Happy, has patterned his life after Willy's and views success as his father does. After Willy finally asks his boss for an in-town selling job and is fired instead, Biff forces him to realize that both of them are failures. Because his insurance is paid up, Willy feels he still can be a success by killing himself and leaving the insurance money to his family. He goes to the garage to start his car, and his wife, Linda, foresees what will happen. Even though she loves him for what he is, she is powerless to stop him.

Many plays that have survived from earlier periods contain universal themes simply because our drives and motives are the same as they were thousands of years ago. *Agamemnon*, written in 458 B.C. by the Greek playwright Aeschylus, for instance, involves unfaithfulness. Clymtenestra takes a lover while her husband Agamemnon is away at war. He returns home with the captured princess Cassandra, and Clytemnestra murders both of them. Unfaithfulness is also treated in many modern plays. Biff, in Arthur Miller's *Death of a Salesman*, discovers his father, Willy, in a hotel room with a woman. Biff's life is greatly affected, first in that he does not graduate from high school. Muriel Resnik treats the idea of unfaithfulness humorously in *Any Wednesday*, in which a business executive maintains an apartment, supposedly for business purposes but actually to house his mistress.

Theatre is an imitation of what we ourselves experience. It imitates but heightens life's experiences. It offers new insights into our feelings. It has relevance for us both as individuals and as part of the human race. We understand our own motives more fully when we see them on the stage. Certainly, most of us never will become murderers, but we recognize that under certain circumstances we may possibly be capable of killing another human being. We can understand and sympathize with Hamlet, for instance, when he avenges his father's death.

When *Hamlet* opens, Claudius has become the ruler of Denmark by killing Hamlet's father and marrying his mother. This scene from Act III shows how strongly Hamlet feels about his father's murderer.

Because of the universality of its theme and characters, Shakespeare's *Hamlet* remains a popular and often produced play. Director, Donald Glaven. *(Photo courtesy of Thurber Theater, Ohio State University.)*

Hamlet   Now might I do it pat, now he is praying;
  And now I'll do't. And so he goes to heaven;
  And so am I revenged. That would be scann'd:
  A villain kills my father; and for that,
  I, his sole son, do this same villain send
  To heaven.
  O, this is hire and salary, not revenge.
  He took my father grossly, full of bread;
  With all his crimes broad blown, as flush as May;
  And how his audit stands who knows save heaven?
  But in other circumstance and course of thought,
  'Tis heavy with him: and am I then revenged,
  To take him in the purging of his soul,
  When he is fit and season'd for his passage?
  No!
  Up, sword; and know thou a more horrid hent:
  When he is drunk asleep, or in his rage,
  Or in the incestuous pleasure of his bed;
  At gaming, swearing, or about some act
  That has no relish of salvation in 't;
  Then trip him, that his heels may kick at heaven.
  And that his soul may be as damn'd and black
  As hell, whereto it goes.

Hamlet, Prince of Denmark
William Shakespeare, c. 1600

Because "the times are out of joint," sin has corrupted the royal court. Hamlet's uncle, Claudius, has secretly murdered Hamlet's father and married his mother, Gertrude. Sworn by his father's ghost to vengeance, Hamlet must first make certain that Claudius indeed is guilty. He does so by hiring a band of players (actors) to reenact the murder. Claudius betrays himself during the performance. Hamlet suspects Polonius of being in on the conspiracy and even suspects Polonius' daughter, Ophelia, even though he has formerly courted her. Ophelia is deeply in love with Hamlet. Inadvertently, Hamlet kills Polonius, after which he is exiled and Ophelia goes mad. Laertes, Polonius' son and a former friend of Hamlet, challenges Hamlet to a fencing match. He puts poison on his swordpoint with the approval of the king. Gertrude accidentally dies of a poisoned drink Claudius has prepared for Hamlet. Hamlet kills Claudius; Laertes kills Hamlet. But Laertes himself dies by the poisoned rapier.

Through such plays as *Hamlet* we learn we are not alone in our feelings; we are a part of a whole. Therefore we can accept ourselves and our feelings more fully.

At least since Greek and Roman times comedy has involved **stock characters,** exaggerated character types. The playwright takes certain traits we can observe in friends, relatives, or neighbors and heightens them. For example, we all have known finicky people and hypochondriacs. Neil Simon combined these two traits and exaggerated them to create the character of Felix in *The Odd Couple.* Hypochondriacs have appeared through history in many other plays, including the French writer Molière's *The Imaginary Invalid* in 1673. The playwrights took what they knew; they imitated life and then built upon the imitation through exaggeration.

> **Stock characters** character types in which a certain trait or traits, such as miserliness, are highly exaggerated.

The Odd Couple
Neil Simon, 1957

Oscar Madison is an extremely sloppy person who lives alone in his apartment after his wife leaves, unable to put up with her husband's messiness. Felix, totally the opposite, is compulsively neat and organized. Felix's wife has just left him, so as the play opens, he moves in with Oscar on a temporary basis. The two men have many problems in adjusting to each other's habits. By the time the play ends, they are adjusting better, and it looks as if the situation will be permanent. Most of the humor in the play comes from the two men learning to live with each other.

The mime is descended from earlier stock characters. *(Photo by Kip Baker and courtesy of Robby Ramsel.)*

A Definition of Drama

Drama all written plays, regardless of their genre or form.

Despite the fact that certain elements have characterized theatre since its beginning, theorists always have disagreed over what constitutes **drama,** or the written play. The French theatre critic Ferdinand Brunetière stated: "I leave the dramatist complete freedom in development. That is where I depart from the old school of criticism, that believed in the mysterious power of 'rules' in their inspiring virtues."

> But the truth is that there are no Rules in that sense; there never will be. There are only conventions, which are necessarily variable, since their only object is to fulfill the essential aim of the dramatic work, and the means of accomplishing this vary with the piece, the time, and the man. . . . Evidently, all these alleged Rules effect or express only the most superficial characteristics of the drama. Not only are they not mysterious, they are not in the least profound. Whether we observe them or not, drama is drama with them or without them. They are only devices which may at any time give place to others. It all depends on the subject, the author, and the public.[5]

Planning a theatrical production begins with a script, or drama. Whether it gives elaborate instructions or a bare outline, the script is the jumping off place for a production. Unlike other forms of literature, a

[5]Ferdinand Brunetière, "The Law of the Drama," in *European Theories of the Drama*, Barrett H. Clark, ed. (New York: Crown Publishers, Inc., revised ed., 1965), p. 381. Reprinted from *The Law of the Drama*, Phillip M. Hayden, trans. 1914.

play script is not a complete piece of art once it is written and revised. Except for "closet drama," plays that are written to be read, not performed, a drama requires the contribution of each theatre artist to bring it fully to life. "The printed script of a play," according to playwright Tennessee Williams, "is hardly more than an architect's blueprint of a house not yet built or built and destroyed." He adds:

> The color, the grace and levitation, the structural pattern in motion, the quick interplay of live beings, suspended like fitful lightning in a cloud, these things are the play, not words on paper, nor thoughts and ideas of an author, those shabby things snatched off basement counters at Gimbel's.[6]

Often directors or actors will say in reference to a script: "It plays better than it reads." What they mean is that an audience cannot receive the full impact of a play by reading it silently. They need the atmosphere of a theatre and the technical aspects of the stage performance. When the set designer adds a visual interpretation, the actors analyze and impersonate the characters, and the director integrates the total production, only then does a script fully communicate the playwright's intention. Plays are written to be presented by actors for the entertainment or enlightenment of an audience; they require a live performance to be complete and aesthetically pleasing. Only under conditions of performance does theatre exist.

Of course, if we read a play and visualize a setting and actors, the script can appeal to us emotionally and aesthetically. A production adds much more, but let us look at the contribution of the script. How does it imitate life? How is it structured? Usually, a play contains dialogue, portrays conflict, and has action and purpose.

A Theory of Drama

According to the Greek philosopher Aristotle in *The Poetics*, the earliest treatise we have on the theory of drama, a tragedy should have a beginning, a middle, and an end. Simply, Aristotle, who recorded his theories in the fourth century B.C., meant that a tragedy should be complete in itself. It should contain everything necessary to understand it. The incidents should exhibit a cause-and-effect relationship, and the dramatic question or problem should come up early in the play. The play should provide a frame for the action or story line, within which the characters and ideas can reveal themselves. The problem should be solved. Although Aristotle was discussing tragedy, the criteria are the same for any play with a plot.

Since the sixteenth century, when Aristotle's writings on drama be-

[6]Tennessee Williams, Afterword to *Camino Real, Where I Live: Selected Essays* (New York: New Directions, 1978, reprinted from the first published version of *Camino Real,* New Directions, 1953), p. 69.

Blithe Spirit is an example of a play with a plot. The play was presented by Summerfun Summer Theater at Montclair State College, with William Goeckler as director; Keith Malick, set design, and A. Neilson Morse, costumer. *(Photo courtesy of Montclair State College.)*

came widely known, he has greatly influenced dramatic theorists and playwrights. But there is a certain amount of disagreement with his views. Some critics think that if a playwright follows Aristotle's definition, the play becomes too artificial.

Most people agree that the audience does need some sense of ending, some feeling that the play has been completed. That is why we rarely see any true "slice of life" drama in the contemporary theatre. Even if a play has no plot line that we can follow, the audience has to feel either some satisfaction or some emotional release when the curtain descends.

Naturalism a theatrical style which attempts to duplicate life, or in effect, transfer actual life to the stage.

All drama has to be selective to provide a feeling of completion. This is true even of **naturalism,** which tries to duplicate life. But current naturalism, like all other theatrical styles, cannot present every detail of life. Nothing would be more boring than to come into a theatre and watch a family just go about their everyday tasks on stage, although even this has been done. Petty details must be discarded. The action, the dialogue, and even the characters have to be condensed. Time has to be compressed, while still resembling life. The dramatist must select the high points or the moments of direct conflict and forget the extraneous material. We call the right to make such changes "dramatic license."

The Story Play

Theatre artists most often deal with the **story play,** or what often is termed the **well-made play.** (See Chapter 5). The major element of this type of drama is conflict. The major character, the **protagonist,** needs or wants something. The protagonist is opposed by the **antagonist,** which may take the form of a person, a group of people, or a force. When the protagonist's needs are established and then opposed, we have the basis for the **motivation,** which leads to the **conflict.** The conflict or struggle continues throughout the largest part of the play. If a central character is well drawn, the audience can easily trace the character's actions to the motivational base, the moment at which the conflict was introduced. Only in poorly constructed story plays does the central character seem to be unmotivated.

Other Types of Drama

In contrast to the story play, other types of plays make drama an elusive form to define. For instance, in some plays there actually is little conflict among the characters. *In White America,* a documentary drama that premiered in 1963, has no main character. When the play was first produced, six actors played a variety of roles. At times they read from the script, and occasionally they moved into specific scenes. Scenes of direct conflict between actors never lasted for more than a few moments. The actors constantly changed from one role to another, outlawing sustained conflict.

There was, however, conflict inherent in the script. The author, Martin B. Duberman, shows how blacks have been treated unfairly in the United States. The play calls attention to the oppression of blacks from slave times to the present. The major conflict is in the minds of the spectators.

Another element of drama is dialogue, but it is not always necessary either. In Jean-Claude van Itallie's *Motel,* the two major characters destroy a motel room. The one-act play, which has almost no conversation, attempts to show the disregard we often have for others' belongings and for other people themselves.

Plays often tell a story or contain a plot line that builds from an inciting incident to a turning point and climax. But many plays, those of the **absurdist writers,** for example, tell no complete story. The aim of such plays is to show the absurdity of the human condition. They often have nonsensical dialogue that tells no logical story. They express the idea that life is neither good nor bad at face value. Only what we choose as moral or immoral makes life good or bad to us individually. An example of absurdist writing is the following excerpt from Eugène Ionesco's *The Bald Soprano:*

Story play a play that has a plot and builds in intensity from an inciting incident to a turning point and climax.

Well-made play in current theatre refers to a play with a plot; historically, a play that presented a particular social problem for which the playwright offered a solution.

Protagonist the major character in a play; generally, the protagonist tries to reach a certain goal and is opposed by the antagonist.

Antagonist opposes the protagonist; the antagonist can be a person or persons, society, a force such as a flood or a storm, or a conflicting tendency within the protagonist.

Motivation the reason for taking any action; why the protagonist in a play attempts to reach a certain goal.

Conflict opposition; antagonist and protagonist engaged in a struggle to triumph over one another.

Absurdism or Theatre of the Absurd a movement of the fifties and sixties in which playwrights dramatized the absurdity and futility of human existence. Generally, absurdist drama is nonsensical and repetitive.

Mr. Smith (still reading his paper.) Tsk, it says here that Bobby Watson died.

Mrs. Smith My God, the poor man! When did he die?

Mr. Smith Why do you pretend to be astonished? You know very well that he's been dead these past two years. Surely you remember that we attended his funeral a year and a half ago.

Mrs. Smith Oh yes, of course I do remember. I remembered it right away, but I don't understand why you yourself were so surprised to see it in the paper.

Mr. Smith It wasn't in the paper. It's been three years since his death was announced. I remembered it through an association of ideas.

Mrs. Smith What a pity! He was so well preserved.

Mr. Smith He was the handsomest corpse in Great Britain. He didn't look his age. Poor Bobby, he's been dead for four years and he was still warm. A veritable living corpse. And how cheerful he was.

Mrs. Smith Poor Bobby.

Mr. Smith Which poor Bobby do you mean?

Mrs. Smith It is his wife that I mean. She is called Bobby too. Bobby Watson. Since they both had the same name, you could never tell one from the other when you saw them together. It was only after his death that you could really tell which was which. And there are still people today who confuse her with the deceased and offer their condolences to him. Do you know her?

Mr. Smith I only met her once, by chance, at Bobby's burial.

Mrs. Smith I've never seen her. Is she pretty?

Mr. Smith She has regular features and yet one cannot say that she is pretty. She is too big and stout. Her features are not regular but still one can say that she is very pretty. She is a little too small and too thin. She's a voice teacher.[7]

For the presentation of a drama we do not even need a stage. Many plays are produced in nothing more than large rooms with a space in the center or at one end.

The Elements of Drama

If we can dispense with conflict, dialogue, plot, and stage, what remains essential to drama?

One ingredient essential to all drama is action. We should think of action as synonymous with life. Any person who is alive is acting and reacting. The characters in a play are doing something; their actions have a purpose. According to Brunetière: "In drama or farce, what we ask of

[7]Donald W. Allen, trans., *Four Plays by Eugène Ionesco* (New York: Grove Press, 1958), pp. 11–12. Reprinted by permission of Grove Press, Inc. Copyright © 1958 by Grove Press, Inc.; also reprinted by permission of John Calder (Publishers) Ltd., London.

the theater, is the spectacle of a *will* striving towards a goal, and conscious of the means which it employs.''[8]

Despite the exceptions, drama usually relies on certain basic techniques, such as dialogue, action, and a plot that leads to a climax and resolution. A playwright, like a painter, generally must work within a certain structure. A painter can choose colors, brushstrokes, and composition but has to apply pigment to a surface. No matter what the dimensions, the surface is still a containing form. The successful artist does not view this limited space as restrictive; such diverse paintings as Gainsborough's *Blue Boy* and Picasso's *Woman with a Guitar* can emerge on a similar canvas. Each differs greatly in style, and neither would benefit from any extension. Similarly, drama and hence theatre has a basic structure, within which exists freedom to experiment, to establish new methods, and to present new concepts.

Aristotle described six elements as essential for drama. They still are worth consideration in reference to contemporary theatre. These elements are plot, character, thought, dialogue, melody, and spectacle.

Plot, the most important element of a play according to Aristotle, is the framework of the action in which the story line develops. It is the progression of the action by means of the other elements.

Character is the major ingredient for the advancement of the plot. Through the characters' speech and behavior the plot is revealed to an audience. The characters most often are the controlling force in a play. Placed in certain circumstances, each character reacts in ways that bring about success or failure. Characters should be both individual and typical. A character has to be an individual to appear believable, but must not be so alien from others as to arouse no identification on the part of the audience. The character must be individual enough to maintain interest but familiar enough to illustrate a general truth.

Character, in conjunction with the other elements, gives the play a universal appeal. The play must affect us personally through an appeal to our emotions. It must provide situations, characters, and events with which we can identify and through which we can learn.

Thought refers to the playwright's ideas. The play should be both specific and general. That means it should be the story of an individual but should have a universal application. According to Aristotle, a play can have several themes or ideas, but only one should be dominant.

Dialogue refers to the speech of each character. It should suit the characters and be consistent with their backgrounds and personalities. It helps establish the tone or prevailing mood of the play and the changing tempos of the various scenes.

Melody refers to the rhythm and flow of the language. The emotional state of the characters and the emotional content of the situation should

[8]Clark, p. 382.

be reflected in the dialogue. The overall rhythm of a play depends upon its emotional content. Basically, the rhythm of a tragedy is slower than that of a comedy. Rhythm influences the audience's response.

Spectacle, the least important element according to Aristotle, is the scenery and background. It is the element over which the playwright has the least control; the director and designers are largely responsible for the visual elements of a play.

There are several functions spectacle fulfills. It enhances the production and gives the audience information. For instance, we can often tell the location and perhaps the historical period and the season through the setting. It aids in creating the prevailing mood and helps to establish character by giving clues to the economic and social levels of the major figures. The scenery sometimes even establishes a character's profession and personality. It demonstrates the tastes of the characters in the color, the architecture, and the furnishings, and shows cultural background through the use of art objects.

Theatre Conventions

Like the drama, the production itself relies on certain established rules. In all ages theatre has followed certain conventions, devices the actors, the playwright, the designers, or the director use to expedite the production. An audience willingly accepts and expects such devices as a type of shorthand.

According to Samuel Taylor Coleridge, a nineteenth-century poet and critic, theatre involves "the willing suspension of disbelief." Those involved in the production of a play attempt to create an illusion of reality through the use of conventions, and the audience completes the illusion by accepting as real what it sees and hears. Although conventions serve a number of purposes, many are conventions of selectivity. They entail implying rather than showing or stating. In exaggerated melodramas, for instance, we know immediately who the villain is because he dresses in black and constantly twists the ends of his moustache. Conventions in the theatre apply to all areas of a play's production and often change from one historical period to another.

Proscenium or Proscenium arch the framing device that isolates the stage area and provides the focal point for the action; the spectators are asked to imagine that they are viewing the action through an imaginary fourth wall.

Acting Conventions

An audience willingly accepts all sorts of acting conventions, from actors' projecting their voices to be heard throughout the seating area to actors rarely turning their backs on the audience in a **proscenium** theatre. Actors in a large theatre make broader gestures than a person normally would in everyday life. They exaggerate so the audience can see and interpret the movements.

Writing Conventions

Playwrights too use many conventions. Most of them are concerned with heightening and condensing material and choosing the high points of a story for the plot of a play. Almost every writing convention falls into this category.

Some specific writing conventions are the **soliloquy,** the **aside,** the **monologue,** and the **flashback.** All are ways of presenting **exposition** (a convention in itself) and feelings on the parts of the characters. A soliloquy shows a character thinking aloud, in much the same way we may talk to ourselves when we are alone. The purpose is to show the character's inner feelings and to let the audience know these feelings in a succinct manner. Without the use of the soliloquy or comparable conventions, we would have to observe the characters in many more circumstances to understand their feelings. An example of the soliloquy is Hamlet's speech, "To be or not to be."

The aside, popular in late nineteenth and early twentieth-century melodramas, allows a character to talk only to the audience so that the other characters on stage "cannot hear" what is said. Often during an aside, the characters not speaking "freeze" until the actor delivering the lines finishes. Often the villain in melodramas would reveal in an aside how, for instance, he planned to dupe the heroine into signing over all her worldly possessions to him.

A comparable convention is the type of monologue (long speech) in which a character speaks directly to the audience, as does the Stage Manager in *Our Town,* when he describes Grover's Corners, New Hampshire. One character also may have a monologue in speaking to another character. Generally, this type of monologue reveals feelings. An example is Edmund's monologue in Eugene O'Neill's *Long Day's Journey into Night,* in which he tells his feelings about the sea.

> You've just told me some high spots in your memories. Want to hear mine? They're all connected with the sea. Here's one. When I was on the *Squarehead* square rigger, bound for Buenos Aires. Full moon in the Trades. The old hooker driving fourteen knots. I lay on the bowsprit, facing astern, with the water foaming into spume under me, the masts with every sail white in the moonlight, towering high above me. I became drunk with the beauty and singing rhythm of it, and for a moment I lost myself—actually lost my life. I was set free! I dissolved in the sea, became white sails and flying spray, became beauty and rhythm, became moonlight and the ship and the high dim-starred sky! I belonged without past or future, within peace and unity and a wild joy, within something greater than my own life, or the life of Man, to Life itself! To God, if you want to put it that way. Then another time, on the American Line, when I was lookout on the crow's nest in the dawn watch. A calm sea, that time. Only a lazy ground swell and a slow drowsy roll of the ship. The passengers asleep and none of the crew in sight. No sound of

Soliloquy a theatrical convention in which a character thinks aloud, revealing his innermost thoughts.

Aside a speech delivered directly to the audience by a character in a play; supposedly, the other characters on stage are unable to hear what is said.

Monologue a long speech delivered by a character in a play, either to the audience or to other characters.

Flashback a theatrical convention in which the audience, through the eyes of a character in a play, is able to see scenes from the past before the time in which the play exists.

Exposition any background information necessary to the understanding of a play; it may be presented through dialogue, setting, and properties.

An actress speaks directly to the audience in this production of *Sexual Perversity in Chicago* at the Marquis Public Theatre in San Diego. Director, Tavis Ross; set design and lights, Bette Ogami. *(Photo by Wanda T. Robin.)*

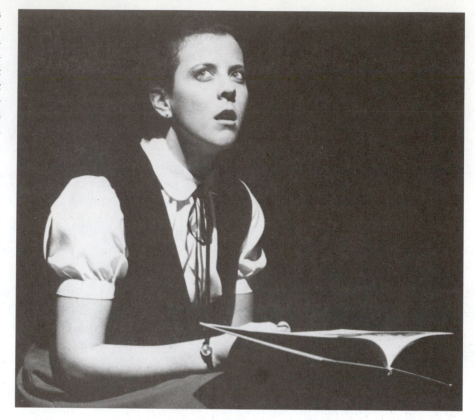

man. Black smoke pouring from the funnels behind and beneath me. Dreaming, not keeping lookout, feeling alone, and above, and apart, watching the dawn creep like a painted dream over the sky

Long Day's Journey into Night
Eugene O'Neill, 1940

The play tells how the past affects the Tyrone family. James Tyrone, who neglected serious acting to become a matinee idol, regrets what he has done but cannot change it. Poor as a child, he now uses his money to buy worthless land rather than to hire good physicians for his younger son and his wife. Mary has become a drug addict after a quack physician gave her drugs. She lost her first baby and spent months in a hospital. Jamie, the elder son and now an actor, is a cynical alcoholic. Edmund, the younger son, recently returned home from the sea, is ill with what the family fears is consumption. As the play progresses, Jamie and James drink heavily and dredge up hurtful memories of the past. Edmund learns he must enter a sanitorium. Mary, who has promised to stop taking drugs, actually is taking them secretly. As the play ends, she appears carrying her wedding dress, attempting to recover the past.

and sea which slept together. Then the moment of ecstatic freedom came. The peace, the end of the quest, the last harbor, the joy of belonging to a fulfillment beyond man's lousy, pitiful, greedy fears and hopes and dreams! And several other times in my life, when I was swimming far out, or lying alone on a beach, I have had the same experience. Became the sun, the hot sand, green seaweed anchored to a rock, swaying in the tide. Like a saint's vision of beatitude. Like the veil of things as they seem drawn back by an unseen hand. For a second you see—and seeing the secret, are the secret. For a second there is meaning! Then the hand lets the veil fall and you are alone, lost in the fog again, and you stumble on toward nowhere, for no good reason.
(He grins wryly.)
It was a great mistake, my being born a man. I would have been much more successful as a seagull or a fish. As it is, I will always be a stranger who never feels at home, who does not really want and is not really wanted, who can never belong, who must always be a little in love with death![9]

Flashbacks are similar to soliloquies or monologues in that they can show the feelings of the character. They can also provide exposition, background information necessary to the audience's understanding of a play, and condense or expedite the story. A flashback is a "scene" that occurred before the play's action begins. Most often the audience members are asked to imagine that they can "see" what a character is thinking as the remembered scene appears on stage. Miller's *Death of a Salesman* contains a number of flashbacks, including the times when Willie imagines Biff and Happy are young again.

An audience knows that events progress faster on the stage than they do in real life. **Dramatic time,** as opposed to chronological time, means that on stage people express their thoughts more explicitly and concisely than people do in everyday life. They leave out unnecessary and distracting details, which ordinarily intrude on conversations. This convention is another means of condensing action. In *Oedipus Rex*, for example, we learn all the events that preceded the action of the play, from Oedipus' infancy to marrying his mother; yet the play takes place in less than a day's time.

An audience will accept almost any character or event if it is in the proper framework. For instance, in *R.U.R.* Karel Čapek portrays a society in which robots exist. In *Motel* van Itallie uses papier-mâché characters that are grotesque caricatures of human beings. Shakespeare introduces ghosts and witches into his plays. The audience is willing to accept these devices because a framework has been established in which they can exist. Only when the author deviates from that framework does a play become unbelievable. For instance, if van Itallie suddenly introduced flesh-

Dramatic time the amount of time represented by a play; an hour onstage may represent any amount of time, although more time usually is represented as having passed than the actual two hours or so it takes to present a play.

---

[9]Eugene O'Neill, *Long Day's Journey into Night* (New Haven: Yale University Press, 1955), pp. 53–54. Reprinted with permission.

Oedipus Rex

Sophocles, c. 425 B.C.

The people of Thebes, stricken by a terrible plague, gather in prayer. King Oedipus assures them he is doing what he can to find what is causing the plague. He has sent his brother-in-law, Creon, to the oracle at Delphi to find out what to do. Creon returns and says that once the murderer of the former king, Laius, is found and exiled, the plague will end. Oedipus consults the prophet Tiresias, who tells him that Oedipus himself is the man who killed Laius. Oedipus protests, and Tiresias further warns that the king is unclean because he is guilty of incest. Alone with his wife, Jocasta, Oedipus tells her he fears that he may indeed be his father's murderer because once he did kill a man who tried to force him off a roadway. He says that he once had a prophecy from Delphi that he would murder his father and marry his mother. Jocasta comforts him, saying that Laius was murdered by a band of robbers. As proof, she summons an old herdsman, the last survivor of the fight in which Laius died. Instead of confirming Jocasta's story, the herdsman admits that Oedipus is the murderer. He also recognizes Oedipus as Jocasta's son, whom he had saved as a baby. Upon hearing the news, Jocasta kills herself and Oedipus puts out his eyes. He appears blinded before the citizens of Thebes and asks to be exiled in fulfillment of the curse placed on the killer of Laius.

and-blood characters into *Motel*, the play would become unbelievable, because a framework already is established in which human caricatures appear.

The events depicted in Shakespeare's *Timon of Athens* would take much more time to transpire than the time it takes to present the play. Director, Eric Christmas; set and costume design, Peggy Kellner. *(Photo by Bill Reid and courtesy of the Old Globe Theatre.)*

Production Conventions

Modern audiences accept many conventions connected with the physical production. For instance, the **setting** is one convention. An audience knows that the living room that appears on stage is not a living room at all but made up of a series of **flats** positioned to bring about a certain effect. They know that nobody's living room is arranged like the one on stage. In a real house furniture is closer together to conserve space. The audience knows that the room on stage is much larger than the one in most homes.

The audience knows that many times a performer uses a property that appears to be the real object but is not. The diamond ring may be a piece of costume jewelry. The letter is only a piece of blank paper. The pistol fires blanks and does not really harm anyone.

The audience also realizes that the lighting is artificial sunlight or moonlight, and that in real life there are more shadows than we see on a stage. The lights on the stage are brighter than those we use at home, and they illuminate a larger area. The audience knows, too, that actors usually wear more makeup than does the person we meet on the sidewalk.

Setting the environment or physical background for a play; the visual symbol of a play.

Flat a frame constructed of one-by-three boards, covered with canvas, painted, and used most often for interior or exterior walls of a building in a stage setting.

Setting is a theatrical convention. *The Basic Training of Pavlo Hummel* was presented at the University of Hawaii, under the direction of Glen Cannon. The set designer was Richard Mason. *(Photo by Francis Haar, and courtesy of University of Hawaii.)*

Throughout history the theatre has been a blending of the talents, artistry, and ideas of many individuals working to bring all the elements of the form together for an audience. Theatre therefore continually evolves, and in that lies its magic and excitement, whether it was the excitement of seeing Shakespeare's new play performed by his company, the King's Men, at the Globe Theatre outside of London during the reign of Elizabeth I, or of witnessing a production of the musical *Mame* where the sets slide on and off stage and a circular staircase twirls around to reach its proper spot.

QUESTIONS FOR DISCUSSION

1. In what ways does theatre approximate life?
2. How is theatre more specific in its communication than are some other art forms?
3. How can theatre help us understand ourselves?
4. What is the relationship of imitation and ritual to theatre?
5. What is the meaning of the statement: "Theatre differs from static arts in that it is temporal"?
6. How does theatre differ from other art forms?
7. In what ways is theatre a combination of art forms?
8. In what ways is theatre a part of our everyday lives?
9. Why does theatre continually evolve?
10. How does the concept of universality apply to theatrical productions?
11. Why is a printed script often not considered an art form in itself?
12. What are drama's essential ingredients?
13. What are the requirements of a story play?
14. What are the six elements, according to Aristotle, that a drama should contain? How is each important?
15. What are theatrical conventions? What purpose do they serve?

SUPPLEMENTARY READING

PLAYS
Ghosts by Henrick Ibsen.
Hair, with book and lyrics by Gerome Ragni and James Rado; music by Galt MacDermot.
Sticks and Bones by David Rabe
The Subject Was Roses by Frank D. Gilroy.
West Side Story, with book by Arthur Laurents, lyrics by Stephen Sondheim, and music by Leonard Bernstein.

BOOKS

Bentley, Eric. *The Theatre of Commitment and Other Essays.* New York: Atheneum, 1967.

Matthews, Brander, ed. *Papers on Playmaking.* New York: Hill and Wang, Inc., 1957.

CHAPTER 2
The Audience

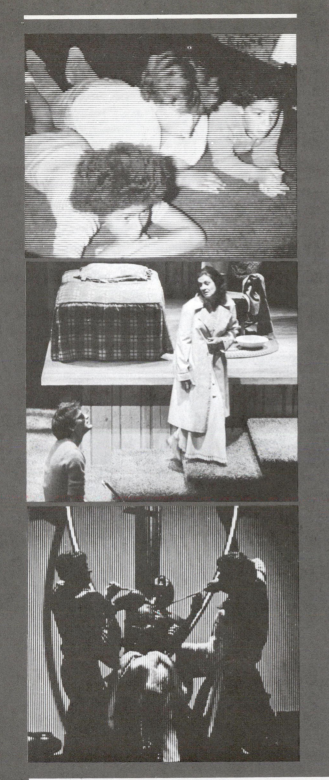

There is an unknown in every theatre presentation: the direct contact between artist and spectator. Even with the same script, setting, and performers, a play differs from night to night. Not only do the performers' attitudes and actions change, but the audience changes as well. Each audience differs from the next; each brings new expectations and attitudes. The result is a different flow between the stage and auditorium. For artists and performers alike, this aspect of going to the theatre is most striking.

Often in the final stages of rehearsal a show is technically near-perfect but lacks life. In most cases, fortunately, the audience supplies the sparkle. Spectators often are surprised to hear this fact. Many of them believe that a production will be the same each time, except that it may continue subtly to improve. This is not the case at all: The performers need the response from the audience as much as the audience needs the flow from the actors. Many times a performer or technician will refer to a "dead house" or ask: "Was anyone really out there?" The size of an audience affects the flow of communication to a certain degree, but even two audiences of the same size will react much differently during two nights of a play's run.

According to the late Noel Coward, a British actor and playwright, "You've got to listen to the audience's reaction, because audiences, as you know, vary at every performance."

The audience has a great effect on an actor's performance. Madeline McGuire appears in a scene from *Sexual Perversity in Chicago* at the Marquis Public Theatre in San Diego. The play was directed by Tavis Ross with set design by Bette Ogami. (*Photo by Wanda T. Robin.*)

A rehearsal shot of *Sugar*, presented by the Little Theatre of Tuscarawas County, Ohio, under the direction of Jill Lynn. *(Photo by Bill Douds.)*

Sometimes you have an equal number of people, one night they're a lot of cods' heads, the next night they're marvelous; and you have to know how to handle them. If they are dull, then you've got to be a little quicker; if they're warm and very responsive, you've got to catch yourself, otherwise they'll lead you astray and make you over-play. In fact, I believe that all acting is a question of control, the control of the actor of himself, and through himself of the audience.[1]

The Importance of an Audience

The direct flow of feeling between audience and artist is what sets theatre and other live arts apart, even from film or television. The immediate presence of performer and audience member has a great effect on both. Philip Burton, stepfather of Richard Burton, and himself an actor, director, and theatre teacher, said once that "unless an actor is able to present a truly imagined and felt character, he is unlikely to hold an audience,

[1]Hal Burton, ed., *Great Acting*. (New York: Bonanza Books, 1967), p. 165.

but there must always be a part of him instinctively sensitive to his effect on the audience and ready to spring into action when he feels he has lost or is losing them."[2] If a production fails to come up to the expectations of either the audience or of the performers, there are certain to be negative results. Each has to feel appreciated. Each has to respect the other. The presence of both audience and performer alters what each one does.

To be successful a theatre production should appeal to the emotions of the audience. In many presentations the audience empathizes or relates to the characters and becomes involved with their struggles and conflicts. In this production of *I Never Sang for My Father* the audience could easily relate to the emotions being portrayed. *(Photo by Gary Anderson of* The Coshocton Tribune *and courtesy of Footlight Players of Coshocton, Ohio.)*

The fact that the production is live and immediate gives theatre its appeal. Audiences enjoy the direct contact with the performers. Those associated with the arts of film, television, and recording recognize the audiences' need for direct contact with the performers. This need accounts for the many personal appearances stars make. To maintain their popularity they must have direct contact with their fans.

Theatre critic Eric Bentley observes that film has many of the same qualities as theatre, including a theatre building, actors, and an audience; but he adds:

[2]Philip Burton, *Early Doors: My Life and the Theatre* (New York: The Dial Press, Inc., 1969), p. 165.

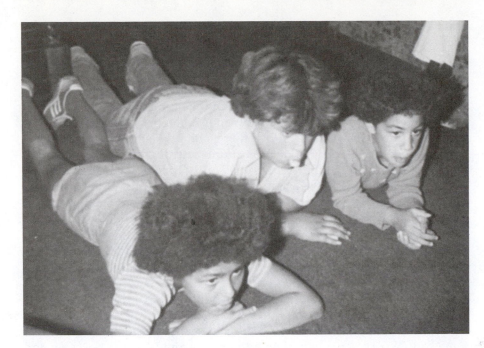

Children enjoy experiencing many forms of theatre, including television. *(Photo by James D. Kitchen.)*

No current flows from celluloid to audience—or, at any rate, no current flows from audience to celluloid. In the movie theatre, we can watch a story and we can admire many things that actors do, but we cannot be caught up in a flow of living feeling that passes from actor to audience and from the audience back again to the actor.

For example, Bentley explains, in the theatre the audience can catch an actor's smile, throw it back, and have it return to them again. This interplay is impossible with a film.[3]

Similarly, it is impossible with television, in spite of various attempts, to simulate live performances. In the early days most television shows were performed "live" before a studio audience. This method had several disadvantages. Despite the live response from those in the studio, the home viewers realized that for them the performance was not live, and they even subconsciously resented it. Moreover, viewers saw shows "raw" and full of mistakes.

Later shows were filmed and still later taped. This method worked better, in that the performances could be more polished. Still, there was something lacking—the response of an audience. The solution was

---

[3]Eric Bentley, *The Theatre of Commitment and Other Essays* (New York: Atheneum, 1967), pp. 59–60. Reprinted by permission of the author.

"canned" or recorded laughter, which was played back during the sequences that those in charge of the production felt would be the funniest. Then critics objected that it is impossible to anticipate at exactly what points a live audience will laugh and how much.

Later still television performances began to be taped before a studio audience. This approach works better than the original "live" productions because the director can tape the show more than once and take the best segments from each taping. Now there are problems in mingling responses from a number of audiences and in catching little inconsistencies of appearance. During a broadcast of *All in the Family*, for instance, shots of Carroll O'Connor showed first that the second button of his shirt was open and then that it was closed. Apparently, for one of the tapings he had worn his costume one way and for the second another way.

Despite attempts to imitate theatre, television is a different medium. Whereas theatre changes from performance to performance, a rebroadcast of a television program is exactly the same the second time as it was the first. Audience responses differ, but the performers whose images appear on the screen have no way of altering what they have done. Performers in live theatre can change what they do.

Actors change before an audience in many ways, some good and some bad. Novice actors who know their lines and blocking perfectly and who have developed a highly believable characterization may "fall apart" when they sense the presence of the "many-legged monster." On the other hand, the presence of an audience often spurs the actors to an excellence in performance they never thought possible. It stimulates them to a greater degree of feeling and communication than they could otherwise experience.

An audience before a show is usually only a collection of individuals. Only later do they take on a specific character. *(Photo courtesy of Montclair State College.)*

When asked if a performance depends on the audience's reaction, Julie Andrews said: "It's almost the biggest part of the challenge. Nobody knows you were good last night except the people who were there. So each night is entirely new and must be good."[4]

The Audience Affects Itself

An audience affects not only the performers but also itself. Whether we call the phenomenon "reinforcement" or "mob psychology," being a part of a group affects each of our personalities. To a certain extent we lose our own identities and inhibitions. Many things we would never consider doing by ourselves we undertake with no hesitation as a part of a group.

In a group we somehow sense what we want and what direction we will take, although our purpose or response may not be fully defined before we join with others. As a group we are willing to experience more of a release of our emotions than we generally will by ourselves or with one or two others. As the French theatre critic Francisque Sarcey puts it: "A crowd laughs more heartily and boisterously than an individual. Tears are readier and more abundant with an audience than with a single man."[5] "An audience . . . feels more keenly than the individuals composing it. It enters more impetuously into the reasons for weeping than the poet gives it; the grief that it experiences is more intense."[6]

That is why, for instance, it is difficult to appreciate a theatre performance if there are few members in an audience or even if they are isolated from one another. Eric Bentley describes it:

> There is something about an audience—that is, about a group of people in close physical proximity with their faces all pointing one way, and their attention—their eyes, ears, hearts and minds—focused upon a single object. There is something about ceasing to be merely an *I* and becoming, under such circumstances, in this *place*, before that *actor*, a part of *we*. There is something about the cosiness and sociability of the whole physical setup. And possibly—though one hesitates to believe it—there is something about its uncosiness, unsociability and positive discomfort.

Despite a lack of knee room and a "shortage of lobby space," Bentley says, "the fact is familiar: an experience is charged by being shared in such company in such a manner." It is then that "the joke *I* impercep-

[4]Roy Newquist, *Showcase* (New York: William Morrow & Co., Inc., 1966), p. 41.

[5]Francisque Sarcey, "A Theory of the Theatre," H. H. Hughes, trans., *Papers on Playmaking*, Brander Matthews, ed., (New York: Hill and Wang, 1957), p. 125.

[6]Sarcey, p. 129.

tibly smile at alone in my study, *we* perceptibly grin at, we perhaps all 'roar' at, in the theatre.''

What's the matter, are we drunk? Boastful—wishing to show off our sociability? Polite—as one would laugh more loudly at a joke made by the president of the board? The less respective motives no doubt enter in, as we are so directly under the noses of our fellow men, so mercilessly exposed and therefore bound to be on our ''best'' behavior; but it is not chiefly the atmosphere of a full theatre, the psychology of *we*, that has put us at our ease, and caused a great deal of good feeling to pour out of us that we would normally suppress. That is, if we felt it in the first place; for much of the good feeling is created by the occasion, by the psychology of *we*. Or perhaps, more accurately, still, while initiated by the *actor* and the *place*, such feeling is constantly *increased* by the occasion, by the psychology of *we*. One speaks of ''infectious enthusiasm,'' and the enjoyment of an audience is a positive contagion.[7]

A smart usher or house manager knows that the spectators are more likely to respond to a performance if they are seated close to each other and close to the performers. If there are several rows of empty seats directly in front of the stage, the members of the audience will tend to retain some of their individual inhibitions. For the audience to merge the members must experience physical closeness.

In the past it often was the practice to hire professional spectators or ''plants'' to attempt to lead the audience to more unrestrained laughter or applause than would be likely otherwise. It still is common for a director or an actor to tell a friend: ''Be sure to laugh a lot.'' To a certain degree the ploy can work, but sometimes the result is forced artificial feedback from one or two isolated areas of the auditorium. An audience does not want to be led; it wants to be free to develop its own character. For this reason, you may attend two performances of a show's run and find yourself responding much differently each time, perhaps even in spite of what you expected.

In other ways a crowd's reaction is different than an individual's reaction. For instance, many times at sporting events violence erupts or tempers flare. Students are thrown through windows at basketball games or pushed from bleachers at football games. People in the collective perform differently than they would by themselves. On a more positive level, this influence accounts for ''team spirit,'' a feeling of belonging, and the security of knowing we behave as others do. The same bonding happens in a theatre experience. That is why, for example, we often hear a burst of laughter at a line that strikes the audience as funny. The members trust each other. Most responses, then, are group responses and are immediate. We trust the other members of the group to react as we are reacting.

[7]*The Theatre of Commitment*, pp. 56–58. Reprinted by permission of the author.

During a production the audience often feels united. This production of *Poor Murderer* was produced by the Old Globe Theatre and presented at the Cassius Carter Center Stage, San Diego. Director, William Roesch; designer, Kent Dorsey. *(Photo by Clifford Baker and courtesy of the Old Globe Theatre.)*

This group response has to occur for the individual audience member to be an integrated part of the production. Just as a play would lack a certain dimension without a set, costumes, or theatrical lighting, so too would it lack dimension if each of us remained the individual rather than the crowd spectator. There has to be a collaboration to reach the ultimate enjoyment or emotional response. The theatre must and can exist only for everyone involved.

If a performance "works," there is a closeness among those involved. Strangers will talk more easily with each other after the final curtain than they will before the play begins. During the play they have established a common ground by sharing a common experience.

The shared experience includes the performers. We feel closer to an actor whom we see on stage.

The theater gains its natural—and unique—effect not from the mere presence of "live" actors, or the happy accident of an occasional lively audience, but from the existence of a "live" relationship between these two indispensable conspirators, signaling to one another through space. When this exhilarating, intensely demonstrative union takes place the walls of the playhouse can barely contain the spiritual excitement that is bred; actor feeds on audience, audience feeds on actor, a fiery, nourishing pulse races back and forth between them.[8]

As the audience experiences a release of emotions, so do the theatre artists. This shared experience adds to our emotional stability because it reassures us we are part of what is happening around us. We are not isolated. For a time we have allowed our souls to touch those of others; we have experienced a total sharing.

In a theatre production there is a constant flow between the audience and the actors. The script is communicated by the playwright to the other theatre artists and the audience. The theatre artists add their interpretations to the script. During the actual presentation most flow and feedback is between the performers and the spectators.

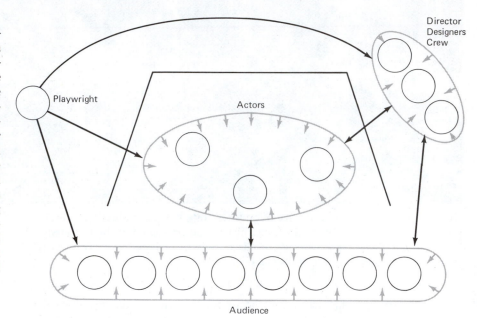

Why Audiences Attend the Theatre

Finding Entertainment

There are various reasons for attending the theatre, but people most often attend for entertainment. Theatre offers them a chance to escape into a make-believe existence and to forget everyday cares. It is a means of relaxation. "From the first it has been the theatre's business to entertain people," playwright Berthold Brecht once said. "It is this business which

[8]Walter Kerr, *The Theater in Spite of Itself* (New York: Simon and Schuster, 1963), p. 68. Reprinted from "What Ails the Theatre," the *Saturday Evening Post*, Dec. 22, 1958.

always gives it its particular dignity; it needs no other passport than fun."[9]

Even though entertainment is the main reason audiences attend the theatre, popular playwrights often are criticized for writing nothing of lasting value. An example is Neil Simon, certainly the most successful contemporary playwright in terms of popularity. His critics complain that his comedies do not say anything, and that in a few years they will be forgotten. Simon's plays do not have deep philosophical or psychological themes, but they need not. Such hits as *California Suite*, *The Sunshine Boys*, *Barefoot in the Park*, and *The Odd Couple* fulfill the audience's need for escapism, as do many other contemporary plays.

Witnessing Change

Another reason for attending the theatre is to learn of recent, present, and imminent change. Theatre, like other arts, not only mirrors the society in which it is produced but often judges the social, economic, and political climate in which it is presented. Henrik Ibsen, the great Norwegian playwright, stated that the artist must be a few years ahead of the average person in thinking. Artists must anticipate what changes will occur in their society. Art gauges the undercurrents of society and predicts the future.

For example, productions such as *Hair*, with its now quite dated issues, led audiences and society toward change. *Hair* foreshadowed what would happen and pointed out changing attitudes about patriotism, the Vietnam conflict, and sex. In essence, the musical is a series of loosely related scenes protesting all sorts of things that seemed "wrong" with established society and its attitudes. Its opening song hails the age of Aquarius, in which love and peace will be the new ruling factors. The play contains a great deal of obscenity, including such songs as "Sodomy," which is just a listing of sexual terminology. The characters advocate the use of marijuana, the burning of draft cards, and the defiance of regulations.

Most theatre productions do not cause change in themselves, but they show what change is likely to occur or already afoot.

Confronting Social Problems

Since World War II, theatre has changed in content and style as it has tried to alert us to the needs of society. For instance, Frank D. Gilroy's *The Subject Was Roses*, produced in 1964, shows the discouragement and disillusionment faced by a young man home from World War II. This

[9]Berthold Brecht, "A Short Organum for the Theatre," John Willet, trans., *Playwrights on Playwriting*, Toby Cole, ed. (New York: Hill and Wang, 1960), p. 74.

A scene from the New York Shakespeare Festival production of *Sticks and Bones* by David Rabe, produced by Joseph Papp. *(Photo courtesy of George Josephs.)*

production foreshadowed the increasing discontent over the Vietnam conflict. A decade later came David Rabe's *Sticks and Bones,* a violent anti-war play that attacks the silliness and hypocrisy of middle-class America. Whereas Gilroy's play uses realistic subject matter, characterization, and dialogue, Rabe's play uses strong new devices: a phantom Vietnamese girl, "present" only in the memory of the returning Vietnam veteran; characters patterned after the Nelson family on the old *Ozzie and Harriet* television show; and dialogue that often is purposely inane or "corny."

Theatre brought forward other social issues by allowing nudity, freedom of expression, and openness of subject matter. Playwrights attempted to make Biblical teachings relevant to modern needs and to get around the traditional church's lack of progress in attracting young people. The result was such plays as *Godspell,* by John-Michael Tebelek based on the book of *Matthew,* and *Jesus Christ, Superstar* by Andrew Lloyd Webber and Tom Rice from an idea by Tom O'Horgan.

At first the theatre often presented problems about isolated individuals or groups far removed from the experiences of the audience. Most of the audience members could empathize with the characters but feel secure in the knowledge that the productions presented someone else's particular troubles. Maybe it would be kind to help, but they could go home after the performance and not worry that the problems would affect them personally.

In recent years, theatre has tried in many ways to come closer to its audience's problems and needs. Earlier plays did not neglect universality or **immediacy,** but more recent theatre has tried consciously to dramatize the concerns of its audience. One group that tried to dramatize the problems of young people was the Living Theatre, popular in the sixties. In its production of *Paradise Now,* the group openly confronted audiences and demanded responses to such issues as war and "establishment" rules. In this respect, of course, the Living Theatre's themes were similar to those of *Hair.* The Open Theatre, under the guidance of Joseph Chaikin, presented such productions as *America Hurrah,* which ridiculed the treatment individuals often receive in impersonal job interviews and protested the disregard we often show for others' property. (See Chapter 1 for a discussion of *Motel,* one of the three one-acts comprising *America Hurrah.*) These two groups received more notice than others that sprang up for a time and presented similar pieces.

Immediacy the quality of a work of art that makes it important or relevant to the time in which it is presented to the public.

Learning about Human Nature

Audiences go to theatre to learn not only about society and its problems, but also about individuals and their personalities. To depict human nature, theatre possesses universality or immediacy. The character Hamlet, for instance, possesses universality; we can understand his hatred and need for revenge. By contrast, the characters of Henrik Ibsen often deal with the immediate concerns of their own time. In *Ghosts,* for example, he portrays Mrs. Alving, a woman who, because divorce was frowned upon at the time, stayed with an unworthy husband, now dead. Written in 1881, the play shows the mental anguish a person may have to suffer in choosing the "safe" route. Mrs. Alving continues to suffer the consequences when she learns that her son Oswald has a venereal disease, inherited from his father. Another ghost remains in the presence of the maid, actually Alving's daughter by another woman. When Oswald tries to have an affair with the maid and then discovers she is his half-sister, the stress causes him to go insane, and he begs his mother to poison him. She cannot.

A scene from *The Royal Hunt of the Sun*. Director, Earl Curtis; scene designer, Louis O. Erdmann. *(Photo courtesy of Kent State University Theatre.)*

Learning from the Past

Audiences seek another kind of learning at the theatre: a play may acquaint us with the past in order to provide new interpretations of the present. Such is the case with Peter Shaffer's *The Royal Hunt of the Sun*, which deals with Pizarro's conquest of the Incas of Peru. Although the play deals with historical events, it also shows what loss of faith can do to us. Pizarro has lost faith in Christianity and wants to believe in the immortality of the Indian emperor, Atahuallpa. The emperor believes that because the Sun is his father, he will be resurrected if he is put to death. Pizarro wants to have faith in Atahuallpa too; but of course, when he kills him, the emperor is not resurrected.

Reaffirming Beliefs

No matter what we stand to learn from a play, the playwright has a better chance of reaching us by beginning with a common premise, something that most potential audience members already believe. For example, if an audience did not feel at the beginning of a production that war is inhumane in some respect, a play with an anti-war theme would have little chance of success.

Audiences sometimes seem to like plays that are nothing more than observations of life. The absurdist movement, which reached its height in

West Side Story

Script by Arthur Laurents, lyrics by Stephen Sondheim, music by Leonard Bernstein; based on an original idea of Jerome Robbins, 1957

Modeled after Shakespeare's *Romeo and Juliet*, the musical tells the tragic love story of Maria and Tony. Leader of the Jets until he turned the position over to Riff, Tony is a New Yorker. The Jets, a white street gang, are determined to keep out Puerto Ricans from their area of Manhattan. The Sharks are Puerto Ricans, determined to dominate their block. The gangs meet at a dance in a neighborhood gym. Tony, still supporting the Jets, goes to the dance and meets Maria, the sister of Bernardo, leader of the Sharks. The two young people fall in love and plan to meet at the bridal shop where Maria works. At the same time the two gangs plan a rumble. Tony persuades them to have just one person from each gang meet to fight the following day. Then Bernardo learns of Tony's and Maria's love and threatens Tony. A major fight ensues, and Tony's friend Riff is killed. Tony, enraged over his friend's death, stabs Bernardo to death with Riff's knife. Then Tony is killed by Chino, Maria's intended husband.

the fifties, stated only that life is absurd. Absurdist plays were reaffirming a belief many people shared, although they had not necessarily thought much about it.

Often an audience is willing to be led in a certain direction but does not want a decision pushed upon it. *In White America*, for instance, implies that something should be done to correct racial prejudice, but it does not try to force any particular action upon the audience. *West Side Story* presents a similar plea for understanding among individuals of different cultural backgrounds by showing how prejudice can destroy. One of the musical's messages is that understanding, caring, and love should begin on an individual basis.

Feeling Emotion

Most important, an audience wants to feel, to experience emotion. The playwright, the designers, and the actors all work together to try to elicit certain responses. A serious play allows empathy or identification more often than does a comedy. There are exceptions, such as the plays of Brecht, which try to keep the audience from identifying with the characters as persons. The purpose is to have the spectators identify more with the situation, and in this way to elicit emotional responses. An example is *Mother Courage and Her Children*.

Usually the spectator feels a wider range of emotions in connection with the characters or situations in a serious play than in a comedy. The latter appeals more to the intellect; it should make us feel, but tie in the feelings with happiness or laughter. The treatment of subject matter often determines whether the play is comic or tragic, or whether the theme is light or serious. Almost any subject can be treated humorously or seri-

Mother Courage and Her Children
Berthold Brecht, 1939

Mother Courage is a traveling merchant who sells to the troops on both sides during the Thirty Years' War. She has learned shrewdness and tenacity to keep her family together and to retain her wagonful of goods, the symbol and actual means of the family's survival. Then Mother Courage loses her entire family as they each become victims of their own heroic actions. Mother Courage herself survives the misfortunes of war and continues to drag her wagon across the battlefields. She never realizes that because she lives off war, she is partly responsible for the deaths of her children.

ously. As we saw in Chapter 1, *Agamemnon* deals tragically with infidelity whereas *Any Wednesday* treats the subject humorously.

Purpose and audience are inseparable in the theatre. An audience brings its own personal viewpoint with it, and this fact accounts for the appeal of plays to particular age groups or segments of society and the wide variety of theatre available today.

Types of Audiences

Every type of play attracts a different audience. There also will be different audiences at certain locations, times, and types of theatres. Those attending a matinee in New York City differ from those attending a Saturday night performance. The former consist largely of women and young people, whereas the latter are businesspeople trying to impress clients, or couples "out on the town."

Across the United States are many types of theatres. Each exists for different reasons, of which audiences generally are aware. (See Chapter 10 for the purposes of various types of theatres.) The type of production that a professional, academic, or community theatre can present in one area of the country may not be acceptable in another. What draws audiences in New York City may leave many empty seats in the South or the Midwest. Moral and sociological outlooks differ from one area to another. A larger city also has a larger potential audience of any particular type from which to draw than does a small community.

Audiences bring all their background, knowledge, and awareness to a theatre production. This experience influences the type of play they want to see. It also colors their perceptions of the performance. They, like the theatre artists, interpret. For this reason, a play may be a success in one area or even for one audience and a failure for another.

The theatre itself can influence or educate the audience. For example, members of community theatres often complain that the audience will not accept unusual endeavors. Maybe so, but the theatre members can gradually raise the standards of the spectators, if they wish.

Engaging the Audience

Symbols in the Theatre

Because theatre is not life but an *approximation of life,* the spectators, as well as the theatre artists, must free their imaginations. They have to realize that the theatre is made up of **symbols,** and nothing in it is "real."

Just as any form of communication involves a series of symbols that make up a code, so theatre shows us the outer manifestations of feelings, beliefs, and ideas. If someone expresses love for you, you can never know exactly what that means. You have to rely on your own feelings and project them to the person speaking. If a person mentions a fence around a backyard, you can only call upon your own memories of fences to understand the meaning. Even if you see the fence, you perceive it in the light of your own background. You are forced to interpret, using your own experience.

You also interpret in the theatre, where symbolism is carried even further. You must push to the back of your mind the fact that in the musical *George M,* the man singing "Give My Regards to Broadway" is not really George M. Cohan, upon whose life the musical is based, but only a symbol of the man. Moreover, the play itself is the result of various people's collaboration on one interpretation of the high spots of Cohan's entire life.

Although they are asked to imagine, spectators have a right to expect that the presentation will help them free their imaginations and lose themselves. Just as we can cry over the heroine's death in a novel, we can experience strong emotion over the "death" of a character in a play, when intellectually we know that nobody has actually died.

When attending a performance of *The Diary of Anne Frank,* we may empathize strongly with Anne because we know she will die. We realize that the play is based on incidents that did occur, and there is a strong basis for our emotion. At the same time we realize that the events depicted occurred while this young Jewish girl hid from the Nazis during World War II, and the performers are only symbols of the actual occurrence.

When we attend the theatre, we know that there has to be a certain amount of background information to introduce us to the characters and situations. We expect such exposition along with other theatre conventions, but still rightly expect to become involved in the production. All the conventions and symbols do become real if we allow them, and if the production has been well planned and presented.

Symbol one thing that stands for another. In the theatre the setting and lights, for instance, represent a background or environment for the action, while the actors symbolize the characters in the play.

Aesthetic Distance

On the other hand, the symbols and conventions should not become too
real. There should be a balance between empathy and **aesthetic distance.**
We identify with characters and situations but still maintain a detachment
from them, so that we can appreciate the beauty of the art form. If we
did not, the play would no longer be a work of art. It would be life; it
would involve us too directly. We would suffer too much or worry too
much or try to offer our help to the actors. Just as there must be a balance
between the artistic and the technical, there must be a balance between
our involvement and our noninvolvement. With part of our minds we
accept what we see as real, but another part keeps us from "preventing a
catastrophe" or "rescuing" a character in trouble.

An audience at a play knows that what is presented on stage is not life but only
an imitation of life. However, the spectators usually identify and empathize with
the characters. The actors, though, can't identify so strongly with a role that they
lose emotional control of their performance. A proper balance between empathy
and aesthetic distance must be maintained as in the case of this performance of
The Ghost Sonata. Director, Kjell Amble; scene designer, Don Powell. (*Photo courtesy of San Diego State University—Dramatic Arts Department.*)

Actors recognize the need for a balance between empathy and aesthetic distance. Noel Coward describes it:

> If you're playing a very strong scene, a moving scene, there is a moment at rehearsal when your words are clear, when you know it very well and it's beginning to flow, there is a moment when you really feel it. This is a very important moment. You cry, you overplay, but you have genuinely felt it. From then onwards until the opening night you have to begin to eliminate, because you cannot afford really to feel, when you're playing eight performances a week, and you're going to give the public their money's worth. Also it is not acting.[10]

In some cases the performers encourage audience participation in a production. Often in children's theatre, the actors want the spectators to warn the hero of impending doom or to boo the villain. During the sixties and seventies there was a move toward involving audiences directly in many productions. Performers sometimes brought audience members to the stage or went into the seating area to talk with them. They were attempting to break down the barrier between audience and actor, to make the spectators experience stronger emotion, or to make theatre more relevant to them as individuals. In many cases this attempt failed because it disturbed the balance between empathy and aesthetic distance. Such experiments sometimes failed, too, because they did not separate art and life. At other times members of an audience felt uncomfortable and embarrassed when asked to assume a role themselves.

The Performance Group tried to involve audiences in the action of *Dionysus in '69*, loosely based on *The Bacchae* by the Greek playwright Euripides. The production was presented in a converted garage in New York City, and the audience was encouraged to sit wherever they wished. At times the performers, in small groups, caressed spectators and involved them in singing and dancing during open rehearsals. The play involved nudity, and audience members also were encouraged to disrobe. Later, the actors themselves began to feel inhibited by audience participation.

There are many ways to reach an audience other than direct participation. The play can strike home in theme, character, or situation. Maybe the playwright has thought through a matter more than most others have. Maybe the playwright challenges the audience to reexamine values, or entertains them by building suspense or making them laugh. What the play communicates must seem important in some way to the audience, even if it is only to relieve tension through laughter.

[10]*Great Acting*, p. 166.

Audience Responsibilities

Learning about Theatre

While the theatre artists do their best to reach them, the audience has half a contract to fulfill. Most important, the spectators have the responsibility of becoming acquainted with theatre. Only in this way can they understand it as an art form. An important aspect of understanding is experiencing. When we become more familiar with something unknown, we generally lose our fear and begin to appreciate it. We are interested in more varied types of theatre presentations once we understand them. The following chapters explain the work that goes into bringing a theatrical production before an audience. They deal with the various elements of a production and how they can be integrated. They discuss some of the rules of the "painter's canvas" of theatre. All of this theory and explanation will take you halfway: for complete understanding and appreciation, you have to experience theatre at first hand.

To pursue theatre as an art form, take as many opportunities as possible to experience a live production. Attend a variety of plays, from current tragicomedy to Elizabethan tragedy. Only in this way can anyone learn to judge the worth of a production; and the more effectively you can judge, the more you can enjoy. A play does not have to be a light comedy to give the audience a good feeling; a well written and well produced tragedy can give equal pleasure.

Paying Attention

An audience also is responsible for paying attention to the total production. The theatre artists are responsible for integrating the production so that no element stands out; the audience should then appreciate the combined elements as a totality.

Because the audience does bring much more than its physical presence to a theatre, it may be difficult at times to view the production without other things getting in the way. There are literally dozens of outside forces that compete for our attention all the time. Maybe we have a headache or are tired. The seat may be hard, the building too warm or cold, or the traffic outside annoying. Most of the time we can block out these annoyances so that they exist only below the level of consciousness. Of course, if our shoes are too tight or have rubbed blisters on our heels, the demand for attention is stronger; but we should try to become involved in the production.

Mental attitudes also compete for attention and affect our theatre experience. We could be worried, angry, or excited about an upcoming event. These feelings affect our ability to concentrate. Maybe we do not like a particular performer, a style of set design, or the physical layout of the theatre. All of these opinions can detract from the total experience.

Still it is up to us as audience members to do everything we can to make our theatre experience worthwhile.

Evaluating the Production

The audience must do its best to enjoy, but it also must discriminate between theatre that is good or bad, mediocre or outstanding. The quality of any type of art involves subjective judgment to some degree, but there are rules that apply to any art form. Occasionally, these rules are broken deliberately to add a new dimension to the production of a play. An audience member should be able to judge when they are broken for effect and when the production has been poorly conceived and executed.

As audience members, we should maintain a balance between pleasure and analytical judgment. A professional theatre critic, for instance, can enjoy an evening at the theatre and later pick out high spots and flaws. It would be rare for an entire production to have no missed lighting cues or altered lines. People are human; they make mistakes. The errors should not be the focal point of a production, unless they occur in abundance.

Asking Productive Questions

It is easy to say we like or dislike something, but it is more difficult to analyze why we feel as we do. To help us in the analysis we can ask ourselves certain questions.

First, is the play easily understandable? Are you able to follow the playwright's thinking, the director's interpretation? Does the play have meaning? Many times a production has a strong emotional appeal or "gut feeling" and defies analysis. Such a production can be successful because it affects us emotionally and changes us in some way, whether by adding knowledge, reinforcing our thinking, or swaying us to a particular side of a social problem. On the other hand, some plays are easy to follow. We have no difficulty in understanding the plot of *Hello, Dolly* by Michael Stewart and Jerry Herman, a love story about a widow who is a matchmaker. She is able to match young men and women happily but has difficulty in finding happiness for herself. The play is entertaining and should make the audience happier for having seen it. It is only when the audience's response is confused or there appears to be no message in the play that either the script or the production is unsuccessful.

Next, did we find the production entertaining, or would we have gained more by staying home and reading an essay on the subject? Was it significant? Was it a true and honest depiction of a theme, a character, or a situation?

We should consider how well the artists each carried out their responsibilities, and how well their efforts were coordinated with the total production. No one element should stand out, but we can be aware of

This review of a San Diego production appeared in the bi-weekly newspaper *Update*. (Reprinted by permission of *Update*, Kevin P. Mullin.)

Devour the Guilt

That our sense of morality, our concept of what is acceptable and what is not acceptable behavior, is imposed upon us by the prevailing "system", can be clearly demonstrated by a number of fairly common examples. Although killing another human being is a crime not to be tolerated under everyday circumstances, mass slaughters are not only accepted but encouraged during wartimes, and while society continues to "frown upon" homosexual behavior, there are "special circumstances" (in prison, or during long and isolated confinements of other natures) where the taboo is conveniently set aside.

There is a catch. Re-entry into "normal" society requires a cleansing process comprised of remorse and, generally, proof that some new arbitrary line has not been crossed. ("I only killed the people I had to kill." "I didn't actually *enjoy* having sex with any of those guys.")

Abe Polsky's *Devour the Snow*, currently being presented in a finely crafted production by the Marquis Public Theater, examines just such a re-entry process after an extraordinary set of circumstances forces a group of forty-eight people into cannibalism. Based on fact, the play is set in 1847 in Sutter's Fort, just outside what is now Sacramento. Ten days have passed since the final survivor of the Donner Party wagon train, trapped high in the Sierra Nevada Mountains for five months by an unexpected snowstorm, has returned. Met with recriminations, on-the-sly charges of murder, and horrific accounts of the relish with which he devoured his "victims", Lewis Keseberg brings fellow party members Eddy and Foster to trial for slander in an attempt to clear his name and start his life afresh.

What results, instead, is a series of wound-opening revelations that leave no one unscarred.

Kent Brisby has directed this play with a calculated dream-like texture that allows the players to slip in and out of a recurring nightmare: Peter A. Jacobs as James Reed, one of the party's leaders whose series of faulty choices was responsible for the tragedy, is an exceptional study in forced reserve, modulating his voice and actions faultlessly to cover the depths of his own guilt; Barry Schear nervously hides Foster's sins until he is forced to reveal them in a breathtaking breakdown; and Kim McCallum is quite simply mesmerizing as Keseberg, wrestling with his past and future, his soul and his sanity in a virtuoso performance.

Quality is a constant within the rest of the cast: Paul L. Nolan, Howard Muhleman, John Warriner, Paty Sipes, Kimberly Garland and Josie Retsch, with only Bill Dunnam missing the rich ensemble. While his character, Fallon, is in every way intended to be an outsider within this dream, Dunnam appears to be the creation of another dreamer altogether in another, far more modern time. The tricks that served him so well in *Who's Happy Now?* are out of place here.

Joseph Dana's beautiful and simple sets and costumes, and Nancy Godfrey's superb lighting design (including a perfectly timed blood-red sunset) are artfully executed examples of technical craft.

Devour the Snow is an unforgettable experience.

—*Kevin P. Mullin*

each element. We can concentrate momentarily on the acting, the scenery, the direction given the actors. How well do they stand up to the production as a whole? How well are they carried out individually, in light of their purpose?

We should ask ourselves how well the production stands up as a whole. How does it compare with other productions we have seen? Does it meet our expectations of what a comedy, for instance, should be? How does it compare with what we expect of theatre as a whole?

In making the comparison, we should analyze the play's impact. Was it a worthwhile production? Was it worth the effort it took to write and produce? We can begin to judge the worth by analyzing the truth of what the playwright says. Is the viewpoint honest? If not, why not? What in the play made us feel the phoniness? Was it the script itself or an element of the production? If it was the fault of the production, what could or should be changed to bring across the writer's message more effectively? If it was the script, what was poor about the writing?

Another question we can ask ourselves is whether or not the production was consistent. Were the characters well drawn, both by the writer and by the performers? If not, what contributed to the weaknesses, and how were they made apparent? Did the action of the play progress in a logical manner, or were there distracting or jarring elements in the writing or production? How could these elements be changed or eliminated? Did the play seem probable?

Next we can consider the significance of the play. Of course, plays are written for different reasons; but in a serious play, was the message of significance to us? How? If it was not significant, why not? Why would a playwright write a play with little significance? Or was it that the theatre made a poor choice in judging its audience? Maybe the play would be important to others, but not to us. We should be able to figure out why the play left us cold, and why it might have worth for others. In the case of a comedy or farce, was it really entertaining? Was its entertainment value the basis of its significance to us? Why or why not?

What comic devices were used? Were they used effectively by the writer and the performers? Comedy requires good timing. How could that be improved? What about the overall pace and rhythm of the production? Did they fit the mood?

Did the director and performers understand what the playwright wanted? Did their interpretation fit our ideas of the play? Did it contribute to our understanding of the play? Did it bring out subtleties of plot and characterization?

Did the play hold our attention? Were we really interested in the ideas, the story, the plot, the characterization? What did not interest us? Why? A major goal of an audience member is entertainment, and to be entertained we must lose ourselves in the story. We must be able to concentrate and suspend our disbelief. If we could not, why not? What distracted us or failed to interest us at the beginning? Was it the basic premise or some other flaw in the writing?

We should be able to sum up everything by asking whether the production dealt with universal feelings, traits, ideas, or characteristics. If not, was it at least timely? Is it important right now? How do we think it will be viewed by audiences in ten years, in fifteen, in fifty, in a hundred?

Most important, how did we feel about the production later? Are we glad we saw it, and would we want to see it again? Theatre does not have to be a one-time experience. Each time we view a painting or listen to a record album we can grow to love it more. Do you feel the production you saw is as worthy as a favorite painting or a favorite piece of music? Any outstanding book should stay with us after we have read it. We want to think about it more fully to assimilate the ideas it contains. Such should be the case with a theatre production. If the play is a comedy, we should remember the funny lines or situations with fondness. Any play should leave us with positive feelings about ourselves, about others, and about the production.

Many times a beginning theatre student will say: "I can never enjoy a play anymore because I keep watching to see how well the actors are doing their jobs, or how many mistakes the lighting people will make." We should be aware of these matters, but we also should learn to watch the total production, and not be concerned exclusively with techniques.

Theatre is a unique form of art. From the beginning it has evolved and changed. There always was and always will be experimentation with new forms and new techniques. During the change the bad is weeded from the good. We should learn to appreciate theatre so that we can judge it for ourselves and so help to eliminate the poorer aspects.

We must understand the unique qualities of theatre and appreciate them. We must realize that each time we see a play it is in a new form that never can be exactly duplicated. We must understand that it took a large number of people to present this art form to us. We must understand that when we view a production, we become one with the artists and other audience members.

We should remember too that an audience can influence the type of production presented. It can support what it likes and stay away from the kind of theatre that lacks appeal. Just as the audience learns from the theatre artist, so should the artist learn from the audience.

QUESTIONS FOR DISCUSSION

1. Why may it be necessary for actors to alter their performances from night to night?
2. Why do you think each audience develops its own specific character and affects itself?
3. What are the various reasons audiences attend the theatre?

4. Why do you think types of theatrical productions differ from one area of the country to another?
5. Why is it necessary for a spectator at a theatre production to maintain a balance between empathy and aesthetic distance?
6. What are the responsibilities of an audience member?
7. What are some of the criteria for judging a theatre production?

SUPPLEMENTARY READING

PLAYS
Agamemnon by Aeschylus.
The Bald Soprano by Eugène Ionesco.
Death of a Salesman by Arthur Miller.
Hamlet by William Shakespeare.
Motel by Jean-Claude van Itallie.
The Odd Couple by Neil Simon.
Who's Afraid of Virginia Woolf? by Edward Albee.

BOOKS
Aristotle. "The Poetics," *European Theories of the Drama.* Barrett H. Clark, ed., newly revised by Henry Popkin. New York: Crown Publishers, Inc., 1965.

Fergusson, Francis. *The Idea of a Theatre.* Princeton, N. J.: Princeton University Press, 1945.

Lawson, John Howard. *Theory and Technique of Playwriting.* New York: Hill and Wang, Inc., 1960.

Lewis, Allan. *The Contemporary Theatre.* New York: Crown Publishers, Inc., 1962.

Williams, Tennessee. *Where I Live: Selected Essays.* New York: New Directions, 1978.

CHAPTER 3
The Actor

The actor generally symbolizes the theatre for an audience and is the theatre artist with whom the audience most often identifies. At the same time, the actor must rely largely on self to convey his or her art. *(Photo by Isabel Kopp.)*

Just as theatre cannot exist without an audience, it cannot exist without an actor. The actor was the first theatre artist in primitive times and still is the one with whom most audience members identify. When we think of the theatre, we usually think first of the performer, then of the stage, the set design, and all the other elements. Without a doubt the actor provides the glamour and personifies theatre for most audience members. It is the actor with whom the spectators linger to talk after a performance. The performer is the one who is congratulated if the production succeeds.

"If somebody asked me to put in one sentence what acting was," Sir Laurence Olivier, possibly the greatest modern actor, once said, "I should say that acting was the art of persuasion."

The actor persuades himself, first and through himself, the audience. In order to achieve that, what you need to make up your make-up is observation and intuition. At the most high-faluting, the

Performers and their art cannot be separated. Many times performing involves more than assuming a character. Hours of discipline, exercise, training, and rehearsal are prerequisites to performing a dance, such as this in an original play, *Hollywood Heartbreak*, presented by the Trumpet in the Land Company of New Philadelphia, Ohio. *(Photo by Isabel Kopp.)*

actor is as important as the illuminator of the human heart, he is as important as the psychiatrist or the doctor, the minister if you like.[1]

Whereas other artists have canvas and paint, or fabric and light with which to work, actors rely basically on themselves. They have few tools with which to work outside their own bodies. Setting, lights, makeup, and costuming provide accessories, but the actor alone is on display. Painters frame and hang their work at exhibits; musicians record songs; authors publish novels; and in this way they gain the attention of the public. Performers exhibit themselves, making their art one of the most direct and intimate and also one of the most demanding.

A ballerina dances; a vocalist sings; a reader interprets a poem or a piece of prose. Actors often use all the arts of other live performers. Once on the stage they have only their training, background, and concentration upon which to rely. A painting can be changed or even discarded if it fails to meet the artist's standards. Actors have only one given moment to convey a message. They have just one chance at each performance to present their art.

Onstage and Offstage Acting

To convey this message, an actor relies on the mimetic instinct (see Chapter 1). This instinct is a part of each of us, but the stage actor develops the ability to imitate further than does the average person. The actor uses

[1]Hal Burton, ed., *Great Acting*. (New York: Bonanza Books, 1967), p. 23.

aspects of mind and body that each of us possesses, but has the potential and desire to develop them to a higher degree. As Michael Redgrave, an acclaimed British actor, once said: "It is a truism that actors are born and not made; another truism that acting cannot be taught. The basis of all acting is undoubtedly instinctive."[2]

Even if acting is instinctive, the person who successfully plays the role of history student in real life may have difficulty playing the role of a serious history student in a stage production. On the other hand, the stage actor who never studied history may successfully portray such a role, relying on other experiences to "feel" the part. The offstage history student probably has more genuine feelings in the assumption of this role. The student is a real person with real goals of becoming a historian, whereas the actor only presents a symbol of a potential historian.

There are other differences between the two types of "roles." When we see actors in a performance, we can be fairly certain that they always are aware that they are acting, that they are playing to a particular audience. Role playing in real life often is an unconscious deed. We usually are serious about our goals, and therefore we do not consider that class participation or preparation is role playing. A student returning home or to a dormitory does not consciously think, "Now I have to assume the role of friend, roommate, or relative." Actors in a play are more conscious of their surroundings. They remember to move in a certain manner, to use properties in a particular way at a particular time, and always to project their voices to fill a large space. They are aware of body placement, the arrangement of the other actors, and what is expected of each as a part of the total production. Role playing is much more spontaneous. In trying to reach a certain goal, unlike the stage actor, we may have several alternative methods. For the actor, generally, the script is written, the action preplanned, and the work done within a certain framework. There is room for the actor's own creative instincts within that framework, an actor is more aware of fitting into an overall scheme than is a ruthless business tycoon who tramples everyone to reach the top. The actor must consider (except in such rare plays as Beckett's *Krapp's Last Tape*, a one-character show) that constantly to dominate the scene means failure for both the performer and the production.

In talking about the stage actor, actress Helen Hayes, often called the first lady of the American stage, said: "What you're doing on that stage is projecting yourself into someone else entirely, into the mind of the author, into the being of the character. You are trying to settle down to be comfortable in that character and speak the author's words. You are merely an instrument for what he is saying."[3]

[2]Michael Redgrave, *The Actor's Ways and Means* (New York: Theatre Arts Books, 1953), p. 30.

[3]Roy Newquist, *Showcase* (New York: William Morrow & Co., Inc., 1966), pp. 204–05.

Actors often must assume roles alien to themselves. Here an actor portrays an animal in the Old Globe Theatre's production of *A Midsummer Night's Dream*, directed by Jack O'Brien, with costumes by Robert Morgan. *(Photo by Bill Reid and courtesy of the Old Globe Theatre.)*

Despite speaking someone else's words, the stage actor at times can be more honest in the portrayal of a particular role than is the person who plays such a role in real life. Maybe the actor strongly identifies with a character and holds the same ideals and beliefs, whereas in day-to-day life each of us often is guilty of being hypocritical or at least of acting as we assume others want us to act.

Because each of us does possess the rudiments necessary to becoming professional actors, it often is difficult to distinguish acting from role playing. In realistic productions the actor who most successfully conveys the impression of life or of being natural is the most successful. Therefore it may seem that there is little difference between "acting" in life and acting on the stage. However, acting and live theatre are not and can never be life, because it takes a great deal of training and concentration to be able to appear natural on a stage. There is an old cliché: "Everyone thinks he can be a writer." The same is true of acting. Because we each use the mimetic instinct and because stage acting appears to be like life, many people think there is nothing difficult about being an actor. All you have to learn is to speak a little louder, and you can do just as well on the stage as the next person can.

Such a belief is totally wrong. To become an actor requires, first of

Good acting fails to call attention to itself. Roy Bowen directed this production of *Skin of Our Teeth* at Ohio State University. *(Photo courtesy of Thurber Theatre, Ohio State University.)*

all, a strong drive to succeed. This drive is a prerequisite to endless training and discipline, involving years of hard work and hours of rehearsal for a single role. Even performers who have acted professionally for years often continue their studies. Just as a ballerina spends years on elementary exercises or a singer practices endless scales, so must the actor keep practicing. The work involves rigorous training and strong dedication.

Tools of the Actor

The training and dedication pay off when the creation of a role in a production appears to be an effortless undertaking. This seeming ease is what makes the acting good. Any art that belabors its medium or draws attention to technique is not good art. We appreciate a piece of sculpture for its beauty, for the freedom and flow of its line. We appreciate acting that involves us in a total production and that fails to call attention to itself. If we stop to think that an actor is performing well, he or she probably is not.

Actors who do perform well have learned to use their minds, bodies, and voices to best advantage. These are the actor's major tools. Only when mind, body, and voice serve a role will the performance possess freedom, the freedom that comes through discipline, work, and dedication. At this point the performance becomes "effortless." Then the actor can draw upon experiences and training, often subconsciously, to present the symbol of another person and draw the audience into a realm of suspended disbelief.

Because the actor and the art are inseparable and they both are on display, created out of what the person is, the actor learns to use the voice, body, and mind to the best advantage.

> It is wrong to suppose as many actors do, that a true inner feeling will inevitably express itself in a true outward form. This will only happen when the voice, the speech, and the body have acquired by rigorous training and discipline a flexibility instinctively at the command of the inner truth, and no physical technique is of any use to an actor until it is so much an organic part of him that he is not really conscious of its employment.[4]

The Mind

As important as any of the other aspects of an actor's mind is the willingness to learn. Actors must understand the techniques of acting, the various styles in which a production can be presented, and how to execute these styles. Then they learn the most effective way to project the emo-

[4]Phillip Burton, *Early Doors: My Life and the Theatre* (New York: The Dial Press, Inc., 1969), p. 165.

tions of the characters they are playing. They project themselves into situations and characters and make them believable.

"The best definition of technique I know," actor Hume Cronyn explains, is:

> that means by which the actor can get the best out of himself. It's as simple and as broad as that—and as personal and private. How do you make use of that instrument which is your voice, that which is your body, all the components of yourself, and that emotional reservoir of experience that must be brought to bear on everything you play? Speaking generally there are two broad approaches. You must become so facile in the use of your physical equipment that it will respond instantly and do what you want it to do. Obviously this means that you must exercise your voice and train it and get it to respond, and understand it almost as one would a musical instrument. Precisely the same is true of your body. This is why I would urge any young actor to work carefully, if he can, as a dancer, and to sing, and to do really quite exhaustive and frightfully dull vocal exercises. All this has to do with form. It is external. Because—and this is the second approach—one can have a superb voice, and marvelous control, a body trained like Nureyev, and still be a bloody awful actor.
>
> Without the inner things—without being able to call on qualities of emotion or spirit—you're stuck with only a husk, a frame, a case. How do you go about developing what should be inside? How can you exercise that inner person, enrich it, make it immediately responsive? This is much more difficult because it's infinitely more subtle.

Cronyn explores an answer to the question he poses:

> There's a physical law called Kirchoff's Law of Radiation, which states that the best absorbers are the best emitters. Actors are in the business of emitting, of giving out, but they can only give out what they've managed to take in and absorb. How one charges the batteries, how one learns and grows in the sense of total artistic appreciation and an understanding of the world we live in and our particular society, is a much more subtle and complex thing. One can't awake in the morning and say, "From now on I'm going to be aware, aware, aware. I'm going to be like a sponge and soak life up." You can't do it mechanically, yet without one's emotional antannae constantly aware of how people behave, respond, and react; without some degree of analysis of your own surging emotions—particularly in the moments when they're ungoverned; you're not growing. You have to find out these things because that's the grist of your mill. All this must be, in turn, lent to the author by being brought to bear on the given emotional conflicts of a play. . . .
>
> It takes a great deal of perserverance to learn real discipline and not have it strangle you, not to fall back on stereotype forms. But the whole struggle which any artist has . . . is this struggle to keep form and content in balance. Very often he doesn't succeed. In

These three productions of O'Neill's *Long Day's Journey into Night* show that the designers, actors, and directors had differing concepts of how the play should be presented. The first production was directed by Bedford Thurman, with Dale Willis as scene designer. *(Photo by C. James Gleason and courtesy of Kent State University Theatre.)* The second was directed by Clyde McElroy with scene design by W. Scott McConnell. *(Photo courtesy of Montclair State College.)* The third production was directed by Glen Cannon, with scene design by Richard Mason. *(Photo courtesy of University of Hawaii).*

some cases one understands the content but has never been able to give it proper form, so that what comes out is a vomiting of emotion, of hysteria, of laughter or tears, without reason, of an inability to involve the audience. The actor cannot play his role and enjoy the audience's privilege at the same time.[5]

What Cronyn means is that actors use their minds in all sorts of ways that may be useful to their art. They learn to observe life; they learn as much about human nature as they can. Then they learn about the theatre: what works or has worked and probably will continue to be of use. They experiment to discover the best ways they can portray any character or emotion or play out any situation. They take their knowledge and apply it to what they have to do in any particular play.

The Body

Much more is involved than the actors' mental processes. They have to have control of their bodies to meet the demands of every play. For example, it is not unusual for an actor to lose several pounds during a particularly demanding performance of a role. The actors' bodies must be in shape to sustain high levels of performance. Actress Sybil Thorndike puts it simply: "You've got to be like iron."[6]

Sir Laurence Olivier, even after years of performing, refuses to rest on his accomplishments.

I keep myself very fit now, I have to. I go to a gym twice or three times a week, not merely to look tremendously muscular, but I have to keep fit for my job. I'm determined to hold on to my job. I love it. But it is no use pretending it doesn't involve a certain amount of overwork, because it does. I've seen a lot of contemporaries get a bit under the weather with such work and I'm determined not to.[7]

Not only does the actor try to stay in shape just to remain healthy and fit, but the demands of a role may require an athletic body. Actors often are called upon to perform exhausting feats, such as sword fighting. In a musical they may do as many as seven or eight intricate dances. Because of these demands, acting is not a "soft" job. The actors have to strive to keep their bodies in top physical shape.

The Voice

Acting also can be demanding on the voice, which must be kept in shape, too. Actors do not all have deep, mellow voices, but they should develop the voices they have to their fullest potential. They should understand how the voice works and learn proper exercises to improve its use.

Actors learn how to portray emotions through various vocal quali-

[5]Newquist, pp. 66–67.
[6]Hal Burton, p. 50.
[7]Hal Burton, p. 16.

Acting often demands great body control, as is evident in this scene from *Scapino!*, directed by Russ Ratsch at Summerfun Summer Theater at Montclair State College. *(Photo courtesy of Montclair State College.)*

ties. They learn to make pitch and volume fit the situation or the character. To be heard and understood they learn projection and precise articulation. They learn various dialects and pronunciations to play a variety of roles. Through proper exercising, much like that of a singer, actors learn to use the voice without straining it. The voice has to have strength and endurance. It has to be flexible to fit a variety of circumstances. The actor has to have complete control over it.

There are many roles that are demanding both vocally and physically. For instance, George and Martha in *Who's Afraid of Virginia Woolf?* sustain a high emotional pitch throughout the play.

Approaches to Acting

Today's theatre puts many demands upon actors. They must prepare to perform in a large variety of styles of plays from the period of Greek Classicism to the present. To fill these demands, there are two major approaches to acting: the **internal** and the **external**.

Internal approach seeking within oneself the emotions and experiences to portray a character in a play.

External approach concerned with the technique of acting; or what outward signs of emotion can be used to portray that emotion.

Shown are three entirely different styles of acting. The first, *The Odd Couple*, requires a fairly broad style; the second, *The Scarlet Princess of Edo*, a Kabuchi theatre presentation, requires a much more formal style, and the third, *Tartuffe*, requires a realistic style. *The Odd Couple* was directed by Kjell Amble with scene design by Don Powell. *(Photo courtesy of San Diego State University—Dramatic Arts Department.) The Scarlet Princess of Edo was directed by James Brandon with scene design by Richard Mason. (Photo courtesy of University of Hawaii.) Tartuffe was* presented at the University of Kentucky. *(Photo courtesy of Theatre Arts Department, University of Kentucky.)*

No matter which approach actors favor, they often need to present highly emotional scenes. This actor appears in *Much Ado About Nothing,* directed by Mack Owen at San Diego State University. *(Photo courtesy of San Diego State University—Dramatic Arts Department.)*

The two approaches have certain ground in common. In either case the actors develop their ability for imagination and observation. They imagine how they would react in certain circumstances, so that they can play any particular role effectively. They observe how other people stand, move, and sit, and how they react to pressure, happiness, anger, and all the other emotions. The performers get into the habit of observing and recording in their memories the way individuals talk and any idiosyncrasies of character that might be transferred to a role. These observations are not confined to a particular age group or economic level but take in as many types of people as possible. The actors do not transfer whole characters or even specific reactions of others to the stage. Instead they modify and mold the characters to fit the part they are playing and to conform to their own limitations.

Tobacco Road seems to lend itself to an inner approach to acting and portrayal of character. Director, Louis O. Erdmann; scene design, Marsh Cassady. *(Photo by C. James Gleason and courtesy of Kent State University Theatre.)*

Here the approaches part company:

It would be not unfair to say that there are, roughly speaking, two kinds of actor: those who primarily play for effect and those who, whether by instinct or method, seek for cause before making their effect. But even this cannot be elevated into a dictum, for those who play primarily for effect—or as we say in the theatre, "from outside"—are by no means unaware that they must indicate, and to some extent feel, the cause or motivation which should precede that bid for effect. Similarly those artists who try to discover primarily the truth of a character are also usually aware to some extent of the effect they are creating.[8]

Michael Redgrave is explaining the two approaches. Those actors who play for effect are using the external method; those who seek the truth of the character are using the internal approach.

The Internal Approach

The internal approach, the elements of which were first brought together and then developed by the Russian director, Constantin Stanislavski, was

[8]Redgrave, p. 13.

a reaction against declamatory and extravagant earlier styles of acting. The earlier styles, for example, relied on certain memorized gestures and posturing to portray each emotion. They were highly artificial, and by today's standards they appear humorous and posed. Stanislavski sought to present dramatic truth through an observation of life or nature. He taught that actors should seek truth of feeling and experience in the characters they play, finding the psychological depth of each role.

Basically, Stanislavski, who founded his system in Russia in 1906, believed that the secret of art was in discovering creativity. He wanted to find the true nature of creativity in the human being and subsequently discover the means for its development. He became increasingly interested in the operation of the subconscious and emotions. He formed the concept of **emotional memory**—remembering how one felt in a particular situation and relating that memory to similar circumstances of a character in a play. In other words, actors need to move, perceive, concentrate, and feel while on the stage. They cannot merely pretend to do so. The internal approach involves feeling and relating emotions, thoughts, and ideas to their outward manifestation.

According to Edith Evans, a British actress, "Almost all the parts you play, if they are well written and if you are suitable to them, you find them, bits of them, in yourself."[9]

Emotional memory remembering how one felt in a particular set of circumstances and then relating those emotions to similar circumstances in a play.

The External Approach

On the other hand, those who follow the external approach are largely concerned with technique. They think it is unnecessary to undertake the study of a role by trying to understand emotionally what a character does and says. It is only necessary to determine what the emotion is and then modify outward, observed signs of this emotion to fit the role. For example, when frustrated, you may snap a pencil between your fingers or pound a fist into the other palm. Actors following the external approach take these observable characteristics and mold them to a particular role. Critics of this approach say that the actors are using "tricks," because they are concerned with effect rather than feeling. They are, of course; but to some degree all portrayal of character involves "tricks" because the actors are aware of the audience and playing to them.

Combining the Two Approaches

When asked whether he "inhabited" a character or looked at the role from outside, actor Ralph Richardson said:

> Part of it is stepping aside and controlling it, that's the first thing. You're really driving four horses, as it were, first going through, in great detail, the exact movements which have been decided upon. You're also listening to the audience, as I say, keeping, if you can,

[9]Hal Burton, p. 129.

This scene from *Something Afoot* seems to lend itself to an external approach in acting and character portrayal. *(Photo courtesy of University of Kentucky, Department of Theatre Arts.)*

very great control over them. You're also slightly creating the part, in so far as you're consciously refining the movements and, perhaps, inventing tiny other experiments with new ones. At the same time you are really living, in one part of your mind, what is happening. Acting is to some extent a controlled dream. In one part of your consciousness it really and truly is happening. But, of course, to make it true to the audience, all the time, the actor must, at any rate some of the time, believe himself that it is really true. But in my experience this layer of absolute reality is comparatively small one. The rest of it is technique, and I say, of being very careful that the thing is completely accurate, completely clear, completely as laid down beforehand. In every performance you're trying to find a better way to do it, and what you're reshaping, the little experiments, may be very small indeed and quite unnoticed by your fellow actors; but they are working all the time. Therefore three or four layers of consciousness are at work during the time an actor is giving a performance.[10]

As Richardson implies, an actor often combines the internal and ex-

[10]Hal Burton, p. 71

Actors have to perform on two levels—one concerned with technical aspects of a production; the other concerned with the truthful presentation of the drama. *Play Strindberg* was produced by the Old Globe Theatre at the Cassius Carter Center Stage, under the direction of Eric Christmas. Set design, Steph Storer; costume design, Lissa Skiles. *(Photo by Bill Reid and courtesy of the Old Globe Theatre.)*

ternal approaches, and no form is entirely pure. Actors do rely on both, although they may lean more heavily toward one or the other. No matter how much actors "feel" a role, they also are aware of the audience. They would not act in exactly the same way if the same situation occurred in real life as in a play. Helen Hayes refers to it this way: "I do not indulge myself on the stage. Sometimes it seems to be more convincing and artistically pure if you don't try to project too much, don't try too hard to convey to the last row; it might be more in keeping to just mumble (if mumbling is indicated in the character's emotion) but you musn't do that. You must share everything with the audience."[11]

On stage the actors have to be concerned with projection, the delivery of memorized lines, their spatial placement in relation to the other actors, and other technical aspects. Therefore they perform on two levels, one concerned with analysis and technique, the other concerned with feelings and veracity and the appearance of life.

Philip Burton, attempting to define what an actor is, cautions against the internal alone:

> He is the one who finds his fullest self-realization by imaginatively assuming the being and actions of fictitious characters for the entertainment of audiences gathered in a theatre. Again I stress the theatre. There is a kind of theatrical training in this country that emphasizes the emotional release in acting to such an extent that audiences become almost an intrusion upon a private rite. To me, this self-indulgence is unhealthy.[12]

There always has been a controversy, since the development of the inner approach, over which method of acting is the correct one.

> The dominant mode of acting [in the modern theatre] has been some modification of the Stanislavsky method . . . , which trains an actor, in effect, to lose his own personality while on the stage and become the character he is playing. This is the extension into the player's art of the realistic style, for just as the realistic stage is thought to become not a symbolic representation of reality but an actual place, so the Stanislavsky actor ceases to be a player representing someone else and is transformed into the character. But while this has been the dominant acting style, the reactions against it have been constant and extreme: Brecht trained the actors in his *Berliner Ensemble* to remember always that they were on stage playing a part, and actors at the Abbey Theatre in Dublin, it is said, were frequently rehearsed in barrels in order to restrict their movements and to force them to concentrate on speaking their poetic lines, thus reminding them that they were no more than voices for the poetry, necessary but ultimately unimportant instruments of the author.[13]

[11]Newquist, p. 205.
[12]Phillip Burton, p. 165.
[13]Alvin B. Kernan, ed., *The Modern American Theatre* (Englewood Cliffs, N.J.: Prentice-Hall, Inc., 1967), p. 16, reprinted from *Classics of the Modern Theatre*, Alvin B. Kernan, ed. (New York: Harcourt Brace Jovanovich, 1965).

Other Approaches

Within the last few years methods of acting have begun to change even further. Part of the new experimentation in theatre can be credited to the Living Theatre of Julian Beck and Judith Malina, who sought to make drama fluid and poetic. They believed that new methods of acting should be discovered for new plays that were being written. Part of the experimentation involved an attempt to convince the audience that they were watching real events rather than the acting out of a play.

Other experimentation was done by Jerzy Grotowski's Polish Laboratory Theatre, which explored thoroughly the nature of acting, giving the actors a technique based on total discipline, thus freeing the mind and body completely. As Grotowski stated: "I believe there can be no true creative process within the actor if he lacks discipline or spontaneity."[14] Grotowski believed that the best approach to theatre and acting as art was to strip them of all nonessentials. That meant there should be no sets, makeup, lighting, or costuming. The actor, through discipline and control, creates these things in the minds of the audience. By controlled movement the actors create whatever they wish the audience to perceive. Impulse and reaction are simultaneous. The actor does not merely desire to perform a certain action but is incapable of not performing it. The skills become involuntary. The goal is to eliminate mental, physical, and psychological blocks. The result is the totally disciplined formation of a role in which all inhibitions are nonexistent and every phase of self is revealed.

Developing a Character

No matter what approach actors use, they develop the mimetic instinct to a high degree and are willing to experiment with it. Such creativity takes many forms. At first, the actor assumes a character. This process may be long and involved. In reading a script the actors see that the exposition or the development of the plot brings out certain character traits. The actors use that material as a starting point and build from there, adding traits, characteristics, and features that are consistent with the character's personality. Such a building of character is a continuing process that may last up to and through the first performances.

As part of the process, the actor places the character in alien situations to see how the character reacts. Often directors will have actors improvise a scene with the character. The scene is based either on the play itself or on an incident entirely divorced from the play. The actor learns how the character is likely to react in a variety of circumstances

[14]Jerzy Grotowski, *Towards a Poor Theatre* (New York: Simon and Schuster, 1968), p. 209.

Just by observing this actress, an audience can easily surmise several things about her character. *Finian's Rainbow* was directed by Louis O. Erdman at Kent State University. *(Photo by· C. James Gleason and courtesy of Kent State University Theatre.)*

and becomes more comfortable with the role. The actors also project how the character reacts emotionally, psychologically, and physically to each situation and to the other characters within the play.

As mentioned earlier, theatre contains many symbols, one of which is character. It is up to the actors to take these symbols and make them truthful for the audience. The actors, working with the other artists, interpret the playwright's overall message as well as their own roles. Their characters have to represent truth, and the actors determine how best to present this truth. Is the character to be represented as true-to-life or not? In Van Itallie's *The Serpent: A Ceremony* (discussed more fully in Chapter 4) the actors switch from role to role and even sometimes appear as themselves. These actors would have a difficult time if they tried to present true-to-life characters, because they switch from one to another so much. By giving their own names and telling the audience about themselves, they say, in effect: "I'm a person who is assuming several roles, but keep in mind that I am not those characters but myself." No matter how the actors present the characters, they represent truth as the actors (with the director and playwright) see it.

Training the Actor

In many ways the new forms of actor training and actor goals look back to ritual and tradition, modify them, and build upon them. Largely, the new movements are reactions against some parts of the old while at the same time embracing some of their aspects. Grotowski's rigorous training exercises, for instance, come from such diverse areas as gymnastic movements, Chinese classical ballet, and yoga.

In the past many actors were trained in the Stanislavski system, or method acting, as it came to be called in the United States. At the same time these actors were generally taught not to go completely inside themselves when assuming a character but to be aware of such things as body placement, vocal projection, and how to move well and speak well. However, with such groups as the Polish Laboratory Theatre, actor training has begun to change in the last couple of decades.

Less traditional forms of training include psychological and emotional exercises to stimulate the senses. Sensitivity training, which began largely as a part of psychological counseling, has proven of value to the actor. In addition to developing sensitivity to self, others, and the environment, such training builds confidence in oneself and in others, breaking down inhibitions. Often the training is closer to role playing than to acting.

Sensitivity training has valid uses in many areas of the actor's development. One exercise, for instance, is to have actors work in pairs. One is blindfolded for a short period of time and must rely on the other for guidance. Not only can this exercise help the actor to develop trust in another person, but it can make keener the senses other than sight.

Traditionally, actor training often begins with classes in such areas as oral interpretation, singing, dancing, and fencing, the last not only as

These acting students are participating in a trust circle, a form of sensitivity training. The person in the middle closes his eyes and lets himself fall into the arms of those in the circle. They, in turn, push him gently from person to person. *(Photo by Kathy A. Oda.)*

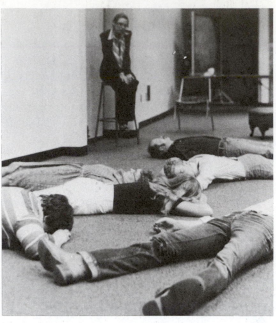

The same group participates in a guided fantasy. The young woman seated on the stool is asking the other students to visualize the imaginary journey on which she is taking them. *(Photo by Kathy A. Oda.)*

Given circumstances the background information provided about a character or the play as a whole. Actors take the given circumstances as a beginning in establishing a character.

an end in itself but as a means of body control. There are some schools that have actors participate in team or individual sports to improve reflexes and reactions and to build stamina.

Sometimes the games move into pantomime. An example is playing basketball without equipment or a gym. Through these exercises actors learn to concentrate on how people actually perform in various situations in that they are forced to simulate.

As another exercise, an actor often is told **given circumstances** or basics and must proceed from there. Given circumstances are the background information that sets a scene and establishes characters. After they receive the information, the actors create the action or carry the scene to its conclusion. The given circumstances could be as simple as being asked to take out the garbage when interested in wathcing a television show, or bursting into an adjoining apartment to complain about the noise of a wild party.

Actors sometimes are encouraged to play the "what if" game. For example, what if I were walking along a lonely street at night and heard a scream? What if I returned home one day and found strangers and strange furnishings in my house? The actors project themselves into imaginary situations and try to determine logically how they would act.

Another aspect of actor training is learning to understand and communicate the subtleties of a character through **body language.** We all project attitudes, emotions and states of physical being through body position and movement. For instance, a man seated in a desk chair with his legs stretched out in front and his thumbs hooked into the side of his belt communicates relaxation and lack of tension. Seeing such a person, we realize that he is in an open, perhaps expansive or friendly mood. If the same man were sitting with arms folded and feet planted on the floor, we would assume that he was not be open to joking or friendly conversation.

According to Richard Boleslavsky, an actor and director directly influenced by Stanislavski, an actor's education has three parts. First is "the education of his body, the whole physical apparatus, of every muscle and sinew." Secondly, is the "intellectual" and "cultural" education. Third "is the education and training of the soul—the most important factor of dramatic action." "An actor," Boleslavsky said, " cannot exist without a soul developed enough to be able to accomplish, at the first command of the will, every action and change stipulated. In other words, the actor must have a soul capable of living through any situation demanded by the author."[15]

Whatever training the actors have or whatever method they follow, they learn to approach a role for the purpose of communicating to an audience. They remain faithful to the message and ideas of the playwright. Whether the actors closely identify with the character and bury themselves under the assumed personality or stand apart and view the character intellectually rather than emotionally, they call upon their skills and training in preparation for playing a role.

> **Body language** the emotions, attitudes, and states of physical being we communicate through body movement and position.

Analyzing a Role

Setting Goals

An actor often approaches a new role by what is referred to in the Stanislavski system as seeking the **spine** or **super-objective**—the essence of the character. The super-objective is always a goal the character wants to achieve. It is expressed as an action and not as a feeling or emotion. In *Death of a Salesman* Willy Loman's super-objective could be that he wants to be a success. He defines success in terms of having money and being

> **Spine or Super-objective** the major goal of a character in a play.

[15]Richard Boleslavsky, *Acting: The First Six Lessons* (New York: Theatre Arts, Inc., 1933), pp. 25–26.

Death of a Salesman was presented at Kent State University under the direction of Earl Curtis, with scene design by Barry Baughman. The role of Willy was played by professional actor Arnold Moss. *(Photo by C. James Gleason and courtesy of Kent State University Theatre.)*

"well-liked." Toward this end he deludes himself into thinking that he is a great salesman and finally commits suicide so his sons will have the money from his insurance policy.

Defining the spine works best with realistic or naturalistic plays whose characters approximate real people. One actor conceivably could discover a different spine for a role than another actor. Often the director helps the actor interpret, but except in premiere productions, the actor has no chance to ask the playwright what the goal of that character should be.

After determining the super-objective, the actor analyzes each individual scene to figure out its specific objective and how it relates to the character as a whole. The goal in each scene may differ, but each contributes to the overall goal of the super-objective.

Material about a character is provided in dialogue of the other characters, in lines the character delivers, and in the character's actions. We

Actors need to understand their character's relationship to the play as a whole. Leonardo Enrique appears as El Gallo in the Marquis Public Theatre's production of *The Fantasticks,* directed by Walter Schoen. *(Photo by Wanda T. Robin.)*

learn much from the way others in the play view a character. The setting also can tell us about the character's present circumstances.

Determining the Character's Makeup

Actors go on to determine as much as they can about their characters by asking themselves certain questions. For instance, what is the character's physical makeup? Some playwrights, particularly those in modern theatre, provide many clues to a character's appearance through a short description in the script at the character's first appearance. Eugene O'Neill sometimes wrote several pages about setting and character. Actors, of course, cannot drastically alter their basic physical types; but they can change age, hair color, and posture, and determine other strong characteristics such as a tic.

Rarely can the actor find complete information within the given circumstances provided by the playwright, but they serve as a starting point. If the playwright provides a little information about the character's physical makeup, the actor builds upon it, adding distinguishing traits.

Determining the Character's Background

Next the actors determine their characters' background. Where were they born? Where did they grow up? What are their educational, sociological, ethnic, and financial backgrounds? What are their present circumstances? The more an actor "knows" about a character the easier it is to act believably. Maybe not much is provided about background, but the actor surmises from what is present what a character's background could be. This process explains why, for example, Laurence Olivier and John Gielgud have played Hamlet in different ways, each effective. Each actor has interpreted the character in a unique way but logically in light of what is known.

Choosing Character Traits to Emphasize

The actors also determine how their characters view the world. What are their basic beliefs about life in general and the circumstances in the play in particular? How are they most likely to react in certain situations? What are their most important personality traits?

Determining background as much as possible helps the actor to define the character's needs and goals within the framework of the play. An actor determines the overall goal first and then breaks the play into short scenes or units to figure out the reason for the actions and reactions in each section. In this way the actor understands how a character builds, how a personality unfolds or is gradually revealed, and where the focus should be in each section.

A character's traits cannot all be presented. Because of time limitations on the stage the actors present only a few of these traits. They decide which are most important to the audience and why. They determine which facets of the character's personality should be emphasized and which deemphasized. Only the actor who fully understands the character and the play makes this choice successfully.

Characters often are a combination of a type and an individual. They show a universal trait, which makes them a type, and they have another, particular trait, which makes them individual. For example, a universal trait is Oedipus' pride, whereas an individual trait is his limp.

Often to individualize a character for the audience, the actor emphasizes a distinctive trait that may not be suggested in the script, but which immediately identifies the character in the minds of the audience. An actor portraying the father in *Long Day's Journey into Night* could have the character play with a silver dollar as a symbol that he has money, or have

A rehearsal for Paul Green's *Trumpet in the Land*, an outdoor drama presented for ten weeks each summer at New Philadelphia, Ohio. *(Photo by Isabel Kopp.)*

him constantly pick up scraps of paper or pieces of string and put them into drawers, to indicate his miserliness.

Determining Relationships

Next the actor determines the character's relationship with the other characters. Does the character like them or hate them? Why? What is the character's self-image? How does the character go about trying to reach goals? How does all this relate to the theme or action of the play?

Compromise often is necessary in view of the overall interpretation of a play. Maybe the director views a particular character in a different light than does the actor. Maybe two actors have clashing ideas about their characters' relationship. The actors must be able to work within the circumstances, environment, and situations upon which they and the director agree.

Adjusting the Interpretation

Finally, the actor determines the atmosphere of the play and the mood of each scene so as to suit the characterization to the prevailing conditions. Although the analysis occurs before or at least near the start of the re-

The actors playing Harvey and Milt in the Footlight Players production of *Luv* must figure out their relationship to each other and to the script as a whole to convey the meaning of the play to an audience. (*Photo by Gary Anderson of* The Coshocton Tribune.)

hearsal period, the actor enters the role with the understanding that the character will continue to build until the play is presented. If not, much of the rehearsal period could be eliminated. Rehearsal involves exploring relationships and projecting the actors more completely into their characters.

Many times actors find that their analysis does not work. Then they need to discover why. Maybe the analysis was incomplete or even wrong. Maybe the interpretation just cannot work for one actor but could for another. Sometimes actors will completely change, at their own instigation or that of the director, the entire characterization.

Building and growth often seem to occur naturally once actors appear on stage together. It is much easier to act well yourself when your fellow actors are doing their best in presenting their characters. When all perform together, it is easier to set the mood and to determine the rhythm and pace of the play as a whole. Some plays require a fast pace to sustain suspense or comedy; others need to go slower for understanding, reflection, or a serious mood.

The Rehearsal Period

After analyzing a role, the actor relies on training or discipline to make the character come to life and appear a three-dimensional being.

Memorizing Lines and Business

The rehearsal period begins with the memorization of lines and **business**—any physical actions taken by the actor as an integral part of the script, for the purpose of portraying and defining character, or of presenting a pleasing picture on the stage. An actor may have no other purpose in moving than to prevent crowding one stage area or to allow another actor easier access to a prop or an exit. The actor makes even this type of movement appear natural and purposeful. Obviously, actors cannot just edge out of the way but must make their moves "in character." For example, an actor playing a drunk could reel or stagger to the proper position. This motion would be "in character," so it probably would not be distracting to the audience.

Actors usually have familiarized themselves during the analysis with the script as a whole and with the progression of ideas within each unit of the play. When they have learned the sense of the scene, the lines become easier to learn and to remember. Directors sometimes have actors who have not yet learned their lines "ad lib" a scene, using the ideas but

Business physical action taken by the actor.

A rehearsal of *Mr. Toad of Toad Hall* for the Children's Wing of Trumpet in the Land, New Philadelphia, Ohio. *(Photo by Isabel Kopp.)*

not the exact dialogue. This exercise has a dual purpose. It helps in characterization, and it gives the actors confidence that they do know the direction of the scene. This exercise can give them a psychological boost.

Cue the final line or action that signals that it is time for an actor to begin the next action or speech.

Along with their own lines, the actors memorize their **cues,** the lines or actions preceding their own lines or actions. If they are familiar with others' lines as well as their own, they have little trouble with mental blocks or with forgetting lines and actions. It is common for actors to say that they were unable to think of their lines until they heard their cue; then they knew exactly what they were to do. Of course, if they use the internal approach to acting, they are not thinking of what comes next but concentrating on what is happening at the moment.

Certainly the actors, in learning the sequence of ideas, must understand their meaning. Otherwise there will be little chance of conveying the playwright's message to an audience. They must understand each other's actions and speeches as well. Actors really react. One person says or does something, and the next action comes as a direct result. Even when actors are not speaking, they listen to what the other characters are saying and react to what they hear. If they do not do so, the audience members will be reminded again and again that they are in a theatre watching a play.

Interpreting Ideas

Another reason for understanding the speeches and scenes is so that the actors can interpret and convey the ideas effectively. They call upon their observation, creativity, and imagination to know how their characters would deliver a particular line or how they would react to a given action. It is then that the actor's body training comes into use, through believable movement and body language that fits the traits of the character. During rehearsal the actors discover what movements are most appropriate and how they can bring them across to an audience.

They must be thoroughly familiar with the ideas in the play to know also how to use their voices effectively. Then they must practice using tone, voice quality, and pitch to convey these ideas.

Success depends on the degree of freshness or spontaneity present in the characterization. It requires hours of training and rehearsal to appear relaxed and spontaneous. The actors must concentrate more fully on their roles at each rehearsal and each performance. College directors often worry that their performers will "peak" before opening night and then will "go stale." This problem does arise, but it should not. For instance, Stanislavski rehearsed a play for months before presenting it publicly. The actors should be able to concentrate enough to make the roles spontaneous rather than robot-like. They can also try to make their characterizations better each night, no matter how long the show runs. Unfortunately, it is common, even on Broadway, to see actors who have played their roles for a long time become automatic in their acting and responses.

Despite immersing themselves in their roles, the actors also remain on the technical level—listening for cues, being ready to meet unexpected audience response, and watching for the occasional fluffs of lines or mistakes of technicians. If they wholly immerse themselves in the role, oblivious to outside changes or interference, they are letting themselves in for disaster. As Michael Redgrave stated:

> We actors frequently like to give the impression that the whole composition is, as it were, inspired from within and that there is nothing of the deliberate about it. This may be partly our vanity, or it may be the very natural and proper desire to conceal our methods or tricks in the belief that if the spectator knew how they worked they would cease to impress or deceive him. Nevertheless the biographies, journals, and letters that actors have left us bear witness to the infinite degree of care, especially over small details. I imagine that the mind processes of the actor at this stage are similar to the work of a detective. He does not set about, like a police inspector, simply to gather every bit of evidence for its own sake or as a matter of routine, but like Sherlock Holmes, or the detective Maigret cre-

Portraying a charac-
ter involves reacting
as well as acting.
(*Photo of* The Red
Shoes, *courtesy of*
Pick-A-Pack Players,
Inc., of Milwaukee.)

ated by the novelist Simenon, he shifts the available evidence
around in his mind rather as one might shift the pieces of a jigsaw
puzzle until by some instinct he finds himself in possession of a
psychological clue or characteristic which will suddenly illuminate
the whole character for him, and help him find the truth.[16]

If actors become completely "carried away" by their roles, they are
not good actors. They will be unable to adjust to others around them,
and they run the risk of reaching too high an emotional pitch that they
will have trouble maintaining. Although in real situations people sometimes do become so angry that they scream and lose their voices, actors
cannot afford to do so. They have to be aware of vocal technique and the
technique of building a scene. By playing at too high a pitch throughout
a scene or an act, they also may lose their audiences. People expect contrasts for emphasis. If the actors reach an emotional peak too early, the
audience may become confused and consequently inattentive.

The actors do have to present believable characters, while still being
seen and heard by the audience. There has to be a balance between the
purely artistic and the purely technical: between credibility and projection. Actors, through training and experience, learn to trust their own
intuition. If they begin to doubt themselves, they will fail in their roles.

[16]Redgrave, p. 40.

They have to be confident that what they are doing is the right thing. They must be able to free themselves of doubts and inhibitions.

Working with the Other Actors

Actors are sensitive not only to their own roles but also to the artistry of the other performers. During rehearsal they come to feel what affects the others. Much to current acting involves the **ensemble concept,** or the willingness of yield to other actors when the script indicates they are the center of focus.

There have been countless tales of performers **upstaging** each other in a literal sense as well as symbolically. Upstaging means that an actor moves further toward the back of the stage, so that others are forced to turn their backs on the audience to look at or to speak to the actor. Thus the upstage actor grabs the center of attention. Symbolic upstaging means drawing attention away from the center of interest through any means such as unwarranted physical activity, playing with a property, or assuming an unusual posture. Most often it is the actor who feels inadequate in some way who resorts to such moves.

Ensemble concept the willingness of actors to subordinate themselves to the production as a whole; having no stars who stand out.

Upstaging actors' drawing attention to themselves to the detriment of the production.

The Actor's Responsibilities

Interpreting the Work of Others

The actor's job then is to create, to interpret, to illustrate, to heighten, and to expand. The work bears the mark of the actors's own personality, because like all artists, actors give of themselves. But actors differ from many other artists in that they are interpreting the work of others. First is the playwright, who provides only clues to the building of a character. Next the director adds another personality. The director usually provides only the basic blocking and interpretation. Last the individual actor develops subtleties of characterization and movement.

Technical Requirements

To do a good job, actors must know all the technical requirements of the stage. They know the stage areas and the implications of various types of movement. They know that curved movement can show indecision, whereas one of the strongest movements in projecting determination is from Upstage Center (the central area near the back wall) to Downstage Center (the area closest to the audience). They understand what body positions indicate to an audience. They know how to balance the stage picture. They know how to fake fighting or eating. Such responses are

almost automatic to seasoned performers, but they all require understanding.

The actors may be called upon to do virtually anything on the stage.
Often they must handle unusual properties. Costumes, particularly those
of a historical nature, often are cumbersome. The setting is unfamiliar.
The actors may need to work with all of these elements, just to get their
feel. They may have to experiment with makeup to gain the right effects.

There are special requirements in musicals, when an actor may have
to sing or dance in addition to portraying a character. Even musicals vary
greatly in their demands. *Earnest in Love,* based on *The Importance of Being
Earnest* by Oscar Wilde, requires a broad style of acting, whereas *The Fantasticks* by Tom Jones and Harvey Schmidt, a musical about love and in-
nocence, is an intimate show with little setting and few characters. Unlike
many early musicals, *Man of La Mancha* (Dale Wasserman, Mitch Leigh,
and Joe Darion), which tells the story of Don Quixote in search of human
goodness, has a serious treatment of theme. It requires more realistic acting than do such musicals as *Sugar* (Peter Stone, Jule Styne, and Bob
Merrill), presented in New York in 1972 and based on the movie *Some
Like It Hot.* Both the movie and the show tell the story of two male musicians who witness Chicago's St. Valentine's Day massacre and join
Sweet Sue's all-girl band, which is heading by train to Florida.

A rehearsal shot of *Sugar,* presented by the Little Theatre of Tuscarawas County, Ohio, directed by Jill Lynn. *(Photo by Bill Douds.)*

Knowing a Variety of Styles

Actors must become acquainted with and be able to perform in a variety of styles—the unadorned movement of classicism, the gracefulness of romanticism, the earthy delivery of naturalism. (See Chapter 4 for a discussion of these styles.) They know that the audience and they themselves generally should be more involved in a tragedy or serious play, whereas both usually should stand somewhat apart from the roles in comedy. They should give the impression that they are sharing the joke with the audience in a comedy, and that they are playing for laugh lines. Still, they must maintain a balance between involvement and technique. Too much exaggeration, if it is inappropriate to a character, can destroy a role, as well as can too much naturalness and the failure to project the voice and actions to an audience by speaking too softly and making movements too small.

Communicating with an Audience

Actors are responsible for communicating a variety of feelings with only a few words or gestures. They are oral interpreters who add their own personality to a written work while remaining true to the original purpose. Unlike the writer or painter, they rely on many others, and many others rely on them to present a successful play. They have a duty to the designers, the director, the other actors, the playwright, and most important, the audience. They must understand their roles and the whole play to fulfill this duty.

The Actor's Rewards and Frustrations

The art of acting is rewarding, and the reward is immediate in the approval of the audience. It can stimulate a person to go beyond what seemed possible.

On the other hand, immediacy can be difficult. Actors are doers who must do on schedule. They must forget outside worries and distractions and proceed with their art. They cannot deliver a few lines, analyze what they have done, leave, come out on stage later, and modify their behavior. All the planning has to be accomplished beforehand.

There are many other frustrations connected with acting. Jobs are hard to find, and only a small percentage of the people who set out to become actors are able to make a living at it. Even those performers who are fortunate enough to land jobs in original New York productions may work only a few nights before the show closes. In professional theatre there are long hours of rehearsal and work at home, memorizing lines and analyzing and developing characters. But when actors do succeed, they realize that their job is one of the most fulfilling undertakings in any form of art.

QUESTIONS FOR DISCUSSION

1. Why do you think well-known actors are idolized?
2. In what way is an actor different from other artists?
3. What does it take to become a successful actor?
4. What is involved in making characters and situations believable to an audience?
5. What are the differences between the internal and the external approaches to acting?
6. It has been said that most acting is a combination of the internal and external approaches. How is this saying true?
7. What do some of the newer methods of acting and actor training involve?
8. What purposes are served by the rehearsal period for a play?
9. Why should actors become familiar with the total script, as well as their own roles?
10. What is the ensemble concept of acting?
11. What kinds of knowledge should an actor have to approach a role?

SUPPLEMENTARY READING

PLAYS
The Importance of Being Earnest by Oscar Wilde.
Long Day's Journey Into Night by Eugene O'Neill.

BOOKS

Boleslavsky, Richard. *Acting: The First Six Lessons.* New York: Theatre Arts Books, 1933.

Burton, Hal. *Great Acting.* New York: Bonanza Books, 1967.

Chekhov, Michael. *To the Actor on the Technique of Acting.* New York: Harper & Row, Publishers, 1953.

Cole, Toby, and Chinoy, Helen D., eds. *Actors on Acting: The Theories, Techniques, and Practices of the Great Actors of All Times as Told in Their Own Words.* New York: Crown Publishers, Inc., 1949.

Duerr, Edwin. *The Length and Depth of Acting.* New York: Holt, Rinehart and Winston, 1962.

Grotowski, Jerzy. *Towards a Poor Theatre.* New York: Simon & Schuster, 1968.

Redgrave, Michael. *The Actor's Ways and Means.* New York: Theatre Arts Books, 1953.

Schechner, Richard. *Environmental Theatre*. New York: Hawthorn Books, Inc., 1973.

Stanislavski, Constantin. *An Actor Prepares*. Trans. by Elizabeth Reynolds Hapgood. New York: Theatre Arts Books, 1936.

CHAPTER 4
Dramatic Structure and Style

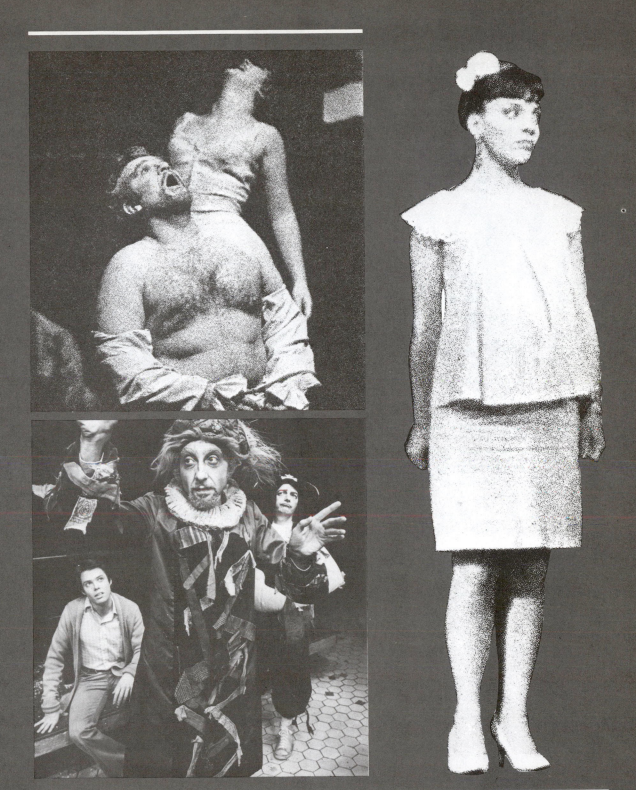

Arms and the Man by Shaw is an example of a story play. Director Craig Noel; setting and costume design, Peggy Kellner. *(Photo by Bill Reid and courtesy of Old Globe Theatre, San Diego.)*

Like all art, theatre attempts to present truth as the artists associated with a production see it. Truth is not only elusive but subjective. The playwright, the director, the actors, and the designers collaborate in communicating their own form of reality through dramatic structure and style. For our part, as audience members we are interested in witnessing truth. As Eric Bentley said: "Would art exist at all if men did not desire to live twice? You have your life; and on the stage you have it again."[1]

The Story Play

Traditional plays have a cause and effect organization. From ancient to modern times this form, sometimes called the story play, has been the most prevalent, and it continues to draw the largest audiences. Very simply, a particular cause or set of causes brings about a particular effect or set of effects. The causes take up the larger part of the play, and the climax shows the major effect.

This type of structure also has been popular in fiction. When we think of a story, we usually think first of being entertained, and second

[1]Eric Bentley, *The Life of the Drama* (New York: Atheneum, 1964), p. 9.

of learning something. Stories are interesting because they deal with people in situations with which we can identify. Readers stay interested because they anticipate the outcome and how it will be accomplished. A story holds our attention because of its unfolding and its revelations. It has a **plot** that keeps us in suspense until the end.

Structure of the Story Play

In the story play a problem is introduced, and the plot leads to its resolution.

> The dramatic approach to reality is, to begin with, a view of life as a condition of disequilibrium, a state of crisis, conflict and change; and dramatic vision encompasses movement toward some new equilibrium, however temporary or tentative, or movement toward a reconciliation that makes survival or sanity possible.[2]

After the problem is introduced, there is a meeting of opposing forces, the protagonist and the antagonist, which results in a struggle. The struggle ends when one of the forces is overcome.

The protagonist is the person who needs or wants something; the antagonist opposes it. The protagonist generally is an individual, although in rare cases, such as Gerhardt Hauptmann's *The Weavers*, it can be a group of people. The antagonist is another person, a group of people, or a nonindividualized force such as nature or economic conditions. It could be a condition of the protagonist, in which case a struggle within the mind of one individual is shown largely in relationships with others. For example, in the comedy *A Thousand Clowns* by Herb Gardner, the central character's conflict centers around whether he will remain a nonconformist and maintain his sense of freedom or get a job and be allowed to continue rearing his nephew.

The story play begins with a situation in which there is a certain balance, or in which the balance has been upset shortly before the play opens. The point at which the balance is upset and the problem becomes apparent is called the **inciting incident.** The protagonist tries to solve the problem, and the suspense, the struggle, and the conflict involved make up the **rising action.** The point at which the action can go no further without something irrevocable happening is the **turning point.** The **climax** occurs when the protagonist either wins or loses. The remainder of the play consists of the **falling action** or **denouement.**

Sometimes the turning point and climax occur at the same time; sometimes they are separated. Suppose two characters have been fighting. One decides to kill the other. The point at which the decision is made

[2]John Gassner, ''The Dramatic Vision,'' in *Dramatic Soundings: Evaluations and Retractions Culled from 30 Years of Dramatic Criticism* (Crown Publishers, Inc., New York, 1968), p. 109. Reprinted from *Impromptu*, 1961.

Plot the progression of a story from the point of attack through the climax and denouement.

Inciting incident the point of a play at which the initial balance is upset and the plot begins to build.

Rising action the building or intensification of the struggle between the protagonist and the antagonist.

Turning point the moment in a plot where the action can go no further without something irrevocable happening.

Climax the high point of the plot; the moment when an irrevocable action occurs that determines the outcome of the play.

Falling action or Denouement the part of a story play that occurs after the climax. It shows the results of the climax.

is the turning point. The killing is the climax. If the decision is carried out instantaneously, the turning point and climax are the same. If there is a time lag, the two are separated.

Exposition

This description covers the basic structure of the story play, but it is over-simplified. Much of the material that is necessary to understand the plot is presented through exposition. The story may begin long before the play opens, but the playwright need not include all the events preceding the inciting incident. We most often learn about these events through dialogue. Thus the "story" includes much more than the plot, which generally covers a short span of time. If a playwright depicted all the events preceding the start of the action, the play probably would be long and boring.

Point of Attack

Point of attack the place in a story where the writer decides to begin the action.

The playwright decides the **point of attack,** the place to begin the play. According to theatre critic William Archer,

> If his [the playwright's] play be a comedy, and if his object be gently and quietly to interest and entertain, the chances are that he begins by showing us his personages in their normal state, concisely indicates their characters, circumstances and relations, and then lets the crisis develop from the outset before our eyes. If, on the other hand, his play be of a more stirring description, and he wants to seize the spectator's attention firmly from the start, he will probably go straight at his crisis, plunging, perhaps, into the very middle of it, even at the cost of having afterwards to go back in order to put the audience in possession of the antecedent circumstances. In a third type of play . . . the curtain rises on a surface aspect of profound peace, which is presently found to be a thin crust over an absolutely volcanic condition of affairs, the origin of which has to be traced backwards, it may be for many years.[3]

Crisis and Struggle

In most plays the action does not build in a straight line to the climax and then fall off for the denouement or the reestablishment of the balance. Generally, the action is a jagged line along which a series of minor crises and struggles are introduced as part of the overall problem. Sometimes these minor problems seem to be resolved but surface later and complicate the rising action. They result in a series of minor climaxes, which

[3]William Archer, *Play-Making: A Manual of Craftsmanship* (New York: Dover Publications, Inc., 1960), p. 58. Reprinted with permission.

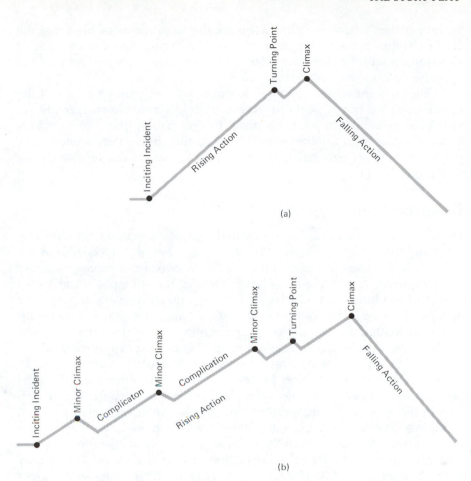

(a)

(b)

The first drawing shows the basic progression of a story play, while the second details the minor crises and climaxes leading to the turning point and major climax. Although each minor climax results in a lessening of tension, the struggle between the protagonist and antagonist is immediately intensified once more.

could be compared to two people fencing. First one attacks and drives the other back; then the second attacks and drives the first back, over and over again until one wins. Each minor crisis somewhat alters the play's direction. Each, usually the result of a new discovery, is introduced by one minor climax and ended by another. An excellent example of this sort of attack and retreat is Anthony Shaffer's two-character play, *Sleuth*, in which one character seems to be winning the battle between the pair until he discovers some trick hatched by the other.

Even in scenes where there appears to be no conflict, it is inherent; it carries over from scenes where it has already been shown. Suppose a man is having trouble at work. He is afraid of being fired. He knows he is the best worker on the job, but another worker degrades everything he does, while taking credit for his accomplishments. Consequently, the protagonist looks bad in the eyes of the boss. The man comes into direct conflict with his co-worker at the office. At home the situation appears to be calmer; but when the man discusses the situation with his wife, the conflict still is present. We know he is fighting against the obstacle of showing his worth to his boss. Maybe in discussing the situation with his wife, he decides what course to take.

Such a scene might belong in a script because it shows a part of the man's character not apparent in scenes with his co-workers. It might reveal how he thinks or what he plans to do, making the audience look forward to the confrontation with the antagonist. Still, every scene of this nature must relate to what is already known. It must not be extraneous to the plot.

Dramatic Action

Dramatic action everything that occurs in a play and advances it toward a conclusion; the motivation and purpose of a play; the physical, spiritual, psychological, and emotional elements that hold a play together.

Dramatic action must be directly related to the opposition of the protagonist and the antagonist. It must be related to what has preceded it in the story. It is the manifestation of the conflict between the protagonist and the antagonist. A man planning how to thwart the attempts of the antagonist to cheat him of an inheritance is using dramatic action, although he may hardly move physically. On the other hand, if a play opened with someone bustling around the stage and putting a room in order, it would not necessarily be dramatic action if no problem had been introduced.

Movement need not be restricted simply because it does not *seem* to contribute to the overall plot. Maybe it accomplishes another valid purpose, which indirectly advances the plot. Often a character is individualized in the eyes of the audience by some characteristic or repeated action. Polishing glasses or pulling on the corners of a moustache may be the outward manifestation of an inner emotion. The establishment of this trait may be important to the interaction among the characters. It may reveal something that explains why a character later takes some larger action.

Dramatic action relates in some way to the central character. Even if the character is not performing the action, it has a direct bearing on his or her situation. Even when the central character is not present, the action is initiated because of this person.

In other words, to build the series of minor crises and climaxes that hold the interest of the audience, the central character initiates an action,

The protagonist in a story play is similar to a racer who must leap various hurdles to reach his or her goal.

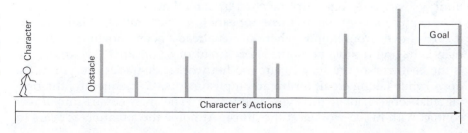

which in turn affects the character. The characters in a play cannot be allowed to be unanswerable for what they do. Once they act, they must be affected by their action. Dramatic action involves a clash of forces and is always reciprocal.

Even when one character seems to dominate, there is an interchange of action. The other person is acting, though maybe not as forcibly. Maybe the character who is being dominated is slowly building up a resentment and later will be in a position to let out that resentment.

Unity

The plot is the arrangement of the dramatic action to build suspense and reach a point of no return. For a successful plot, the action must be probable. It must fit the framework of the play and be consistent with the personality of the character who performs the action. It must contribute to the overall effect of the play. In other words, a play should have **unity**.

Unity a harmony in the way all the elements of a play combine.

One way unity is achieved throughout the play is by having all the action relate to the central character, whether or not the character is on the stage. Other sources of unity are the cause-and-effect relationship and the basic ideas that run through the play.

Unity can be maintained through a careful preparation for future events. Although some events may be unexpected, they must be logical in the framework of the play. The action is organized to gain a specific, unified response from the audience.

At the same time a play should be varied to maintain audience interest and sustain suspense. Variety may be provided by contrast among the types of characters, by changes in emotional pitch, or by changes in location.

Proportioning the Acts

Keeping the balance between unity and variety is a challenge. Playwrights must consider how each act fits into the total script. The plot should progress neither too much nor too little in each act. If there is too little change, the play will lag. If there is too much, there will be nothing to hold interest in succeeding acts.

In a three-act play all the groundwork for the audience's understanding probably has been laid by the end of Act I. Each of the first two acts ends on a high point to build audience anticipation for what is to follow. The first and second acts cannot end with all hope gone or the central character defeated. Although the protagonist is in a tight spot, the audience should have hope that the person may escape, at least for a while, before ultimately winning or losing. For instance, in *West Side Story* after Tony kills Maria's brother Bernardo, we can still hope that everything will turn out well for the young lovers. Our hope is reinforced when Tony tells Maria, in his song, that he will take her to a place where

West Side Story was presented by San Diego State University under the direction of C. E. Stephenson. Director, Don Powell. *(Photo courtesy of San Diego State University—Dramatic Arts Department.)*

they both can be free. The hope is further reinforced through an imaginary scene in which the warring gangs, the Jets and the Sharks, hold out their hands in friendship to each other.

To keep the audience interested, the playwright should not divide the acts into too many scenes in which a blackout or a curtain is needed to show the passage of time or to allow changes in the setting. If there are too many breaks, the play seems disconnected. There are plays, especially musicals, where the setting shifts from one location to another quite often, but the designer usually works out the changes to take a minimum amount of time without any break in the action.

The playwright also must consider when the climax should occur. If it is too early, the remainder of the play will seem dull or unnecessary. If it occurs too late, the audience will feel cheated, because there will not be enough time for the reestablishment of the balance. The climax should be delayed as long as possible for suspense but should come early enough for the falling action.

The Falling Action

The falling action or denouement, sometimes called the unraveling, shows any results of previous action. The climax begins to show the answer to the question asked when the problem was introduced; the falling action finishes answering the question. It may answer more fully how and why a certain event occurred. It may show the effects of the resolution upon the characters. It ties up all the loose ends. If the play is a comedy and the protagonist triumphs, we as audience members want to enjoy the triumph too. In a tragedy when the protagonist suffers defeat, we in the audience want to respond.

For that reason Miller included the cemetery scene at the end of *Death of a Salesman*. In this falling action, we see the different ways Happy and Biff have reacted to their father's death. Happy is determined to "succeed" on his father's terms. Biff recognizes the errors of Willy's search for success. We can assume that Biff's life will be better because he has come to redefine success.

Other Kinds of Dramatic Structure

Thematic Structure

Although the story play still predominates, several other types of dramatic structure are popular. One is **thematic structure,** in which a play is unified around a particular theme. It may have a multiplicity of scenes, all dealing with the same basic issue or situation but unrelated in continuity or characterization. In such a play, we seldom empathize as much with the characters, but the message sometimes is brought out in a more straightforward manner than in a story play.

The play with a thematic structure often is **episodic.** It has various situations that deal with the same subject matter but take place with different characters in different locations. On the other hand, some of the absurdist plays such as *The Bald Soprano* deal with a single set of characters but show no real progression of events. The lack of plot reinforces the theme of life's absurdity. Another example of a play unified around a theme is Brecht's *Mother Courage and Her Children*. The play shows Mother Courage's blind reliance on war to provide a living for her family and makes a strong statement for pacifism.

Sometimes a play will link a series of individual segments even more loosely. It may consist of short sketches. James Thurber's *A Thurber Carnival* begins and ends with a "word dance," music interspersed with one-liners. The rest of the show is tied together only in that it contains short sketches written by Thurber and based on his prose, including "The Secret Life of Walter Mitty" and "The Night the Bed Fell."

Thematic structure the organization of a play unified around a particular idea or theme.

Episodic structure a series of loosely related events that make up a play.

Ritual as Dramatic Structure

A number of plays in recent years have sought to present ritual as dramatic structure. To some extent, the playwrights are looking backwards to the beginnings of theatre for their form. (See Chapter 1.) One of the first persons to advocate such a return to ritual was Antonin Artaud of France. His book, *Theatre and Its Double*, published in 1938, contains his ideas for changing theatre to bring about social change more directly. Playwright Jean Genet, born in 1919, also believed in ritual. In his play,

A ritualistic beating is administered to the Marquis de Sade in this production of *Marat/Sade* at Kent State University. The director was Bedford Thurman, with scene design by Mary Ann Fruth. *(Photo by C. James Gleason and courtesy of Kent State University Theatre.)*

The Maids, two maids perform charades as the lady of the house and act out her symbolic murder. Peter Weiss' *Marat/Sade* is ritualized: the inmates of an asylum act out their crimes in a primitive, symbolic, manner in the course of participating in a play on the French Revolution.

Ritual has a certain structure, a pattern that is performed over and over again. Ritual adds security in everyday tasks. A person often performs a set pattern of activities before retiring for the night—checking the gas burners on the stove, locking each door, turning out the house lights, and so forth. Such ritual gives comfort and a sense of continuity. We are secure in knowing that our world is ordered. David Storey emphasizes the idea of ritual for comfort in *The Changing Room*, where the members of a semiprofessional rugby team perform patterned locker-room behavior.

Experimentalists such as Artaud and British director Peter Brook view ritual as a means of evoking strong emotions. They believe that ritualistic and primitive movements put people in touch with the dark places in their souls and the basic patterns of human nature. Ritual also allows the actor, like the primitive priest, to lead the audience to participate in the performance and thus become a part of nature.

On the other hand ritual occurs as pattern or repetition in such plays as *Waiting for Godot*. Each of its two acts progresses in the same manner. The play, like *The Changing Room*, illustrates **circular structure.** The two main characters spend their time waiting for someone who never arrives. The play opens and closes in the same manner, without anything of con-

Circular structure a type of organization in which the action of a play shows no real progression from one point to another but ends as it began.

Waiting for Godot
Samuel Beckett, 1952

It is early evening on a country road that is endless. Estragon and Vladimir are waiting for a person named Godot. They complain about life, pretend repentence, and fall asleep to have nightmares. They wake up and quarrel and wonder what to expect of Godot if he comes. Pozzo, a pompous taskmaster, comes down the road with Lucky, a near-idiot through being a slave and ever obedient. Now forced to think, Lucky pours out a mixture of theology and politics before he stumbles down the road with Pozzo. In Act II, Estragon and Vladimir trade hats, recite what they think is humorous poetry, play slave and master, and argue about the past. Pozzo and Lucky come back, the former blind and the latter dumb. Neither of them remembers who he is or was. Godot sends word that he won't come today but he certainly will tomorrow. Vladimir and Estragon know they should move on, but neither does, so they just go on waiting.

sequence happening to the characters. *Our Town,* to an extent, follows a circular pattern too, showing that life is a continuing process, about the same at one period of time as at another. The play begins with the Stage Manager acting as narrator telling us what is to come. The play ends with the Stage Manager relating what has transpired and showing that it is similar to what will continue to happen to the characters.

Waiting for Godot was directed by Paul Antonie Distler, with setting and lights designed by Randolph W. Ward, and costumes by Richard E. Donnelly. (Photo courtesy of Virginia Polytechnic Institute and the State University, Theatre Arts—University Theatre.)

Episodic Structure

Another type of organization in drama is episodic structure, in which events are expanded rather than condensed. Although this structure is by no means new, it has been used differently in recent years. An older example is the dramatization of *Uncle Tom's Cabin* in which George L. Aiken included widely separated scenes for excitement. The melodrama often switches locations and characters. It contains several loosely connected stories, with most emphasis on the love story of Eliza and George Harris, on Tom's relationship with Little Eva, and on the cruelty he suffers at the hands of Simon Legree. Altogether, the play contains thirty scenes and a great number of characters.

A modern example of a play with episodic structure is van Itallie's *The Serpent: A Ceremony*, which constantly switches from recent and even current times to Biblical times, encompassing events from the Garden of Eden, to the assassinations of John F. Kennedy and Martin Luther King,

Orpheus Descending is another example of a play with a plot. (*Photo by C. James Gleason and courtesy of Kent State University Theatre.*)

Jr., to the here and now of the individual performers, who state their names and tell about themselves. Van Itallie's play combines many of the ideas prevalent in current theatre. It begins with a ritualized procession to the rhythm of the actors beating upon their bodies. The characters often are symbols much more than individuals. There is no continuity of action; time and place switch from past to present abruptly, and to a large extent the actors improvise.

Such plays show that although most spectators still prefer the traditional, plot-structured play, and many playwrights continue to write in this vein, new writers are moving toward theatre that allows us to explore our inner selves more fully and to draw our own conclusions.

Unstructured Drama

At the greatest extreme is unstructured drama. Its advocates claim that life is unstructured, and therefore theatre should be the same.

The **happenings** of the sixties are the best examples. Happenings sometimes combined many art forms, such as film, painting, and theatre. Seemingly unrelated occurrences came together in an almost uncontrolled format. One of the early advocates of the form was John Cage, who wanted each person at his happenings to be aware of what was occurring and judge it independently. Later, people laid more groundwork for the happenings, even preparing outlines, but there rarely were rehearsals. There was little or no separation of audience and performer; the spectator was to become an integral part of the happening. The purpose was to break down any separation of life and art. Each happening was performed only once.

Critics argued that the presentations had no value; they were not art but only a mish-mash of elements. Even though the happenings may not have been important in themselves, they did help point the way to newer forms of drama.

Happenings a type of unstructured theatre presentation, generally involving the audience, in which there was little planning; the purpose was to break down the separation of life and art.

Theatrical Styles

Besides structure, a distinguishing characteristic of drama is style. In the theatre it often is difficult to separate style from structure. Style is closely associated with the manner in which the playwright or any other artist views life.

We speak of style in two different senses. First is an artist's personal touch. One artist can write or paint in the style of another, but the style of a great artist is unique. Such an artist looks at the world from a special angle, to which others can relate.

A theatre production represents reality by a particular set of conventions. Think of painting: certain groups of painters portray the "real world" they see by using perspective; others embody truth in distortion.

One group of painters conveys reality by showing surface details and textures; another by breaking every scene into dots of colored light or abstract designs. Plays have style in this broad sense too. For example, some groups of playwrights express their themes by means of realistic scenes, some by idealized scenes, some by symbolic places and characters. Style in this second sense provides the key to understanding a presentation.

Nowadays we can see plays in many styles. As one critic points out:

> A Greek tragic dramatist in the fifth century B.C. wrote in a tradition which prescribed the use of certain poetic meters, limited the number of characters who could appear on stage at one time, made obligatory the provision of odes and dances for a chorus, and directed that the plot must be drawn from heroic legend and the myths of the distant past. Modern dramatists work in no such dramatic tradition, and they have been left entirely free to choose subjects and invent new dramatic styles. The result has been a bewildering number of styles: realism, naturalism, poetic drama, symbolism, expressionism, the epic theatre, the theater of the absurd, and surrealism, to name only the most prominent among them. As a result of this freedom, modern plays have taken nearly every possible shape and size, ranging from imitations of Elizabethan tragedy in blank verse to modified Japanese Noh plays; from sprawling plays which take half a day to perform and seek to encompass all human life . . . to brief one-act "anti-plays" which prove the impossibility of finding any meaning in life except its meaninglessness.[4]

During certain historical periods various styles became popular. **Romanticism,** with its freedom in action and characterization, was a direct revolt against the rigid rules of Renaissance **neoclassicism.** Later, the Industrial Revolution brought about a lessening of the power of the upper class. Consequently, theatre moved away from romanticism and its lofty ideals to a more realistic view of life.

Realism is difficult to define. Each playwright who writes in the realistic mode and each designer of realistic sets must rely on a personal perception of reality. Within the broad category of realism we still can see differences from one artist to another.

No matter what the style, the theatre shows the artist's attempt to present truth. A production in the realistic style tries to present life as it is, whereas nonrealistic styles are more allegorical or abstract. An example of the latter is the morality plays of the medieval period. In these plays Everyman, the symbol of every living person, travels through life encountering other characters such as Vice and Evil. There are symbolic

Romanticism a style characterized by freedom, gracefulness, and a belief in humankind's basic good.

Neoclassicism a style popular during the Italian Renaissance, with a strict five-act format and a completely unified production.

Realism a style that attempts to present life as it is, but selectively; not all details are presented but only those that are essential for the audience's understanding of the play and for the establishment of the mood.

[4]"The Attempted Dance: A Discussion of the Modern Theatre" from *The Modern American Theatre*, Alvin B. Kernan, ed. (New York: Prentice-Hall, Inc., 1967), pp. 5–6. Reprinted from "Introduction" to *Classics of the Modern Theatre*, Alvin B. Kernan, ed. (New York: Harcourt Brace Jovanovich, 1965).

A scene from the off-Broadway production of *The Fantasticks*, the longest-running musical in theatre history. *(Photo courtesy of Martha Swope.)*

or allegorical characters in the modern theatre also. El Gallo in *The Fantasticks* is a symbol of "life to be lived." He serves as narrator and as companion, teacher, and guide to the boy, Matt, helping him experience life and become mature in his outlook.

The writing and scenic styles of a production should complement each other. Some plays demand a particular approach in production, whereas others can be done in a variety of ways, depending on the director's interpretation of the script.

Representational and Presentational Styles

Although theatrical styles vary, they fall into two overall categories, **representational** and **presentational.** Representational theatre leans toward realism, whereas presentational theatre is nonrealistic.

In representational theatre the dialogue, setting, characters, and action are represented as true to life. The action on stage shows the audience as clearly as possible the same kind of world they supposedly could see outside the theatre. However, because the actions occur as part of a

Representational style a broad category of style that is stage-centered; the actors make no acknowledgement of the audience, but try to duplicate life.

Presentational style a broad category of theatrical style which is audience-centered; the actors, director, and designer make open acknowledgement of the audience.

Butterflies Are Free, presented here by the Footlight Players of Coshocton, Ohio, is a representational play. (*Photo courtesy of Gary Anderson of The Coshocton Tribune.*)

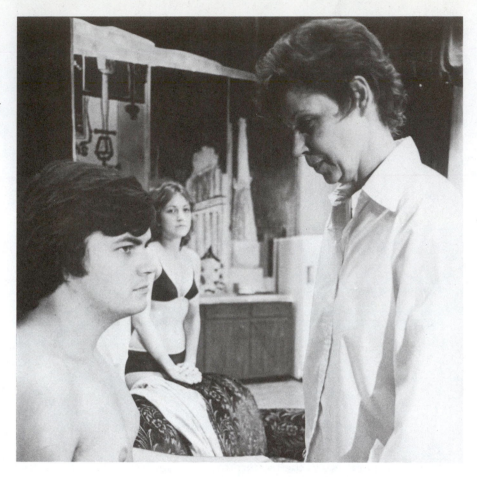

Fourth wall the imaginary wall that exists between the actors in a representational play and the audience; through this wall the audience sees the action.

Naturalism a theatrical style which attempts to duplicate life, or in effect, transfer actual life to the stage.

patterned play, representational theatre must fall short of depicting life as it is. Therefore we should only think of the representational style as a closer approximation of life than the presentational.

There have been many attempts to represent life in its entirety on stage, from having the actors turn their backs on the audience at will to transporting peeled-off wallpaper to the set of a production. André Antoine, who founded France's Théâtre Libre, attempted to create an environment on stage that would reproduce life in every detail, even to deciding shortly before a production which **fourth wall** would be removed for the audience. For one production he hung real carcasses of meat on stage.

Despite all attempts at the actual representation of life, actors speak memorized dialogue, the director plans the movement, and the play takes place in a space specifically set up for a production. Even **naturalism**, the most extreme of representational styles, has to be selective. Audiences at a production of Jack Kirkland's *Tobacco Road* know that the action takes

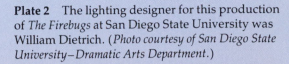

Plate 2 The lighting designer for this production of *The Firebugs* at San Diego State University was William Dietrich. (*Photo courtesy of San Diego State University–Dramatic Arts Department.*)

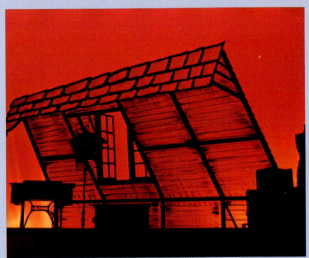

Plate 1 An aerial view of the Trumpet in the Land Amphitheatre at New Philadelphia, Ohio. (*Photo by Jim Coutts.*)

Plate 3 The lighting designer for this production of *Buried Child* at the Marquis Public Theatre in San Diego was Nancy L. Godfrey; set designer, Chuck McCall. (*Photo by Wanda Tritten Robin.*)

Plate 4 This backdrop for *Beauty and the Beast* was designed by W.N. Reed at San Diego State University. (*Photo courtesy of San Diego State University–Dramatic Arts Department.*)

Plate 5 Don Powell designed this setting for *Death of a Salesman* at San Diego State University. (*Photo courtesy of San Diego State University–Dramatic Arts Department.*)

Plate 6 This actor stands on an artificial mountain designed by Daniel Hannon for the outdoor drama *Trumpet in the Land*. (*Photo by Bill Douds.*)

Plate 7 This setting for *The Night Thoreau Spent in Jail* was designed by W. Scott MacConnell when the show was presented at Montclair State College. (*Photo courtesy of Montclair State College.*)

Plate 8 This box set (see floor plan on p. 196) was designed by Don Powell for a production of *Ghosts* at San Diego State University. (*Photo courtesy of San Diego State University–Dramatic Arts Department.*)

Plate 9 This actor is working with a life-size puppet, an example of unusual properties actors may have to use in a theatre production. (*Photo by Bill Douds.*)

Plates 10 and 11 Two scenes from *A Thurber Carnival*, presented by the Little Theatre of Tuscarawas County, Ohio. The women wore leotards and the men black slacks and sweaters as their basic costume. When they had to change roles to become one of many characters each played, they simply substituted a costume accessory, such as the slacks worn by the actress seated on the platform or skirts and kerchiefs for the women and vests for the men in the "Word Dance" scene. Jill Lynn designed the costumes. (*Photo by Bill Douds.*)

Plate 12 Unusual costumes for this production of *Jeezmoh*, a rock opera, were designed at the Marquis Public Theatre in San Diego by Joseph Dana. Lights, Bette Ogami; set design, Joseph Dana. (*Photo by Wanda Tritten Robin.*)

Plate 13 Professional designer Joseph F. Bella designed this costume for the Verdi opera, *Falstaff*, presented by the Washington Opera at the Kennedy Center. (*Photo courtesy of Joseph F. Bella.*)

Plate 14 This costume was designed by Joseph F. Bella for a production of *Tartuffe* at the Philadelphia Drama Guild. (*Photo courtesy of Joseph F. Bella.*)

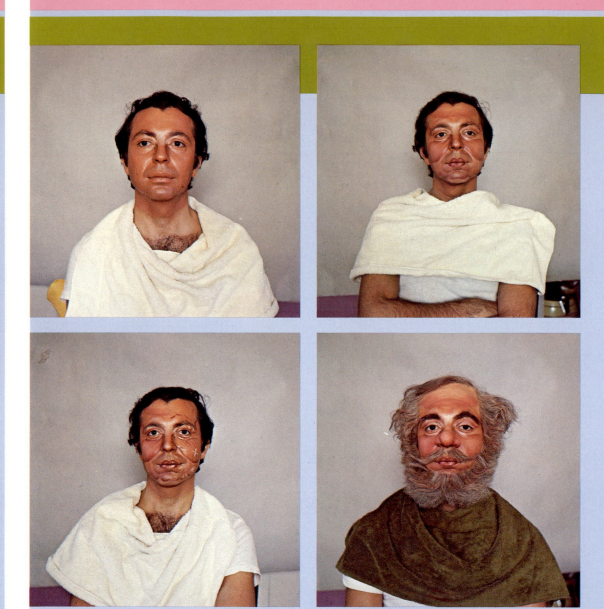

Plates 15, 16, 17, and 18   This actor is being made up for the role of Falstaff.
Make-up, Performer's Make-up; wigs, Ira Senz, Inc.; photographer, Susan Meyer.
*(Copyright © 1971 by Watson-Guptill Publishers. Reprinted by permission of
Watson-Guptill Publications.)*

place on a stage that is covered with a few inches of sawdust or dirt that only represents poor southern land and is not the land itself.

Whereas the representational style is stage-centered, the presentational style is audience-centered. Actors in a representational play make no open acknowledgement of the audience, but in a presentational play they do. They admit the audience's existence and even talk directly to the spectators. Many readers theatre productions, in which the actors read or recite a script without performing any actions, fall into this category, as do plays in which the characters deliver monologues directly to an audience. Often the stage is bare, or elements of setting suggest rather than portray a place. If scenery is used in a presentational production, it usually is nonrealistic. Ancient Greek productions were largely presentational; there was little scenery, and the chorus, in particular, often spoke directly to the audience. The actors wore masks and probably made broad movements. Productions in the public theatres of Elizabethan England also had many elements of the presentational style because, apparently, little or no scenery was used.

No style is pure. *Our Town,* for example, is presentational in that it calls for no scenery, and from time to time a character speaks directly to the audience. It is representational in that on occasion the actors move into specific scenes, such as the one at the soda fountain. This scene is both representational and presentational: in it the Stage Manager assumes another role, whereas George and Emily, the two young people who

Although the subject matter certainly isn't "representative" of life, *Dracula* is a stage-centered or representational play. This production was presented at Ohio State University, under the direction of Maureen Shea. *(Photo courtesy of Thurber Theatre, Ohio State University.)*

grow up next door to each other, later fall in love, and marry, keep the same roles that they have throughout the play. Another example is musical theatre, which is presentational in the use of singing and dancing but often representational in the dialogue.

Even in a play that would be classified as representational, the actor usually plays to the audience. Unless there is a reason or a specific effect desired, the performers on a picture-frame stage do not turn their backs on the spectators. Furniture is not placed across the front of the proscenium opening. All the other styles of theatre, such as naturalism, **expressionism,** and **symbolism,** are offshoots of these two styles and lean more strongly to one or the other.

Expressionism a style that presents the inner reality of the major character; the audience witnesses the workings of the character's mind.

Symbolism a style that presents life in terms of allegory; it depicts subjective or internal reality, determined by the playwright.

Style is sometimes determined in part by the type of structure in which the play is produced. It would be difficult, or at least ineffective, to present *Hello, Dolly* in the type of theatre that would lend itself to a production of *The Fantasticks.* The latter is intimate and demands a small stage and auditorium: the former is expansive and involves room for much more physical movement. We explore structures for theatre in Chapter 7.

The audience at a representational play tends to view the production as realistic, so they can identify and empathize with the characters and situations. A danger in this style is that if there is too much detail in trying to depict life either in the setting or the script, there is no focal point for the audience, and the production will lack any meaning. Unnecessary details take time and attention away from the important aspects of the plot, theme, character, or action.

On the other hand, the actors, the playwright, and the designers of a presentational play acknowledge the presence of the audience and do not try to mask the fact that a play is taking place in a theatre structure. It does not matter if the audience views the play as lifelike. This style proclaims that theatre comes from life but definitely is not life. Presentational theatre can fail to communicate if carried to extremes, because it can become too separated from life.

Naturalism

The most representational of styles is naturalism, which tries to present life as it actually is. In pure naturalism an attempt is made to include everything found in everyday life. In writing, this style means including all the details of conversation and physical movement. In setting, it means including everything that we would find in an actual dwelling or location. It also means that even properties that the actors never use must be authentic. All windows must open, all fireplaces must work, and all costumes must be made exactly like clothes in everyday life. Of course, there can be no such thing as pure naturalism; not everything in life can be duplicated exactly for the theatre, nor can life exist on the stage as it does outside the theatre.

Realism

Realism is close to naturalism in that it attempts to convince the audience that they are viewing life, but realism is selective. It does not try to include every detail, but anything needed to convey a mood or atmosphere or to portray character, whether or not it is used in the play. One realistic setting is the cluttered living room in Kaufman and Hart's *You Can't Take It With You.* It shows that the occupants live haphazard lives, but the clutter need not be mentioned.

Realism in writing means that the dialogue is made to sound lifelike, but it is weeded of extraneous detail. Although it has more direction, the dialogue attempts to present the actors as real people in real situations.

The actors in a realistic play do not recognize the presence of an audience. Nevertheless they must play to the audience, projecting lines to them and making sure they can be seen at all times. Their actions also are selective.

The action in *The Hound of the Baskervilles* is presented in a more realistic manner than is the case with audience-centered plays. The setting contributes to the realism. Director, Atlee Sproul. *(Photo courtesy of Colgate University/Summer Theater, Hamilton, N.Y.)*

Expressionism

A style that is more audience-centered, though still it has elements of the representational, is expressionism, which began in Germany shortly before the beginning of the century. Such a play shows the protagonist's inner self. The play deals with the internal reality of the mind. The setting is supposed to express how the character views life. Expressionism is a close meshing of styles of writing and set design. It attempts to have the audience see reality as the protagonist sees it, or to present inner feelings externally. The style is extremely subjective in its treatment. August Strindberg of Sweden, with such dramas as *A Dream Play* and *The Ghost Sonata*, was largely responsible for the expressionistic movement in theatre.

Symbolism

Symbolism began earlier than expressionism. Current playwrights largely ignore it, except to use certain of its elements in plays of other styles. In symbolism the playwright tries to present truth by internal or subjective means. Life is presented allegorically. Myth and legend often form the basis of such plays, most popular during the last two decades of the nineteenth century. The playwright attempts to evoke a mood that indirectly suggests reality, because truth, according to the symbolists, cannot ever be understood or communicated directly. Therefore nearly everything stands for something else. Undefined forms or unidentifiable locales are used as settings only to convey a general impression. Truth is expressed through analogy; concrete statement is replaced by suggestion.

The outstanding writer of symbolic drama was Maurice Maeterlinck, with such plays as *The Intruder,* written in 1891, and *Pélleas and Mélisande,* written in 1893. The latter, on the surface, is a simple story of a young woman who falls in love with her husband's younger brother. When the husband kills the brother, the woman dies of grief. But the plot is secondary to the ideas. There are recurring uses of water, light and darkness, and height and depth to suggest or imply hidden feelings and meanings.

Other Styles and Treatments

Impressionism is a style of design, exclusive of any conditions demanded by the script. The designer and the director determine what they want to stress most in the setting and apply this element to the physical production. For example, in the Broadway production of Tennessee William's *Cat on a Hot Tin Roof,* Brick and Maggie's bedroom was constructed to resemble a boxing ring because the two characters quarreled constantly. Such a concept in setting is not demanded by the script but was applied externally, pointing up the conflict between the two characters.

Theatricalism, formalism, and constructivism sometimes are called styles, although they really are only treatments of other styles. With **theatricalism,** the designer breaks down any suggestion of a fourth wall and

Impressionism a style in which the designer and director determine what they wish to stress most and apply this element to the setting; the style deals with the design exclusive of the script.

Theatricalism a treatment of a play in which audience members are constantly reminded that they are in a theatre; the fourth wall is broken down and the audience uses its imagination in the matter of setting.

This setting illustrates constructivism in that only what is necessary to the action of the play is shown in the construction of Brick and Maggie's bedroom, which has no walls, in this production of *Cat on a Hot Tin Roof.* Director, Bedford Thurman; scene designer, Mary Ann Fruth. *(Photo courtesy of Kent State University Theatre.)*

Formalism using the physical appearance of the stage rather than a designed setting; using only what is absolutely necessary, for example, ladders instead of houses in *Our Town.*

Constructivism including in the setting only those elements that are necessary to the action of a play.

allows the audience member to use imagination in the matter of setting. The viewers are constantly reminded that they are in a theatre. Often there is no attempt to disguise lighting instruments or backstage areas, and sometimes actors enter and exit through the audience. **Formalism**, which overlaps theatricalism and impressionism, uses only what is necessary to the actor and only because it is there. For instance, rather than flats, drapes may serve for concealment or for exits and entrances. **Constructivism** uses only those elements of setting that are necessary to the action of the play. Only part of the interior of a room may be built, and a ceiling light may hang directly from an overhead railing.

Other minor styles have developed but have failed to last beyond a few years. They are important only in that they brought about freedom to experiment or mix styles in current theatre.

Style in the Modern Theatre

New movements in the theatre have made it difficult to separate style from dramatic structure or even from genre. A type of theatre that has developed in recent years explores current issues. There is not anything new in this concept, except perhaps the manner of depiction. These plays

There was a mingling of styles and types of construction in this production of Pinter's *No Man's Land* at the Marquis Public Theatre in San Diego. Director, Minerva Marquis; design, Nancy Levinson; lighting design, Bette Ogami and Nancy L. Godfrey. *(Photo by Wanda Tritten Robin.)*

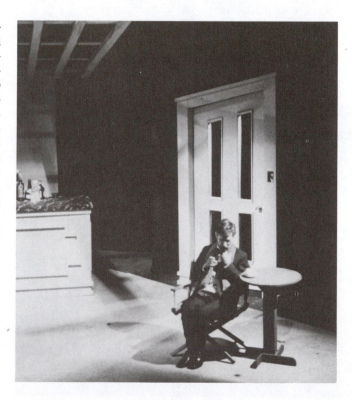

The Glass Menagerie contains elements of various theatrical styles. Betsy Gauerke played Amanda in this production by the Footlight Players of Coshocton, Ohio. (*Photo courtesy of Gary Anderson of* The Coshocton Tribune.)

often are much more subjective than other types of drama, particularly in reference to the issues the playwright is discussing. Because of this open bias, there is the risk of audience alienation. Included would be the type of street theatre that is political in nature. Often presented by radicals, it is held on street corners or in empty outside spaces with the purpose of persuading the audience to a particular viewpoint.

Musical theatre in the past was called "musical comedy," but recent musicals such as *Fiddler on the Roof, Man of La Mancha,* and *West Side Story,* often are serious in their treatment of subject matter. It has become impossible to treat musicals as a single style or define for them a single dramatic structure. All are similar in that they contain elements of singing and dancing; but they can be comedies, farces, melodramas, or tragedies, and they can come in many different formats.

There is a great overlapping of styles in the modern theatre. Many realistic plays, such as Tennessee Williams' *The Glass Menagerie,* contain elements of symbolism and expressionism. Even *Death of a Salesman* contains nonrealistic flashbacks or expressionism in showing the workings of Willy's mind. It is becoming more apparent, as Max Reinhardt (a German director who lived from 1873 to 1943) taught, that each play requires its own individual treatment. Modern theatre has become eclectic in its approach. It selects any combination of styles on the basis of how well they create the theatre artists' view of life.

The Glass Menagerie
Tennessee Williams, 1945

Tom Wingfield is narrator and character in this "memory play" that takes place when he was a young man in St. Louis. He brings back memories of his mother Amanda and his sister Laura, before he left the drab apartment across the alley from a dance hall. Tom held down a monotonous job in a warehouse. Amanda, a former southern belle who longs to live in the past and tries to force its standards on her children, keeps a tight rein on Tom and Laura. Tom's sister, who is crippled, lives in a dream world with her collection of glass animals, her favorite of which is a unicorn. Amanda forces Tom to invite a co-worker to be a "gentleman caller" for Laura, a shy girl who could not stay in business school because the pressure was too great. The caller, Jim, whom Laura knew in high school, is trapped like the other characters. He cannot get ahead and nearly falls into the trap of Laura's dream world. Tom has managed to flee his mother, but he cannot escape the memory of her and his sister and their hopeless existence.

QUESTIONS FOR DISCUSSION

1. In what way is truth communicated through dramatic structure or style?
2. Why do you think the story play is the most popular structure?
3. What are the characteristics of a story play?
4. What is thematic structure?
5. How can ritual be used as dramatic structure?
6. What is the difference between realistic and nonrealistic styles, between representation and presentation?
7. Why is it impossible to have true naturalism on the stage?
8. What is the difference between realism and naturalism?
9. What is the difference between expressionism and impressionism?
10. How does symbolism differ from impressionism?
11. Explain the various ways of treating style.
12. In what way is theatre eclectic?

SUPPLEMENTARY READING

PLAYS
The Changing Room by David Storey.
The Glass Menagerie by Tennessee Williams.
Man of La Mancha, with book by Dale Wasserman, lyrics by Joe Darion, and music by Mitch Leigh.
Mother Courage and Her Children by Berthold Brecht.
You Can't Take It With You by George S. Kaufman and Moss Hart.
Waiting for Godot by Samuel Beckett.

BOOKS

Clark, Barrett H., ed. *European Theories of the Drama.* Newly revised by Henry Popkin. New York: Crown Publishers, Inc., 1965.

Bentley, Eric. *The Life of the Drama.* New York: Atheneum, 1964.

Esslin, Martin. *The Theatre of the Absurd,* revised ed. Garden City, New York: Anchor Books, 1969.

CHAPTER 5
The Playwright

The playwright, unlike the other artists of the theatre, works alone most of the time. "With the exception of a self-indulgent misanthrope, no one is quite so much alone as a writer unless, of course, he owns a collaborator, in which case no two people are quite so much alone together."[1] Although there is a direct working relationship among the other theatre artists, the playwright, working in solitude, begins the creative process that results in a production before an audience.

Because a play begins as one person's work, playwrights have more freedom than any of the other theatre artists. They can express what they wish. Their own observations, experience, background, and sensitivity are the only limiting factors of their work.

Improvisation or Improvisational theatre building a scene or a play on the spur of the moment with little pre-planning and no script.

The playwright creates the raw material of the play. The writer and the actor, along with the audience, are the only absolutely essential artists of the theatre. The actor cannot exist alone, except as the performer-playwright who creates the script in performance. Even in **improvisational theatre** the idea has to come from somewhere. An audience may suggest a line or a situation the actors build into a play. Then the performer and the audience member collaborate in the "writing."

Although plays such as *Hatful of Rain* and *Godspell* have been created by group improvisation, and some plays, such as Van Itallie's *The Serpent: A Ceremony*, have been produced from outlines upon which the actors elaborate, most theatrical productions involve a completed script to which others add their interpretations. Each line and each action are recorded.

For this reason, playwrights generally are well acquainted with the medium for which they are writing. They draw upon their knowledge much as actors do. The playwright's job compares with the actor's in that both assimilate a diversity of material into a production. Both select, heighten, and expand.

Choosing the Audience

Sometime near the beginning of the writing, playwrights decide why they want to write and whom they want to reach. Often this is a subconscious decision. They know whether they want to write for a touring company that performs in elementary schools or for presentation in an off-Broadway theatre.

> Some people may exclaim: "Why should the dramatist concern himself about his audience? That may be all very well for the mere journeymen of the theatre, the hacks who write to an actor-manager's order—not for the true artist! He has a soul above all such petty considerations. Art, to him, is simply self-expression. He writes to please himself, and has no thought of currying favour with an au-

[1]George Oppenheimer, ed. *The Passionate Playgoer: A Personal Scrapbook* (New York: The Viking Press, 1958), p. 221.

dience, whether intellectual or idiotic." To this I reply simply that to an artist of this way of thinking I have nothing to say. He has a perfect right to express himself in a whole literature of so-called plays, which may possibly be studied and even acted, by societies organized to that laudable end. But the dramatist who declares his end to be mere self-expression stultifies himself in that very phrase. . . . The drama has no meaning except in relation to an audience. It is a portrayal of life by means of a mechanism so devised as to bring it home to a considerable number of people assembled in a given place.[2]

No matter what its purpose, a play should have meaning for at least most of the audience. It may express universality in its characters, reinforce a general belief, or present situations with which the audience is familiar.

Characterization

Choosing Characters

After deciding upon the type of audience they want to reach, playwrights can begin writing. There is no particular way to begin. Some writers start with a theme, some with a section of dialogue, others with a situation or a setting. Many playwrights feel as Edward Albee does:

> I'm not a didactic writer. I don't start with thesis, and then create characters, and then create a situation to illuminate the predicament. I don't work that way. Writing, for me, is something of an act of discovery, of discovering what I'm thinking about.
>
> I really don't know the origins. They're difficult to trace. With the exception of *The Death of Bessie Smith*—which I wrote for specific reasons after reading, on the back of a record album, how Bessie Smith died—I can never remember the specific origin of the plays I write. When I discover that I am thinking about a play I've already gotten the idea for a play. As for the exact moment it came to me— it's awfully hard to answer.[3]

Often a writer does begin with a character, who may be based on a real person or a combination of persons. Tennessee Williams says:

> My characters make my play. I always start with them, they take spirit and body in my mind. Nothing that they say or do is arbitrary or invented. They build the play about them like spiders weaving their webs, sea creatures making their shells. I live with them for a

[2]William Archer, *Play-Making: A Manual of Craftsmanship* (New York: Dover Publications, Inc., 1960), p. 9. Reprinted with permission.
[3]Roy Newquist, *Showcase* (New York: William Morrow & Co., Inc., 1966), p. 19.

Protagonists in a story play can be thought of as walking through a maze in trying to reach their goal. The inciting incident places them in a situation from which they try to escape. They are opposed by the antagonist, which constitutes conflict. The action then is made up of a clash of opposing forces, and through the events, the playwright presents the theme. After working through the maze, the characters either win or lose the struggle to reach a particular goal.

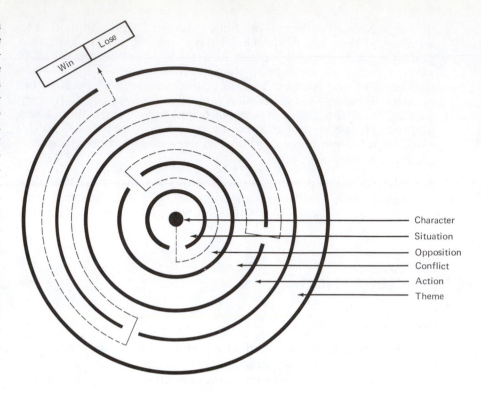

year and a half or two years and I know them far better than I know myself, since I created them and not myself.[4]

A developing character may suggest other elements for the play. Suppose the character is self-centered. The playwright thinks of a situation in which to place the character so that the extent of selfishness can be revealed. Then the playwright chooses other characters with whom the central character can react. The situations suggest the conflict, from which the remaining elements of the play develop.

Knowing the Characters

Most plays focus on one character, even though others may be on stage as much or have as much dialogue. The playwright analyzes every detail to make the character believable—background, attitudes, interests, and the important facets of personality.

A playwright should know how a character is likely to react in any type of situation. If threatened, will this person retreat or lash out? Is the character easy or impossible to defeat? Even though a play probably will

[4]Tennessee Williams, "Critic Says 'Evasion,' Writer Says 'Mystery,'" *New York Herald Tribune*, April 17, 1975. Reprinted in Tennessee Williams, ed., *Where I Live: Selected Essays* (New York: New Directions Books, 1978), p. 72.

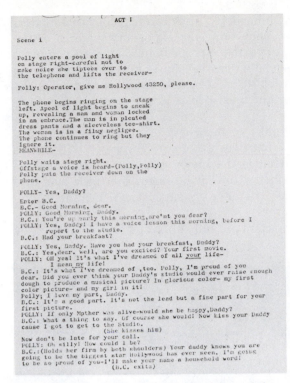

A page of the script and a page of one of the songs from the original musical, *Hollywood Heartbreak*. The script was written by Clyde Ventura, with song ideas by Ventura and David Gibson. Debbie Wright, David Gibson, and Terry Mace wrote the music, with the lyrics by Clyde Ventura. (*Used by permission of David Gibson. Copyright, 1976 by David Gibson, Terry Mace, Clyde Ventura, and Debbie Wright.*)

focus on only one character, the playwright should know all the important aspects of all the leading characters, so they appear to an audience as three-dimensional human beings.

After they analyze the major characters, playwrights determine the relationships among them. What do they think and feel about each other? How do they react to each other? Why do they react this way? What makes them the kind of people they are? Unless it is an unusual play in which characterization is not important, the writer must create leading characters whose actions can be understood, though not necessarily condoned. However, the playwright may know the characters well and still not understand them completely. Williams says that although he knows his characters better than himself, "they must have that quality of life that is shadowy."[5]

After developing the main characters, the playwright decides what traits the audience should see. Novelists can write pages about personal-

[5]Williams, p. 72.

ity and background, motives and actions. They can explain these matters in detail. Playwrights cannot. They bring out expository material or describe character only through appearance or dialogue. Novelists can write books as long as they like. A playwright has about two hours of playing time, which makes it impossible to concentrate upon more than a few personality traits. The playwright must decide which ones are most important.

Often the playwright thinks of the characters, as does the actor, in terms of goals or drives. What does each want the most? What does each hope to accomplish? What is the major goal that can be realistically explored and opposed in the time it takes for the three acts of a play to progress on the stage? The answers suggest which traits to emphasize.

Although the major characters are fully analyzed and developed by

Long Day's Journey Into Night has been called a character study. The personality of each of the four major characters is explored and revealed throughout the play. Here John Duggan plays Edmund while Ann Shepherd appears as Mary in the Playmakers Repertory Company production. Director, Tom Haas; set and lights, Bobbi Owen. *(Photo by Michael B. Dixon and courtesy of the Playmakers Repertory Company.)*

the playwright, the minor characters are not. If they were, there would be a danger that the audience would identify too strongly with them to the neglect of the major characters. There are certain auxiliary characters a playwright often includes in order to advance the play, but they are considered only as dramatic devices. Suppose that a character in a play is a landlord. His function is to provide conflict for the main character, who is behind in the rent payments. There is little need for the audience to identify with him or even to understand the kind of person he is. Two examples of plays with auxiliary characters are *Death of a Salesman* and Simon's *Barefoot in the Park.* In the former Ben, Willy's successful brother, is a symbol of Willy's own lack of achievement; and in Simon's play the delivery man is included only to bring expensive gifts from Corie's mother. The gifts are the mother's way of showing Corie all that she has given up by marrying Paul, a struggling young attorney.

Choosing Scenes for the Characters

Once the playwright has determined which character traits to explore most thoroughly, it is time to choose scenes that will reveal these traits. We can learn about characters by seeing the kind of place in which they live or spend time. We can learn about characters by hearing what others say about them. We learn the most, however, by seeing them in action. In everyday life we learn the most about people not from what is said about them but from what they do and how they react to their environment.

For example, try to describe someone you know to a friend, including impressions as well as physical appearance. Arrange for your friend to meet that person; then ask how well your description matched the friend's impressions. The point is that we cannot learn much about someone just by hearing a description. Others' views are colored by their perceptions and personalities. We must actually see a person to find out important or outstanding qualities.

In a play we learn most about the characters through what they do and how they react to situations they encounter. How do they meet crises or handle conflicts? How do they react to other characters? Each time they are opposed, we learn more about their emotions and psychological makeup.

A playwright may begin writing the first draft of the script by placing the central character in a situation where action is required or where goals are opposed and drives thwarted. When the opposition becomes the strongest, the most important qualities of the character will be revealed. Another objective in revealing character in this manner is to hold the audience's attention. The best way to do that is to make the audience want to know how the character will respond to a particular set of circumstances.

Revealing Character

A character does not usually undergo any massive change in outlook or personality during the progress of a play. What does happen is that the character's personality is gradually revealed. If the audience were to see the total character at the beginning of a play, there would be little interest in the play's outcome.

Any revelation, however, must be logical in view of the character's personality and background. Characters may change their minds, their course of action, or even their goals, but such changes are brought about by something already inherent in their personalities. The changes result only from seeds already growing within. In Lorraine Hansberry's *A Raisin in the Sun*, Walter, like many poor people, defines success in terms of money. Therefore he aggrees to take money from Karl Lindner in return for not moving into an all-white neighborhood. Lindner serves as a spokesman for the community, which tries to bribe the black family into not moving there. Later Walter reverses his decision and finds success in "becoming a man." The seeds of this self-respect and pride already were present in Walter's character.

The climax of any good play must be a logical outcome of the major character's makeup. A person viewing *Barefoot in the Park* knows that the two leading characters will "live happily ever after" because they love each other despite differences in opinion, style of living, and background. A similar idea can be found in the comedy *Mary, Mary* by Jean Kerr. Mary's basic need is to be loved for what she is, without having to play the role of a sensible person. Bob's need is to be loved and cared for; to be dependent upon someone. The conflict in the play deals with the two characters learning to accept things as they are. The conflict superficially seems to be between Mary and Bob, but it really is between the characters and themselves. In the end, instead of fighting against themselves, Bob and Mary learn to accept things as they are and to live with them.

Because an audience often is aware of what the ending of a play will be, the real suspense is concerned with how this outcome will be achieved. The characters should control the action; the plot should not be imposed upon them. At the same time the progression toward a climax must be plausible and clear. The main character should want something, and the play should be the story of an attempt to achieve it.

Theme

Often a playwright sets out to depict a character rather than to dramatize a theme. The theme comes to life only as the other elements of the play develop. For example, if the writer starts with a character, what the character says and does may determines the theme.

On the other hand, a writer may want to deal with a certain subject, to bring it to the attention of an audience. The writer's feelings determine the approach to the theme.

Defining Theme

Theme is synonomous with idea. It is what a playwright wants to say to an audience. It does not have to be a profound discovery. It can be a reexamination of something that everyone knows, but which the playwright wants the audience to rethink. It could be the restatement of a universal truth, or a reinforcement of something upon which the writer and the audience agree.

Theme is tied closely to audience response. How does the writer want the audience to feel after the final curtain? Why? Maybe the writer wants only to call attention to something worth learning or remembering. Maybe the writer wants the audience to reexperience an awareness of a sociological problem or to take a look at its own values. Whatever the theme, the audience will be more willing to accept it if the members are, at least, in partial agreement with the playwright.

Making the Audience Feel

Sometimes theme is merely an observation of life. Often a writer will only lead the audience in a particular direction, allowing them to interpret and draw conclusions.

> It is the task of the dramatist to co-ordinate his play, through the selection of episodes and speeches, that, though he himself is not visible, his point of view and his governing intention will impose themselves on the spectator's attention, not as dogmatic assertion or motto, but as self-evident truth and inevitable deduction.[6]

If a theme intrudes upon the progression of a play, the audience may resent it. The playwright should make an audience feel emotion and thus respond to theme.

To appeal to an audience a play has to have elements that are recognizable. There has to be a common ground upon which the audience and playwright can meet. Even a writer who lives in California has much in common with a person who lives in Switzerland. No human being is totally alien to any other. Nearly everyone experiences anger, love, hatred, disgust, and fear. We have all been in similar situations. There is an old saying: "There's nothing new under the sun." Every emotion that we can feel has been felt before. No situation or action is unique; because there have been other, similar situations and actions. We can restate the theme of many plays as a common expression or adage. For example, the theme of *Our Town* could be: Don't let life pass you by.

[6]Archer, p. 115.

Making an Individual Statement

Playwrights know that audiences relate the action on the stage to their own backgrounds and personalities. Just as children learn by watching others, so do audiences learn through observation. Both theatre and life are related to the mimetic instinct; there would no such thing as imitation if there were no need to relate others' actions to our own lives.

On the other hand, each person's background is different from everyone else's. The chain of events that makes up one person's life differs from the chain of events for anyone else's. Your perceptions of the world and your interpretation of events are slightly different in some cases and very different in other cases from others' views. That difference accounts, in part, for the difficulty police often have in obtaining a description of a robber. Each witness describes the thief differently. Our mental attitudes color our perceptions.

In one of the stories in *Welcome to the Monkey House* Kurt Vonnegut,

An audience usually has little trouble relating to the humor in Moliere's plays, such as *Tartuffe*. *(Photo courtesy of the University of Kentucky, Theatre Arts Department.)*

William Gillette was a popular American playwright/actor during the nineteenth century. *(Photo by Pach, courtesy of the Billy Rose Theatre Collection; The New York Public Library at Lincoln Center; Astor, Lenox and Tilden Foundations.)*

Jr., writes about a society that attempts to make everyone equal to everyone else by handicapping those who have outstanding abilities or attributes. The handsome or beautiful wear masks, and the intelligent have their thoughts interrupted electronically. The physically strong have to carry added weight, and television announcers have speech problems.

The idea of such a society appears ridiculous to us. We need a sense of personal identity. We do not want to stand out because of any defect, but we want to be recognized for our outstanding qualities. No matter what the basis for consideration, no one person is exactly the same as any other. It is these differences that provide interest for an audience.

The playwright has to maintain a balance between what is common to everyone and what is unique to the individual. Audience members want to see characters and situations with which they can identify, but which at the same time have enough suspense or mystery to hold their attention.

Each playwright interprets life differently than anyone else. All make statements, call attention, or make people aware of things they otherwise might fail to see. Writers should remember that what they are presenting is based on the way they see life. They are lending us their eyes.

Through selectivity, playwrights teach us to see what they consider important. They exaggerate; they ignore other viewpoints. They condense time and action, emphasize character traits, and edit the dialogue. They are selective in order to express the theme or to bring across the character. Playwrights write the way they feel.

Plays as Adaptations

Many plays, of course, are adaptations of other works. Often musicals are based on straight plays. Examples are *Hello, Dolly*, based on Wilder's *The Matchmaker*, and *My Fair Lady* (Lerner and Loewe), based on Shaw's *Pygmalion*. Many plays or musicals are based on novels. Steinbeck's *Of Mice and Men* became a play. Recorded history often provides the sources for plays. The many outdoor dramas across the United States restage history. William Gibson's *The Miracle Worker* is based on the life of Helen Keller. Numerous plays are based on the Bible. *Death of the Hired Man* is based on Robert Frost's poem of the same name. The source material can take almost any form.

When playwrights base their drama on earlier works, they have different thematic considerations than when they write original works. If they are writing a historical play, they cannot grossly distort history. If they are using older plays, as Anouilh did in basing his *Antigone* on Sophocles' *Antigone*, they cannot totally distort the original story, although they may provide different emphasis and add their own ideas. In many ways the work is easier than beginning with an original idea; often the characters, the theme, and the setting already are provided. On the other hand, playwrights may feel restrained by what already exists, or they may have trouble deciding what is most important in the novel or historical accounts they are using and how to bring it out.

Like any other playwrights, the writers who adapt their material from other sources perceive life in their own way. They still have a great deal of freedom to do what they feel is best and show us what they think is true.

Hello, Dolly was presented by Carnation City Players and directed by Delbert Walker. (*Photo courtesy of Delbert Walker.*)

Dialogue

Dialogue and Conversation

Just as character or theme can be the starting point for a play, so can dialogue. The idea for a play might come from a conversation the playwright overhears or imagines.

When conversation becomes dialogue in a play, the playwright strives for clarity, appropriateness, and naturalness. Dialogue usually sounds much like everyday speech, but diverse audiences must understand it. There is no clear-cut definition of everyday speech. People in each part of the country have different vocal patterns and inflections. Even people who grow up in the same area and have similar backgrounds speak differently. How then can the playwright determine what is natural and appropriate?

The dialogue must be appropriate and natural for the characters. It must fit their personalities. A stuffy character should speak in a more formal, stilted manner than an uninhibited, outgoing character, even though the same nuances of dialect may be present in the speech of both.

In conversation, educational background and environment also determine in part the way a person speaks. Many American-born residents of New York's Chinatown, for example, speak English with a Chinese accent. This accent is natural, because they imitate the speech patterns of parents and relatives. The extent of schooling often determines speech habits. The playwright observes such connections. The way a character speaks can tell much about personality and background.

Making Dialogue Selective

Although dialogue and conversation are similar, it would be highly impractical to transfer actual, recorded conversation to the stage. The playwright is selective. Because most conversations are social, they tend to ramble and quickly change direction. Dialogue has to make a point to understand, even when a character uses improper grammar or speaks with an accent. It must make the action and the characterization clear.

In making dialogue selective, most playwrights avoid long speeches because they can slow down the action and make a scene static. There are exceptions in some of the plays by O'Neill and Shaw; but the major device for advancing a plot is action, which implies reaction and interaction. Characters speak to each other and react to each other's statements. An actor who is obliged often to stand and listen while another makes long speeches may have difficulty in portraying a role. *Long Day's Journey into Night* does have speeches that go on for several pages, but the play is long enough for all four major characters to reveal their feelings and beliefs.

Making Dialogue Understandable

No matter whether it is long or short, the speech of any character must be readily comprehensible to an audience. Unlike the reader of fiction, the playgoer does not have the time to reflect upon each speech after it is delivered. A play need not be shallow, but the subject matter and circumstances have to be clearly presented. Dialogue has to hold the audience's interest and be concrete. It must help advance the plot.

Dialogue should advance the theme of the play as well. Largely through what is said the audience is able to tell the direction the play is taking. The theme usually does not call attention to itself; the dialogue points us to it.

Determining the Mood

Through a combination of dialogue, setting, and treatment of subject matter an audience absorbs the overall mood of a play. The language, the sentence structure, and the interaction of the characters should tell the audience whether any scene is comic or tragic, nostalgic or mocking. A playwright changes the mood from one scene to another through the use of dialogue as well as through the turn of events. Generally, the more passive the emotions, the longer and smoother the speeches. The higher the emotional pitch, the more staccato and abrupt the dialogue.

Building the Action

In conversation and in life there is a natural ebb and flow. Such should be the case with dialogue. Even when two people are in a lengthy, heated quarrel, the emotion does not remain at one pitch of intensity throughout. The characters become angry, lose some of their anger, and then become even more intense. A scene builds to a peak and then falls off again. Strong emotion cannot be maintained for a long period of time. Either the audience will become too emotionally drained to follow the action, or the intensity will lose its meaning. There is no way to build further, and there is likelihood that the scene will appear flat. Intensity has to be highlighted to have meaning.

Contrasts are needed for impact. A character attacks, retreats, and attacks again. The final attack evokes more emotional involvement and power. An example of this pattern is the quarrel between George and Martha in *Who's Afraid of Virginia Woolf?* The entire play is highly emotional, but there are breaks in the intensity to highlight the emotion.

A play usually consists of a series of small climaxes building to a single large climax. Individual scenes follow the same structure. Not only is there contrast within a scene, but one scene in its entirety is at a higher or lower emotional pitch than other scenes in the play.

Playwrights make certain that they don't place too much material in one scene or even in one speech. Too many important elements, too much background information, too much intensification in a single speech are wrong. A play builds slowly. Writers cannot present their audience with too much at once. Even if the spectators did not lose interest, they would not absorb important elements if they came one right after another.

Using Physical Activity

Sometimes the playwright supplements dialogue with directions. Pantomime or physical activity can be even more effective than dialogue itself. For example, in *The Miracle Worker* the major character, Helen Keller, who is blind and deaf, has no lines until the end of the play.

When a character becomes frustrated and angry, the playwright often allows the audience to see the character venting emotions through action rather than talking about them. A character in a state of mild anxiety may constantly straighten paintings or move papers on a desk. A character experiencing strong anxiety could slam a fist into the wall or smash furniture.

Identifying with the Characters

Dialogue and gesture alike must convince not only the audience but the writer. It would be difficult, if not impossible, to create scenes the playwright does not feel. Writers identify with their own characters and become involved with them. In effect, while writing, authors often become each character in much the same way actors become the characters they are playing. In *The Writing of One Novel: The Prize* Irving Wallace says that when he stops writing to eat dinner with his family, he often is somewhat shocked not to see his characters sitting around the table. He has identified so closely with them that they have become real people. The same thing happens with a playwright who wants to present characters realistically. Only if the writer feels can the characters in turn feel, and this feeling will come out in the dialogue.

Arranging the Dialogue

After the dialogue is written, the playwright goes through each scene to arrange the material. Now is the time to cut unnecessary detail or interject additional dialogue for clarity. The task is difficult, because now the writer has to be completely analytical, while retaining the feeling of each scene. Like the actor, the playwright performs on both the feeling and technical levels. If dialogue is added, the writer makes certain that it fits into the style of the scene and that it meshes with the way the characters are expressing themselves.

The next task is to judge the overall effectiveness of the dialogue. Does it portray personality as well as it should? Does it sound as natural as possible? Does it suit the character and the feeling in each instance?

Finally, the playwright checks the sound of the dialogue. Playwrights recognize that good writing style is not necessarily good speaking style. The spoken word, even in formal situations, is less formal than is the written word. In speech we put less importance on sentence structure and pay less attention to slight errors in grammar. Slang is used more often. By becoming aware of actual conversations, playwrights learn the differences. Then they apply what they have learned to their writing.

Writing the Script

There are some writers who state that when they sit down to write, they put on paper whatever comes to them, without having any kind of outline. These people are in the minority. Usually it takes time for an idea to germinate and to grow. Most writers have some sort of an idea about the progression of events, the theme, or even the type of resolution. Some prefer to work out an intricate synopsis before ever starting to write. Others have just a minimal outline, whereas some rely only on notes. There are even writers who prefer to think through the entire play before putting down a word. According to Edward Albee, "All playwrights work differently." He continues:

> When I'm writing I work, more or less, in two parts. I think about a play at least a year before I start writing it down. The actual writing is rather brief—three months for a long play, four hours of work each morning, six days a week. I do some revision in the afternoon. But other playwrights work very differently. . . . The only awful thing about being any kind of writer is that one is not engaged in a nine to five job working for somebody else. One is one's own boss, and one is quite alone, and one's self-discipline must be enormous.[7]

As we saw, a writer often begins the planning of a play with an analysis of the characters and their relationships. The writer then may plan out the type of setting. Some writers find it enough, for instance, to indicate that the action takes place in a lower middle-class apartment in Manhattan. Others find it better to have the entire setting in mind, because then they can visualize the characters and the actions clearly.

Marc Connelly describes his collaboration with George S. Kaufman on the play *Dulcy* like this:

> All our free hours were spent on building the outline of the play. George and I established working methods then that we followed through all the years we worked together. Having decided that our play should be in the mood of a warm but satiric comedy, we first fumbled about trying to visualize characters and plot progression. As Dulcinea—immediately shortened to Dulcy—was to be a girl of eccentric impulses, we saw possibilities in her engaging as a butler a convicted thief, out of jail on probation. She also was the kind of

[7]Newquist, pp. 28–29.

Rae Randall and David Little in the world premiere production of *Sherman, The Peacemaker* by James Reston, Jr. The play was produced by the Playmakers Repertory Company, under the direction of Tom Haas, with setting by Gibbs Murray, lights by David M. Glenn, and costumes by Bobbi Owen. *(Photo by Julie Knight and courtesy of Playmakers Repertory Company.)*

girl who would invite, among ill-assorted weekend guests, an ego-maniac movie producer, so we invented one she had met at a dinner party. Quickly the characters, their development, and the narrative progression were sketched in great detail. Within a few days we had a completely articulated synopsis of about twenty-five pages. We then individually chose scenes for which we had predilections, wrote drafts, and then went over them together for improvement.[8]

Planning the Exposition

One element playwrights often plan ahead of time is expository material. Generally they can work out most of it along with the character analysis; but because exposition is so important, the writer may write down all such material separately to be sure everything necessary is included. Because it has to be included where it is logical and does not intrude on the progression of the plot, exposition may be written into the script in an analytical manner after the first draft is completed.

We usually consider exposition in terms of background information

[8]Marc Connelly, *Voices Offstage: A Book of Memoirs* (New York: Holt, Rinehart and Winston, 1968), pp. 59–60.

pertaining to character, but it may also deal with the opening situation of the play. What are the general economic conditions, not only of the characters, but of the world in which they exist? What are the social conditions? Where does the action take place? Is there anything the audience needs to know about that location? Is it a desolate farmhouse, easily accessible to pranksters or thieves? Is it a slum area where stepping outside can mean being assaulted and beaten? What are the prevailing attitudes of the general population? What are the general feelings of the time? How do the central and secondary characters' feelings mesh with what the country or the world in general believes?

If the play takes place in another time or location than the one in which the audience lives, what are the prevailing conditions of this time and place? Are the natural laws the same as we expect in our world and in our own time? Setting forth exposition of this sort is really establishing a frame of reference.

After deciding what is necessary for an audience to know, a playwright sometimes ranks the expository material in order of importance. The basis for the ranking is what we needed to know immediately and what can wait until later. In this way the playwright prepares to weave material into the script skillfully and gradually. What an audience needs to know, for instance, at the beginning of the second act, may not have been necessary for them to know at the beginning of the play.

Finally the playwright has to figure out how to present the exposition. There are many techniques: in *Our Town* the Stage Manager tells the audience about Grover's Corners, speaking directly about the town's geography, history, and people; in *Death of a Salesman* the audience learns by flashbacks. If the technique can be presented believably, it can be used. It need only seem logical and call no attention to itself.

Planning the Action

Another element that can be planned out ahead of time is the action or plot of the play. Some playwrights record their plans in outline form, whereas others write a skeletal synopsis or scenario, using actual dialogue and action that they will fill out in greater detail when they write the first draft of the script.

Although it may seem that much of the work of writing a play is finished with the completion of the preliminary outline and the writing of the rough draft, the work is just beginning. It is rare for a writer to complete the first draft and have a finished product. It may take five or more drafts before the writer feels satisfied. There may be a need to rearrange the scenes, to cut sections or speeches, or to add new scenes and dialogue to give the play clarity. Even when the playwright is satisfied, the producer, the director, the actors, and the technical people may suggest or insist upon additional alterations.

Considering Practical Questions

Throughout the writing and revising, the playwright considers whether the script is practical to produce. When there is a scene change, the writer must know enough about scenery to make such a change possible without great difficulty. Playwrights should know enough about the styles of production to be able to determine what will work best for them. They must visualize how their play can be presented.

If the play finally is accepted for production, most often the writer will be required to attend rehearsals. Only then can the writer tell how well the play flows and if it accomplishes what it was meant to do. Many times the revisions continue until opening night or later, until the play is as fine as possible.

QUESTIONS FOR DISCUSSION

1. Why is the playwright one of the artists without whom theatre cannot exist?
2. What are some of the ways writers can start working on a play?
3. Why is it necessary for playwrights to know their characters thoroughly? What kinds of things should playwrights know about them?
4. Why is character usually important to the development of a play?
5. What are the characteristics and functions of good dialogue?
6. How do playwrights begin writing down a play?

SUPPLEMENTARY READING

PLAYS

Antigone by Sophocles.
Barefoot in the Park by Neil Simon.
Mame, with book by Jerome Laurence and Robert E. Lee and music and lyrics by Jerry Herman.
The Miracle Worker by William Gibson.

BOOKS

Archer, William. *Play-Making: A Manual of Craftsmanship.* New York: Dover Publications, Inc., 1960.

Baker, George Pierce. *Dramatic Technique.* Boston: Houghton Mifflin Company, 1919.

Cole, Toby, ed. *Playwrights on Playwriting.* New York: Hill and Wang, Inc. 1960.

Grebanier, Bernard. *Playwriting.* New York: Thomas Y. Crowell Company, 1961.

Langner, Laurence. *The Play's the Thing.* New York: G.P. Putnam's Sons, 1960.

Smiley, Sam. *Playwriting: The Structure of Action.* Englewood Cliffs, N.J.: Prentice-Hall, Inc., 1971.

CHAPTER 6
Dramatic Genre

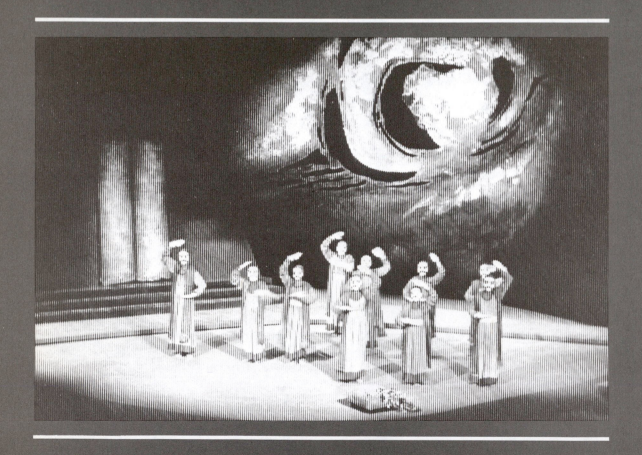

Genre means the form in which playwrights treat their subject matter. Usually the treatment is closely related to the writer's outlook on life. Is it optimistic or pessimistic? Does the writer view life in comic or tragic terms? The outlook determines somewhat the purpose in writing, and this purpose in turn ties in with the treatment of a particular subject or theme.

No writer views all of life in the same manner. Each person views some matters as ludicrous, some as above ridicule, and others as unworthy of any kind of treatment. Even temporary feelings during one period of life may determine the treatment in a particular play.

In modern theatre it is becoming more and more difficult to categorize plays. There is a strong overlapping of genre. There are comedies that have tragic elements, and tragedies that contain elements of comedy. If we use Aristotle's definition of tragedy as a genre that "shows noble actions of noble men," we have a few modern tragedies at all. There are plays that are serious in theme but do not end in the death or defeat of the protagonist, as does traditional tragedy. An example is *The Glass Me-*

This chart illustrates the relationship among the various genres of drama. Tragedy is the direct opposite of comedy. Melodrama is closer to tragedy than to comedy. Farce is close to comedy in that it is humorous, but its scope and format are much more rigid. Tragicomedy generally is closer to tragedy in that it deals with a serious subject or theme. There are also miscellaneous forms or plays that do not fit any genre. Any of these genres can be represented by both straight (nonmusical) and musical plays.

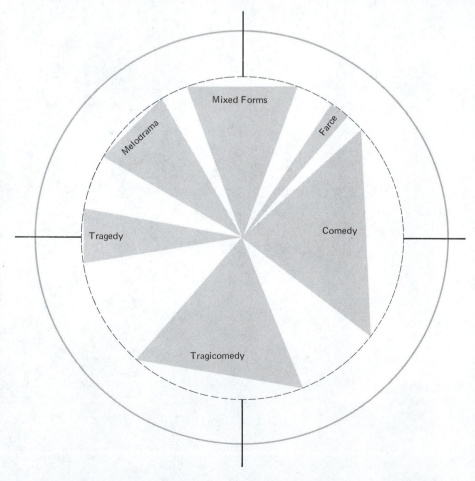

nagerie. The four characters are trapped by circumstances and their own limitations. The audience feels compassion for them, but there is no point of defeat in the play. The defeat has started long before the play opens.

The modern writer is free to experiment with a combination of forms. The theatre has become more accepting of new treatments and the breaking of old patterns. We can have such plays as *Oh Dad, Poor Dad, Mamma's Hung You in the Closet and I'm Feelin' So Sad*, which the author describes as a "pseudoclassical tragifarce in a bastard French tradition."

We need not worry that modern plays are so mixed in genre. As theatre critic Walter Kerr says: "The moment we succeed in consciously patterning our theater, in making it do precisely what we think it ought to be doing, we are apt to paralyze it."[1] All we need ask is that any drama should depict the truth of the human condition as the playwright sees it. Whether this depiction takes the form of comedy, farce, tragedy, melodrama, or a mixed genre does not matter.

Basically, there are two methods of treating subject matter, the serious and the comic. Within these broad categories fall all the various labels of plays. Serious treatment contributes to empathy, comic to aesthetic distance. (See Chapter 2.) An audience can be reached by making it feel what the character is feeling. This treatment prevails in most serious plays or in tragedies. Audiences also can be reached by an appeal to the intellect. Comedy often is funny because of aesthetic distance. Although in many comedies we do identify with the characters, it usually is to a lesser degree. In real life falling and breaking a leg would not be funny. In a comedy it might be.

The author must establish a framework that is appropriate to the genre. However, as Eric Bently explains, a fine play transcends its framework:

> . . . Plays are generally about the big people, though what they say applies to the little people. And there is a converse to this proposition: that when a great playwright, such as Chekhov, presents the littleness of everyday life, he manages to suggest—as indeed he must—the largeness of everyday life, the size of those fantasies which range from the secret life of Walter Mitty to the chivalric musings of Don Quixote.[2]

Tragedy

The purest form for the serious treatment of a theme is tragedy. In tragedy the audience comes to identify with the protagonist, whereas in comedy they often feel more detached from the characters. Tragedy presents

[1]Walter Kerr, *The Theater in Spite of Itself* (New York: Simon and Schuster, 1963), p. 19. Originally appeared as "Cheers for the Uninhibited U.S. Theater" in *Life* Magazine, Feb. 7, 1959.

[2]Eric Bentley, *The Life of the Drama* (New York: Atheneum, 1964), p. 7.

protagonists who struggle against overwhelming odds and are defeated. They meet death or destruction while attempting to overcome whatever obstacle lies in their paths.

Aristotle's Definition

According to Aristotle, tragedy "is an imitation of an action that is serious, complete, and of a certain magnitude; in language embellished with each kind of artistic ornament, the several kinds being found in separate parts of the play; in the form of action, not narrative; through pity and fear effecting the proper purgation of these emotions."

Many theatre scholars believe that the only true form of tragedy is that which conforms to Aristotle's definition. According to them, tragedy must deal with problems that are highly serious and profound. Often it deals with basic human nature. Tragic characters battle a flaw in themselves or evil in others. They struggle against forces greater than they.

Tragedy, Aristotle said, is serious in nature. Its purpose most often is to teach us and to make us feel, through our responses to the characters and their struggles. Tragedy often investigates human values by presenting truly heroic characters with whom we can identify. Because of the elevated spirit of tragedy, the language must be on a high plane.

To have the greatest impact, Aristotle insisted, the tragedy must be presented in the form of action. Only if we see a tragic character's actions can we empathize, feeling compassion and sharing the suffering. We grieve at the character's defeat. This response is what Aristotle means by pity. Fear is the anxiety aroused in the play. This anxiety should carry over to our concern for all human beings.

Catharsis the purge of emotions; the release of emotional tension.

The "purgation of emotions" means that there should be a **catharsis,** a release of all emotional tension, leaving us tranquil. We find this release by identifying with the tragic protagonist. All human beings are similar. We each possess, at least to a degree, the ability to feel or act as others do. When the tragic protagonist pursues a goal to the end, we feel that strength and persistence in ourselves. If the character's actions are affirmative, we too feel the capacity for affirmation. If the character suffers greatly, so can we. We can even feel superior, because we have structured our lives in such a way that we will never have to face the conflicts the character does. For that reason we also feel safe. Above all, tragedy maintains our faith in ourselves as a part of the human race. Even when tragic characters die, their heroism continues to live. Not their death, but what the playwright says about life itself is important. The issues, the heroic adherence to the dictates of conscience, and the reaffirmation of our belief in humanity are the vital aspects.

Even though we suffer with the protagonist, we find aesthetic beauty in the total conception of the drama, which gives us pleasure or satisfaction. Tragedy is concerned with grandeur of ideas, theme, characters, and action, and grandeur is aesthetically pleasing. Through the tragic character we come to terms with our own deaths. We accept the beauty of trying actively to improve the lot of humanity, rather than passively accepting our doom.

Truth in Tragedy

The writer of tragedy has to be a skilled analyst of human nature to bring to life truthfully the inner self of the protagonist. Although the conflict concerns human welfare, universal themes, and general problems, the workings of the protagonist's mind are the most important aspect of a tragedy. It is how the character reacts deep within to exterior events that gives us tragedy. When we hear of the death of another person, we may feel pity. But the more we know about the person's character, the more compassion and sorrow we feel. We can read of a plane crash that killed a hundred people, but unless we know one of those killed, it does not affect us strongly. It is up to the writer to make us feel for and care about the tragic protagonist.

The writer makes us feel that we are experiencing the struggles of a person close to us. Even though they are morally good, tragic protagonists are imperfect. We see the characters' weaknesses as well as their strengths. They appear to be human, and we can relate to their problem.

Except for the loftiness of the drama, the tragic playwright shows life as it is. Tragic protagonists must face the consequences of their a actions. We know they will be defeated; no fate will intervene. In this respect the genre is true to life. As the characters discover new insights into themselves, we discover new insights into ourselves. We know that

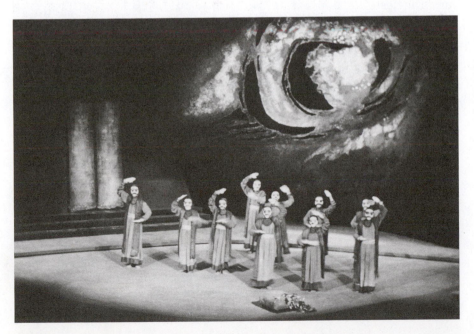

Aristotle based his theory of drama on *Oedipus Rex* by Sophocles. Director, Earle Ernst; scene designer, Richard Mason. *(Photo courtesy of University of Hawaii.)*

Coriolanus, a Shakespearean tragedy, was presented at the University of Hawaii. Director, Glenn Cannon; scene designer, Richard Mason. *(Photo courtesy of the University of Hawaii.)*

there cannot always be happy endings, but we can take satisfaction in our struggles.

Just as in life, the innocent often suffer in tragedies. Ophelia goes mad and commits suicide because Hamlet, the man she loves, kills her father. Oedipus' children are left without parents. In this respect also tragedy shows a close relationship to life. Society or individuals suffer many times because of the actions of others, even though the suffering seems unjust. Tragedy points out the injustice of life and the suffering of humanity. It shows cruelty and despair; but it also shows the heights to which the human being can rise.

Some tragedies can be interpreted with the view that fate causes the downfall of the protagonist, whose defeat has little to do with character flaws or with human errors. For instance, *Oedipus Rex* has been interpreted in two different ways. One is that Oedipus' downfall is preordained, proven by the fact that the oracle at Delphi tells him what will happen to him. He has no choice, no matter what he wants himself. The other theory is that the oracle, still with supernatural powers, only is able to see into the future. It foresees what will happen to Oedipus, but the tragic hero is free to find out who murdered the king (his father) or just drop the matter. Oedipus has free choice, and the gods are not controlling his actions.

Modern Tragedy

Few tragedies throughout history have reached the Aristotelian ideal, but it is a matter of viewpoint what in more recent historical periods constitutes tragedy. If we consider that tragedy occurs when a basically good person commits an irrevocable act because of a particular character flaw, the genre encompasses many more plays than those that follow the strict Aristotelian definition. Even Willy Loman, although by no means a noble character, has a certain nobility in wanting to achieve success for his family. His basic flaw is equating success with money, which finally causes his death. We are able to pity him and fear for him. Willy is a reflection of our society, a common salesman who is a symbol of the American dream of getting ahead. We identify with his feelings and flaws, with his concerns and problems. Such is the case with many modern plays. We feel compassion for Blanche in *A Streetcar Named Desire* and for the foolish Don Quixote in *Man of La Mancha*. They suffer and so do we. When we view the plays in which these characters appear, we feel a sense of aesthetic beauty, an elevation of the spirit. We do not leave the theatre depressed and frustrated.

Our tragic figures are not of noble birth. Because our society is not the same as that of ancient Greece, we cannot conform to Aristotle's ideal in that respect, unless we base our tragedies on past historical periods. Nevertheless modern tragic characters, like Tony in *West Side Story*, fight for what they believe. They still are basically good. They still pursue the only course of action that is consistent with their own moralities. We still question why injustice and evil surround them and why the innocent are made to suffer. We still can identify with our tragic characters and feel the grandeur of their efforts.

In other words, the characters in modern tragedies are noble in their motives if not in their births. In modern society we do not automatically hold well-born members in high esteem. Instead we identify with the character of high principle who is the symbol of the best in ourselves. In ancient Greece the rulers were symbols of society and above reproach. That is why they appear as the major characters in tragedies.

Whether we feel that crowned nobility or nobility of spirit is what makes for tragedy, we have to agree that the protagonists in tragedy are of heroic stature. They are people who are basically good but have a flaw or blind spot that causes them to err in judgement. They can follow several courses, but the only moral alternative is to accept defeat. The struggle they suffer often deals with their own integrity, and the audience should empathize with them in their decisions. Only through experiencing the struggle in its entirety can the audience see that even in defeat, there is triumph. They have overcome temptation and stand by their principles.

Cultures change, society progresses, and theatre is a part of the whole. The final test is whether the modern tragedies bring about a purgation of the emotions of pity and fear and leave us uplifted.

Comedy

The opposite of tragedy is comedy, which seeks to arouse joy or scorn rather than pity and admiration. Its premise is that we should laugh as well as feel sorrowful. Usually we are made to laugh at ourselves and our institutions, taking ourselves less seriously.

Comedy of manners a play that deals with the foibles or amoral characteristics of the upper class.

Of all dramatic forms comedy has the most variety. It can be the subtle **comedy of manners**, which relies on the intellect, or it can be the physical slapstick of the Three Stooges. Comedy even has been defined as any play that has a happy ending. Most often comedy shows a deviation from the norm of everyday life, although it often concerns itself with mundane, everyday problems and the pettiness of day-to-day living.

The purpose of evoking laughter differs from play to play. Maybe the writer wants to teach us not to take ourselves so seriously, or to release us from the tensions of life. Maybe the playwright wants to remind us of our own frailties but show us that they are not so serious as we think. The writer's purpose may be to correct a social injustice or to poke fun at a particular human fault. The idea is that if we can laugh at ourselves or at others, the fault is not so serious as it first appeared. We can correct social and personal flaws if only we laugh at them. In most comedy situations, characters, and actions are exaggerated to show humankind, as Aristotle said, worse than it really is. The purpose is to show us the necessity for a balanced society and to keep us from gaining too high an opinion of ourselves. In fact, pride has been the subject of many plays, both comic and serious. Often pride makes a character hang on to eccentricities no matter what happens. Because it is corrective and does celebrate a rebirth of society, comedy often ends in marriage. An example is Shakespeare's *As You Like It*, in which Rosalind masquerades as a boy until she is sure Orlando loves her.

Deviation from the Norm

The humor in a comedy can come from treatment of character or situation. It forces us to view objectively any deviation from the norm. Any subject matter can be used if it can be treated in a humorous light. It is only if the deviation becomes too painful that the comedy ceases to be funny. It would be cruel and unfunny to treat physical deformities or handicaps as sources of comedy. More often the things over which we have control or our views of uncontrollable forces comprise the subject matter.

Eccentricities of character can be humorous. In the 1600s the French playwright Molière ridiculed extreme greed in *The Miser*. Other eccentricities that might be the basis of comedy are hypocrisy, laziness, or overwhelming ambition.

Unusual situations can be the basis of a comedy. Comic protagonists may become involved in situations with which they are unable to cope or

These two comedies were presented by the Old Creamery Theater Company, a professional group from Garrison, Iowa. The actor in Moliere's *The Miser* is Pat O'Brien, while Susan Scott, Kim Anderson, and Jeffrey Hartig appear in *Charlie's Aunt*. *(Photos courtesy of Old Creamery Theater Company.)*

The Miser
Molière, 1669

Harpagon, a widower and the father of two grown children, is ruled in all his actions by his miserliness. This characteristic frustrates his children and also makes Harpagon the target for anyone who recognizes his all-encompassing passion for money. The children scheme to choose their own mates because their father was ruled by his greed in choosing for them. Harpagon's son Cléante thus becomes his father's rival for Marianne. Finally, Cléante forces his father to choose between the girl and his missing money box. He, of course, chooses the latter. The play includes chases and beatings for comic effect and has one scene where Harpagon plans a party but wants to spend very little money on it.

which are outside their knowledge and experience. Examples are an office worker posing as a diplomat, or a janitor posing as a psychiatrist. Comedy mocks our desire to be what we are not, or to place too much importance on our goals.

Although comedy usually deals with deviation in a normal society, the Theatre of the Absurd often has shown "normal" individuals in an insane, abnormal world. Thus it criticizes society. Whether society or the individual is viewed as normal, comedy begins with an idea in which normalcy is somehow reversed.

Comic Devices

Unlike tragedy, comedy must end happily. The protagonist must win. If not, the audience would feel guilt or shame for having laughed at the central character. It is therefore important that a comic frame of reference be developed. If it is not, the audience may not know how to respond. Viewers should realize that what they are seeing is not to be taken seriously and that they are not to identify too strongly with either the character or the situation, unless it is a matter of laughing with instead of at the character. If a character involved with forces beyond control views the dilemma in a humorous light, then we can laugh along.

In many cases comedy does not hold up across the years so well as tragedy. Many comic devices depend on the here and now. There are often allusions to current society, trends, and individuals within the play's framework.

Despite the fact that much of the comic writing of the past has lost meaning, writers of comedy still rely on certain devices or techniques that have proved successful for centuries. These comic devices help establish a comic frame of reference. For instance, if something funny happens right away, the audience knows the type of play to expect and feels free to go on laughing.

Let us look at six comic devices: **exaggeration, incongruity, automatism, character inconsistency, surprise,** and **derision.**

Exaggeration is the intensification or enlargement of a particular characteristic or situation through overstatement. Most people are not as miserly as Harpagon in Molière's play, nor are most people as finicky as Felix in *The Odd Couple.* Exaggeration can encompass many of the other devices by heightening or intensifying them.

Incongruity refers to opposite or differing elements seen together, usually in deviation from the norm. It would be comic to show a man wearing a tuxedo and a T-shirt.

Automatism refers to a person's acting like a robot rather than like a human being. It includes a visual or verbal gag repeated time after time and becoming funnier and funnier. Many comedians have been identified with certain phrases. The late Jack Benny could get a laugh every time he folded his arms and said: "Well." Often automatism is funnier when variations are introduced. Suppose for the first three entrances a character walks into a heavy floor lamp. On the fourth entrance she approaches the lamp carefully to see that she does not bump it. Someone calls her, and she turns her head to listen. She murmurs a reply and walks into the lamp.

Character inconsistency shows a trait that does not seem to fit the rest of a character's personality. This device is used effectively in *Arsenic and Old Lace.* The two old aunts are the personification of goodness, except that they murder lonely, old men.

Surprise can encompass many of the other devices. It is the unexpected. We know that each joke will have a punch line, but the humor comes when we hear a line we do not expect. This device also includes much of the verbal wit in comedy. The pun, the wisecrack, or the insult can surprise us. In *The Importance of Being Earnest* the audience expects to hear a criticism when Jack admits to Lady Bracknell that he smokes. Instead she says it is a good thing he does, because a man needs an occupation.

Derision is laughing at people and institutions. Writers often deride hypocrisy, pomposity, or ineptitude. The object is to deflate egos or to cause discomfort and reduce status. Derision can be effective, but it fails to have the desired effect when it becomes too bitter. Often, then, the audience identifies with the intended victim. Mere sarcasm inflicts pain by ridiculing faults or conditions that cannot be corrected.

Closely related to derision is **satire,** sometimes classified as a subgenre of comedy. Satire also ridicules, but for the purpose of reform, and it is gentler than sarcasm. Gilbert and Sullivan's *H.M.S. Pinafore,* for instance, is, among other things, a satire on the British Navy.

Ridicule and laughter can be dangerous. The playwright should establish a framework in which the situations, characters, and actions are truly funny, without being cruel.

Exaggeration humor through overstatement and intensification.

Incongruity humor through showing differing or opposing elements together, such as tennis shoes with a formal gown.

Automatism a visual or verbal gag that is repeated many times.

Character inconsistency comedy that results from a trait that does not seem to fit with a character's personality.

Surprise humor through the unexpected.

Derision making fun of people or institutions for the purpose of social reform.

Satire gentle mockery for the purpose of reform.

The 19th-century English melodrama, *East Lynne*, was directed by Jim Bob Stephenson with scene design by Robert Riedthaler. *(Photo by C. James Gleason and courtesy of Kent State University Theatre.)*

Types of Comedy

It is tricky to distinguish the many types of comedy. There is so much intermingling that comedies often defy categorization. Nevertheless, the types range from high to low. These terms do not imply that one is better than the other, but only that the appeal differs. **High comedy** appeals to the intellect, using verbal wit, whereas **low comedy** is largely physical.

According to playwright S. N. Behrman: "The immediate concerns of the characters in a high comedy may sometimes be trivial; their point of view must never be. Indeed, one of the endless sources of high comedy is seriousness of temperament and intensity of purpose in contrast with the triviality of the occasion."[3]

High comedy
humor through verbal wit that appeals to the intellect.

Low comedy
humor that relies on physical actions.

[3]S. M. Behrman, "Query: What Makes Comedy High?" *The New York Times,* March 30, 1952.

High comedy encompasses comedy of manners, in which the excesses and foibles of the upper class are the targets. The writer of such comedy usually is not suggesting a change in the pretensiousness, but only pointing it out.

At the other end of the spectrum is **burlesque,** which relies on beatings, accidents, and often vulgarity. The situations and characters are highly exaggerated.

Romantic comedy usually is gentle in showing the complications the hero and heroine face in their quest for living "happily every after." **Situation comedy** places the characters in unusual circumstances, whereas **character comedy** deals with the eccentricities of the individual.

All these types of comedy have some common ground. First, they establish a comic framework. Second, the humorous aspects are exaggerated, both in writing and performance. More than any other genre, comedy relies on timing. Third, the characters tend to be more stereotyped than characters in tragedy. Often the writer is concerned with plot involvement rather than with characterization.

Even though tragedy generally is more lasting, comedy is as valuable. We need to laugh to release tensions, and comedy allows us to escape everyday monotony. It is corrective. It shows us that our own problems are not unique, and thus it draws us closer to others.

Melodrama

A third major genre is melodrama. Like comedy it often ends happily. Like tragedy it treats a serious subject, and the audience identifies with the protagonist. Here the resemblances end. Rather than exploring a character's inner being, melodrama presents one-dimensional characters, either all good or all bad. When it deals with the painful and the serious, the subject matter is exploited only for its theatrical value. Melodrama often appears to show three-dimensional characters in conflict, but the struggle usually is only surface, and the audience knows that good will triumph. Action generally is much more important than characterization.

When melodrama was at its height of popularity during the last century, it offered the most sensational and exciting scenes. An excellent example is Aiken's version of *Uncle Tom's Cabin.* The play contains scenes of great terror and suspense, such as Eliza's crossing the ice. Tom is too good to be true, whereas Simon Legree is the personification of evil. Like much melodrama of the nineteenth century, the scenes are episodic and often unrelated, except chronologically. It also is full of sentiment, as in the scene of Little Eva's death.

Other favorites, such as *Under the Gas Light* and *Ten Nights in a Barroom,* played year after year in theatres across the country. There was almost always a happy ending, with the hero and heroine declaring their love for each other and the villain defeated or confined to prison. Melodrama was constructed so that escape was inevitable but only at the last

Burlesque a type of low comedy that relies on beatings, accidents, and vulgarity for its humor.

Romantic comedy a comedy whose humor lies in the complications the hero and heroine face in their love for each other.

Situation comedy a comedy whose humor derives from placing the central characters in a comedy in unusual situations.

Character comedy a play whose humor directly involves the actions and eccentricities of the central character.

possible moment. Audiences "oohed" and "ahed" as the hero arrived just in time to save the heroine before the cotton press descended to snuff out her life.

Melodrama offers entertainment and escapism, but it can bring the plight of individuals and groups to the attention of the audience. Within recent years melodrama has become more realistic. The characters are less stereotyped, and sometimes the play does not end happily. There is still exaggeration and scenes of suspense and high excitement. Modern melodramas range from Shaffer's *Sleuth* to Maxwell Anderson's *The Bad Seed*, which is about a little girl who is evil.

Outwardly melodrama has changed, but basically it has the same appeals: a virtuous hero or heroine, a despicable villain, and sensationalism.

Farce

A fourth genre is farce, which is similar to melodrama in that coincidence or fate can play a large part in the outcome. Farce is more similar to comedy than to tragedy. The primary purpose is entertainment. The appeal is broad, and it takes little imagination or intellectual effort to follow

The Paisley Convertible, a farce, was presented by the Little Theatre of Tuscarawas County, Ohio, under the direction of Delbert Walker. *(Photo by Bill Douds.)*

the plot. Like melodrama, farce has stock characters who are one-dimensional. The plots are highly contrived and rely on physical actions and devious twists to hold the audience's attention. The play contains no message of significance, and the progression shows only how the major characters manage to release themselves from entanglements. Throughout the years the form has changed little.

William Butler Yeats describes farce this way:

> A farce and a tragedy are alike in this, that they are a moment of intense life. An action is taken out of all other actions; it is reduced to its simplest form, or at any rate to as simple a form as it can be brought to without our losing the sense of its place in the world. The characters that are involved in it are free from everything that is not a part of that action; and whether it is, as in the less important kinds of drama, a mere bodily activity, a hairbreadth escape or the like, or as it is in the more important kinds, an activity of the souls of the characters, it is an energy, an eddy of life purified from everything but itself. The dramatist must picture life in action, with an unpreoccupied mind, as the musician pictures her in sound and the sculptor in form.[4]

[4]William Butler Yeats, "Language, Character and Construction," in Toby Cole, ed., *Playwrights on Playwriting*, (New York: Hill and Wang, 1960), p. 37. Reprinted from *Plays and Controversies* (London: Macmillan & Co., Ltd., 1923).

Because many farces are concerned with illicit sexual relationships and infidelity, they have been criticized for their immorality. However, farces neither condone nor condemn illicit sex. They are amoral in their outlook. The aim is to provide laughs for the audience by presenting a pattern of humorous actions.

The success of a farce relies heavily on the actor and director. They must present ludicrous actions and deliver gags and absurdities of speech. A farce that is delivered well in one language probably could succeed before an audience that speaks only another, because much of the humor is visual. Farce uses many of the devices of comedy: automatism, incongruity, derision, and physical violence.

The plot often relies on misunderstanding. In a modern farce, *The Paisley Convertible* by Harry Cauley, a young married couple believes that each has become involved with a former lover. The misunderstandings are further complicated when a former girlfriend, Sylvia, spends the night at the man's apartment. Often farce relies on mistaken identity, deception, and unfamiliar surroundings. The characters are victims of their vices, and when caught, appear ridiculous. An example is Georges Feydeau's *The Happy Hunter*. The title has a double meaning: the protagonist wants his wife to think he is hunting game, when actually he is "hunting" illicit female companionship. The action is highly improbable and the entanglements almost beyond imagining.

Tragicomedy

Throughout the history of theatre in the West there has been a mingling of the comic and the tragic. There is some humor in Sophocles' *Antigone* and in several of Euripides' tragedies, all written during the fifth century B.C. in Greece. Many of Shakespeare's tragedies contain scenes of comic relief. Probably one of the most familiar is the gravediggers' scene in *Hamlet*. There is even more mixing of comic and tragic elements in Shakespeare's *Troilus and Cressida* and in his romances. During the late sixteenth and early seventeenth centuries in Italy, France, and England, there was a further mixing of comic and tragic elements, and by the eighteenth century, sentimental comedies were "comic" only in that they ended happily.

Within the past few decades the term *tragicomedy* has been applied to various types of drama. The term is a paradox. A protagonist who is a truly noble figure cannot appear comic. Neither can a humorous character possess the scope of a tragic hero. Nevertheless some plays mix many of the elements of tragedy and comedy. Often the term is applied to absurdist plays. There is a great deal of controversy over what the form really is and when it began to be a new form. Some theatre scholars suggest that we discard the term altogether and call such plays tragic comedies or comic tragedies. One's viewpoint hinges on a matter of definition.

Pinter's *The Birthday Party* is an example of tragicomedy. Director, Lynn Bohart. *(Photo courtesy of San Diego State University—Dramatic Arts Department.)*

At any rate it takes a skillful playwright to mingle the serious and the comic effectively. Tragicomedy is one of the most difficult genres. The playwright must advance the plot without totally confusing the audience. The play must reflect the way life itself intermingles the tragic and the comic. Often the writer of tragicomedy will present a situation that appears to be comic, and later let the audience realize that it is serious.

Harold Pinter's *The Birthday Party* is a total mingling of the comic and the serious, and some scenes even can be taken either way. Pinter called the play a "comedy of menace." During the second act, a birthday party is held for Stanley. Goldberg and Lulu are necking, Meg and McCann are talking, and Stanley is ignored. The purpose is to point up the lack of contact among people. The situation appears funny, but its point is sad.

Likewise it is humorous that the characters in *Waiting for Godot* spend their lives waiting for nothing. At the same time the message is

The Birthday Party

Harold Pinter, 1958

The action occurs in a cheerless rooming house run by Meg and Petey. Stanley, a pianist who has sought refuge from the world, is one of the boarders. Two men who seek lodging in the house suggest that a birthday party be held in Stanley's honor, even though it isn't his birthday. During the course of the party, the two men destroy Stanley's personality and leave him speechless before they take him to their big, black car waiting outside. It is never made clear why the two men are after him.

serious when we think that much of our lives is spent in anticipation of something that never occurs.

Eugène Ionesco said he wants his audience at times to view the tragic as comic and the comic as tragic. Although such plays as *The Lesson*, *The Killers*, and *Rhinoceros* present an unhappy outlook on life, they are written in such a way as to be amusing. One reason is that Ionesco often employs automatism. Examples are the repetition of nonsensical lines in *The Lesson* and the discussion about Bobby Watson in *The Bald Soprano*. (See page 26.) To point up the comedy Ionesco wants ludicrous situations to be played with deadly seriousness.

Often in tragicomedy the audience is jolted from comedy to horror, as happens in *Who's Afraid of Virginia Woolf?* Whatever method the writer chooses to mingle the elements, the genre is well established.

A dance from the original production of *Oklahoma*, choreographed by Agnes de Mille. *(Photo courtesy of the Billy Rose Theatre Collection; The New York Public Library at Lincoln Center; Astor, Lenox and Tilden Foundations.)*

A Raisin in the Sun was presented at Kent State University with Louis O. Erdmann as director and designer. (Photo courtesy of Kent State University Theatre.)

Other Forms

Many modern plays defy classification in any genre. Some are serious plays that have more depth than melodrama but lack the scope of tragedy. An example is Lorraine Hansberry's *A Raisin in the Sun*, which deals with human dignity. The protagonist, Walter Lee Younger, changes his outlook on life and thus succeeds in keeping his dignity.

Often in modern plays the characters are three-dimensional, and we can empathize with them, but their actions are neither serious nor tragic. Often, too, modern characters are people with ordinary problems. In *Cat on a Hot Tin Roof* Big Daddy is stereotyped, but he is neither all bad nor certainly all good. Such too is the case with Maggie and Brick. Big Daddy will die, but the younger people are reconciled. The play is by no means humorous, yet neither does it end in defeat. In a sense Maggie and Brick are triumphant, but the play is not totally melodramatic in that the action is plausible. Such is the case with many plays in current theatre.

Musical Theatre

Music has been part of the theatre since its earliest days. Before the development of Western civilization, dance and chant arose as essential elements in the survival of the community. In the execution of more effective war policy, propitiation of the gods, or initiation of the young into religious rites, music preceded spoken theatre. In ancient Greece, not only in the broad farces of Aristophanes but in the tragedies as well, music and dance were used extensively. Movement to musical accompaniment was part of a total experience.[5]

Originally called musical comedy because the plots were always happy if not truly humorous, musical theatre in recent years has treated almost every conceivable subject matter in almost every conceivable way. So the form is not precisely a genre, nor can it be classified as a style. Perhaps it is closer to genre in that it always contains certain elements, music and dance, as an integral part of the plot.

> The straight dramatic play may attempt to bridge man's loneliness and isolation; the musical does so. The play may reach for the unknown, the disturbing, the nature of discontent; the musical reinforces the joy of living, the escape from realism, no matter how realistic it may strive to be. It has been said that if children are not present in the matinee audiences, no musical has a chance of success. The dramatic play remains, even today, confined largely to naturalism and verisimilitude, a portrayal of the drabness of life with all its anxieties. The musical opens onto the world of opulence, fantasy, and make-believe.[6]

Musical theatre is the United States' most unique and important contribution to the world of theatre. It has its basis in several different sources, including the extravaganza, the burlesque show, the minstrel show, and vaudeville and variety shows. The extravaganza consisted of spectacular scenic effects, singing, and dancing, and often was based on mythology. The burlesque show, as originally presented, was a musical parody or satire of a play or other entertainment. The minstrel show, in large part, was originated by Thomas "Daddy" Rice and consisted of white men with blackened faces presenting comedy, music, and dance. Vaudeville and variety shows too were a series of unrelated acts of all types presented on one program.

The Black Crook, presented in 1866, generally is considered the first musical, although it came about through accident. A ballet troupe had been scheduled to dance at a theatre that was destroyed by fire. Because the dancers had no place to perform, they were put into a romantic melodrama, by Charles M. Barras, *The Black Crook.* The presentation bore little resemblance to the musicals of today, but it did set the tone for using spectacular scenery and dancing girls, which carried into the various "follies" of the early part of this century and into some of the early musical comedies.

Whereas the dancing girls were only incidental to the story of *The*

[5]Allan Lewis, *American Plays and Playwrights of the Contemporary Theatre* (New York: Crown Publishers, Inc., 1965). p. 214.

[6]Lewis, p. 213.

Black Crook, recent musicals use dancing and singing as an integral part of the plot. One person who did a great deal to bring about the development of musical theatre was George M. Cohan. Two of his early productions were *Johnny Jones* in 1904 and *Forty-Five Minutes from Broadway* in 1906.

It wasn't for more than a decade, however, that the musical theatre began to come into its own. One of the earliest musicals was Jerome Kern's *Show Boat,* presented in 1927. Then in 1931 came *Of Thee I Sing,* a satire on politics and campaigning. These productions were followed by *Porgy and Bess* in 1935 and *Pins and Needles,* a revue presented by the International Ladies Garment Workers' Union. The latter satirized current events and politics and constantly was updated during its long run. *Porgy and Bess* was based on the play *Porgy* by Dubose and Dorothy Heywood, with lyrics by Dubose Heywood and Ira Gershwin and music by George Gershwin. Still popular, the show was revived in 1977 and won a Tony Award.

The popularity of musical theatre continued to grow as the form changed and developed. Another milestone was the presentation in 1940 of *Pal Joey,* a play that dealt with dishonest characters involved in blackmail and adultery. The book was by John O'Hara with music by Richard Rogers and lyrics by Lorenz Hart.

Up to the 1940s the dancing still consisted in large part of chorus girls presenting precise routines. In 1943 the role of dance changed with the opening of *Oklahoma!* Based on the play *Green Grow the Lilacs* by Lynn Riggs, it became Broadway's biggest hit to that point. The big dance numbers of previous musicals were replaced by a unique form of ballet. The choreographer Agnes de Mille, explains the style:

> Everyone in the ballet was a character in the play, so that the style of the ballet was the style of the play. It was of a piece, so to speak, and the dancers were of the texture of the play and in style and in content with the rest of the play. This was new, as was the caliber of the dancers, all the dancers, not just the leads.
>
> I didn't particularly intend to break with tradition. You see, I hadn't seen many musicals because I couldn't afford to go to them, so I didn't know enough about traditions to break any purposely. It just seemed to me to be the right way to do things.[7]

Oscar Hammerstein II and Richard Rogers collaborated on *Oklahoma!* Hammerstein wrote the book and lyrics, and Rogers composed the music. The two men collaborated on many later musicals which became hits. *Oklahoma!* was followed by *South Pacific,* based on James Michener's book *Tales of the South Pacific.* This production set the precedent for dealing with serious themes in musicals.

For the next several years most musicals were romantic in nature. Among them were such hits as *Annie Get Your Gun* (book by Herbert and

---

[7]Roy Newquist, *Showcase* (New York: William Morrow & Co., Inc., 1966), pp. 95–96.

Dorothy Field and music and lyrics by Irving Berlin), *Brigadoon* (Lerner and Loewe), and *Finian's Rainbow* (book by E. Y. Harburg and Fred Saidy and music by Burton Lane).

Since the fifties, with productions of such musicals as *My Fair Lady*, musical theatre has encompassed all types of ideas and treatments of subject matter. *Fiddler on the Roof*, which opened in 1964, shows the destruction of the society of the Eastern European Jew. Then in 1966 *Cabaret* presented a look at the attitudes and decadency of pre-World War II Germany. In 1968 another innovation came in, *Hair*, which had no plot. It protested war, the draft, and racism and combined various types of music.

One of the biggest hits of recent years has been *A Chorus Line* (conceived by Michael Bennett; book by James Kirkwood and Nicholas Dante; music by Marvin Hamlisch and lyrics by Edward Kleban), unique in that it presents the story of dancers auditioning for parts in a musical. The audience learns something about each actor when the director-choreographer asks them to tell about their lives.

Like straight plays, musicals have their basis in many sources.

A scene from *42nd Street*, a recent Broadway musical. (*Photo courtesy of Martha Swope.*)

Some, such as *Annie* and *It's a Bird, It's a Plane, It's Superman,* are based on comic strips. *Mame* (book by Jerome Lawrence and Robert E. Lee; music and lyrics by Jerry Herman), is based on the play *Auntie Mame,* which in turn is based on Patrick Dennis' novel of the same name.

No matter what the source, musicals draw the largest audiences of any type of theatrical entertainment in the United States.

QUESTIONS FOR DISCUSSION

1. How would you define genre?
2. Playwrights each present the truth of the human condition as they see it. Why is this consideration so important?
3. What are the characteristics of tragedy?
4. On what premise is comedy based? What are the aims of comedy?
5. What are the characteristics of the various types of comedy?
6. What devices might a playwright use to establish a comic frame of reference?
7. What are the characteristics of melodrama? Of farce?
8. What is tragicomedy?
9. Why is musical theatre usually considered the United States' most important and unique contribution to world theatre?

SUPPLEMENTARY READING

PLAYS
The Birthday Party by Harold Pinter.
Cat on a Hot Tin Roof by Tennessee Williams
A Chorus Line, with lyrics by Edward Kleban; book by James Kirkwood and Nicholas Dante; music by Marvin Hamlish; conceived, choreographed, and directed by Michael Bennett.
The Happy Hunter by Georges Feydeau.
Oh, Dad, Poor Dad, Mamma's Hung You in the Closet and I'm Feelin' So Sad by Arthur Kopit.

BOOKS
Engel, Lehman. *The American Musical Theatre.* New York: The Macmillan Company, 1975.
Kerr, Walter. *The Theatre in Spite of Itself.* New York: Simon & Schuster, 1963.
Laufe, Abe. *Broadway's Greatest Musicals.* Revised ed. New York: Funk and Wagnalls, 1977.
Lewis, Allan. *American Plays and Playwrights of the Contemporary Theatre.* New York: Crown Publishers, Inc., 1965.
Rahill, Frank. *The World of Melodrama.* University Park, Pa.: The Pennsylvania State University Press, 1967.

CHAPTER 7
Theatrical Space

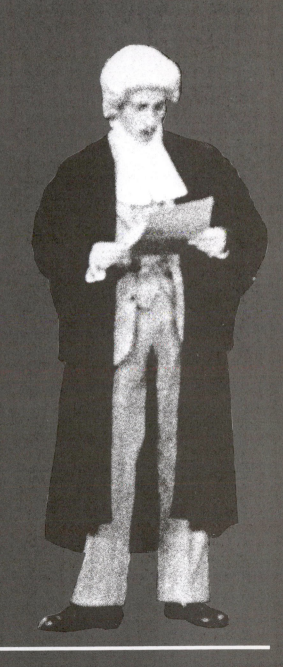

Theatre springs up everywhere. You can find it in barns, warehouses, banquet rooms, and churches. In Los Angeles, Manhattan, Pittsburgh, Minneapolis, and dozens of other communities large and small, plays go on in parks, in vacant lots, on street corners, and in open fields. Look for theatre in cultural centers, retirement homes, basements of private homes, and fraternal lodges. Theatre can exist in any space large enough for the performers and the spectators.

Most of us tend to think that going to the theatre means entering a specific structure designed only for the purpose of presenting a live production; but theatre began and even now exists in much simpler environments. In the last couple of decades there has been a move to bring theatre to the people who wouldn't have the means or inclination to attend a theatre otherwise. This concept of bringing theatre to the people is nearly as old as theatre itself. Throughout history traveling performers have gone from community to community or house to house to present short plays. During the Middle Ages theatre was presented in churches, in pageant wagons on the street corners, and in courtyards.

It is generally believed that ancient Greek theatre began in an open space at the bottom of a hillside. There was no stage or scenery, and only later was a building (*skene*) added so the performers could change costumes and make their entrances and exits. Even during the Renaissance, when interest in scenic design was high, architects concentrated on adapting existing buildings rather than constructing new buildings to house theatrical productions. Actually, the only requirements for a theatre are that the audience be able to see and hear and that the performers have enough space to present the play.

Structures Affect Expectations

To a great degree the type of theatre structure affects audience expectations and even helps determine the type of audience. Many people who stop to watch a performance in a community park might not don their best clothing to attend a professional production at a nearby cultural center. Theatres draw different audiences because of their architectural features. As a general rule, the more ornate the theatre, the more exclusive the audience. In recent years new theatres have leaned toward simplicity of design to attract more varied audiences and to focus on the performance itself instead of on the gold-leaf designs bordering the walls. The architecture of the theatre has a bearing on what play is successful. Mountain Playhouse in Jennerstown, Pennsylvania, is a stock theatre in a converted barn. The setting is quite different from the Vivian Beaumont Theatre at Lincoln Center for the Performing Arts, and from the old opera houses of the nineteenth century with their intricate carvings and statues in recessed niches. Audience expectations and moods differ in each of these theatres.

Basically, there are four different forms theatre takes structurally: proscenium theatre, arena stage, thrust stage and found space or environmental theatre.

The Proscenium Theatre

The traditional type of theatre that still outnumbers all others is the **proscenium theatre.** The proscenium or proscenium arch frames the stage in much the same way a painter frames a landscape. The audience members, seated facing the opening, are asked to believe that they are viewing the action of a play through an imaginary fourth wall.

Scenery

Because there is a psychological as well as a physical separation of audience and actor, a setting can be portrayed more realistically in a proscenium theatre than in any other type of structure. With this type of stage

Proscenium or Proscenium arch a picture-frame stage; the framing device that isolates the stage area and provides the focal point for the action. The audience views the action through an imaginary fourth wall.

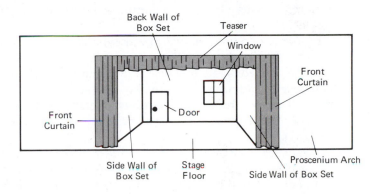

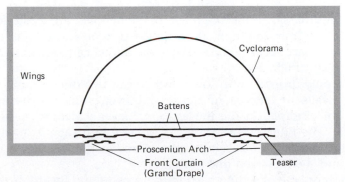

Proscenium arch—frames the set on top and sides
Teaser—a short top curtain that masks flys paces and lighting instruments
Battens—pipes from which lighting instruments and drops are hung

The top part of this figure shows the front view of a proscenium stage. The bottom part shows the stage area and wing space or backstage areas. The semicircle represents a cyclorama, which can frame the action for outdoor scenes.

Box set a setting that generally represents an indoor location and is constructed of flats.

Flats wooden frames covered with canvas and painted, usually to resemble sections of an interior wall.

Backdrop theatrical canvas painted and hung with weights at the bottom; usually stretching across the stage.

Teasers short curtains that are used to mask the lighting instruments and fly space in a proscenium theatre.

Tormenters curtains hung at either side of the stage to mask the backstage area.

Fly space the area behind the top of the arch and above the floor of the stage.

Wings flats that stand independently and are placed a short distance apart from the front to the back of a stage; also the areas to the right and left of the playing area in a proscenium theatre.

the scenery that is used most often is a **box set,** or **flats** fastened together to look like the interior walls of a room or several rooms. The flats are frames made of one-by-three boards, usually covered with canvas and painted. Flats can be constructed with doors, windows, or fireplaces.

Often the scenery for a proscenium stage looks as much as possible like an actual, specific location. The box set offers further realism by providing an environment in which the actors can perform. The setting surrounds them.

Sometimes other kinds of settings are used in the proscenium theatre. The **backdrop** or **drop,** usually theatrical canvas that stretches across the stage, is weighted at the bottom and painted to represent either indoor or outdoor scenes. With drops, top curtains called **teasers** and side curtains called **tormentors** mask the backstage areas and the **fly space,** the area behind the top of the arch above the floor of the stage. At other times **wings,** or flats that stand independently, are placed at intervals from the front of the stage to the back. Sometimes the latter type of scenery, called the *wing and drop* (because the flats extend into the wing or side areas of the stage), is used for unspecified locations. It is painted in neutral shades for various changes of location, which the audience is asked to imagine.

Drops are useful because they can be flown. This term means that they are taken into the fly space, which often is at least as high again as the stage area itself. Musicals, for instance, often require quick changes of scenery. It is simple to raise one drop quickly and silently and lower another. The drops attach to rods called **battens,** which can be raised and lowered in a matter of seconds using a system of ropes and pulleys called the **counterweight system.**

The disadvantage of using backdrops with side curtains is that the actors now must play in front of the scenery; they cannot be part of the scenic environment. Therefore this type of scenery lends itself better to presentational productions. Wing and drop settings can be used as interiors, but they aren't as realistic as box sets. Usually, if they represent interior scenes, it's for period plays written before the development of the box set.

Scrims or semitransparent cloths sometimes are used for drops. When lighted from the front, they appear opaque and the audience sees a painted surface. Backlighting allows the audience to see through them, creating a dreamlike effect.

Not only drops can be flown, but so can two-dimensional set pieces such as walls or cutouts of trees, and even some three-dimensional pieces. For example, in the musical *Once upon a Mattress,* based on the fairy tale "The Princess and the Pea," a large bird cage is used, and the "bird" is a person. The cage can be stored in the fly space until it is needed and then lowered into place.

Another type of setting used in the proscenium theatre is the **wagon stage,** a set constructed on a platform that can be rolled on and off stage. It sometimes fits into grooves in the stage floor. The wagon can be effec-

The photos show three types of scenery used on a proscenium stage. The first is a box set, the second a backdrop, the third wings. The top photo is from the Old Globe Theatre's production of *Witness for the Prosecution.* Director, David L. Hays; scene design, Kent Dorsey. *(Photo by Clifford Baker and courtesy of the Old Globe Theatre.)* The backdrop is from a production of *Of Mice and Men,* designed by Don Powell at San Diego State University. *(Photo courtesy of San Diego State University—Dramatic Arts Department.)* The wings were used in the Little Theatre of Tuscarawas County's production of *Sugar.* Director, Jill Lynn, scene design Rich Jagunic. *(Photo by Bill Douds.)*

Battens rods to which drops or other scenery is attached to be raised and lowered in a proscenium stage.

Counterweight system a system of ropes and pulleys used to fly scenery in a proscenium theatre.

Scrims Semitransparent cloths usually serving as backdrops; when lighted from the rear they look semitransparent; when lighted from the front they look opaque.

Wagon stage a platform on castors that can be wheeled on and off the stage.

Raked stage a stage that slopes upward from front to back.

Apron or Forestage the area of a proscenium stage that extends in front of the grand drape.

tive for quick scenery changes when the theatre has a large enough wing space for storing wagons not in use. Wagons aren't practical when space is limited or when many scene changes are required. Wagons can be large enough to cover the width of the stage, or smaller for intimate scenes.

Other elements sometimes have been added to proscenium stages to provide further spectacle. Most, however, have not remained in use long. One is the elevator stage. The stage itself is an elevator that can raise and lower entire sets. Another type, still in use in some theatres, is the revolving stage. A circular portion of the stage floor is constructed on top of a shaft, which is run by a motor and rotates the cutout portion of the stage floor. Two sets can be constructed back to back and changed quickly.

The revolving stage can also be used in other ways. For instance, when Ray Bradbury's play *Fahrenheit 451* had its world premiere at San Diego State University in the early 80s, William R. Reid designed a set that could be adapted, largely through rear-screen projection, to many locales. At several points in the play two of the characters strolled from one locale to another. To provide the illusion of covering distance, the stage revolved as the two actors "walked".

The designer in a proscenium theatre plans the setting and placement of furnishings so that the audience can see all of the set from any seat and the view isn't distorted. The designer also tries to present a balanced or aesthetically pleasing set. Not every setting has to be ornate or "pretty"; the beauty comes in the set's providing a proper environment for the actors without appearing unbalanced. In other words, the designer has to consider sight lines. Most box sets are wider at the front of the stage than they are toward the back so that people in any part of the auditorium can see the action on all areas of the stage.

The actor also must be concerned with being seen and heard at all times on the stage. Although actors don't usually play openly to an audience in a proscenium theatre, they have to make sure not to turn their backs and to project their lines.

Stage Areas

When proscenium theatres first came into existence, during the Italian Renaissance, stages were **raked** or sloped gradually upward toward the rear wall of the theatre. That's why we use the name *upstage* for the area furthest from the audience. The area closest to the audience is *downstage*. *Stage Right* is the portion of the stage to the right of an actor facing the audience, and *Stage Left* is to the actor's left. The other portions of the stage draw on these terms. For example, *Down Right* is the part of the stage closest to the audience and nearest the right side of the stage. *Up Center* is the portion closest to the back wall and in the center of the stage.

In most proscenium stages there is an **apron** or **forestage** that projects out in front of the proscenium arch. It can be almost any size. The further out it projects, the more playing space there is near the audience.

UR up right	UC up center	UL up left
RC right center	C center	LC left center
DR down right	DC down center	DL down left

This drawing shows the areas of the stage. UR, for instance, is up right, while DL is down left. Thus it is easy to determine all the other areas.

Forestages are used particularly for presentational plays, and sometimes they even are constructed as part of the setting.

Advantages and Disadvantages

One of the greatest advantages of a proscenium stage is the variety of special effects that are possible. Since the stage and auditorium are separate, the front curtain or **grand drape** can be closed to mask (hide) changes and to indicate the end of an act. Any number of settings or set pieces can be flown in, wheeled in, or changed by hand. Properties can be stored backstage and taken on when needed. Because the backstage area is masked, the actors can wait immediately offstage to make their entrances.

A disadvantage of a proscenium stage is the psychological and physical separation of the audience and actor for certain plays, particularly of the presentational type. According to Richard Southern: "The cardinal problem about the proscenium-arch convention is that it creates a line. It is no more than ordinarily difficult to play *behind* that line; but it is very difficult indeed to discover in what tone to handle a passage where you propose to *cross* that line."[1]

Grand drape the heavy, front curtain in a proscenium theatre.

The Arena Stage

Arena staging is a type of theatre structure in which the audience surrounds the action. Although this type of structure sometimes is called theatre-in-the-round, the playing area most often is a square or an oval. It has historical precedent in the arena-style theatres of ancient Greece,

Arena stage the type of stage in which the audience surrounds the playing area.

[1]Richard Southern, *The Seven Ages of the Theatre* (New York: Hill and Wang, 1961), p. 275.

Moliere's *Tartuffe*, designed by Owen McEvoy, is nearly set for opening at Seton Hall University's arena theatre. *(Photo courtesy of Seton Hall University.)*

where the audience nearly surrounded the action. Southern comments:

> Theatre in the round means three things; the first is obvious—it is a theatre where the audience completely surrounds the action on all sides. The second follows from this but is not so immediately obvious—it is a theatre where it is quite impossible to give the effect of a painted picture come to life. The third is that, speaking in general, it is a theatre which has no stage. Thus it can be properly be called an *arena theare*.[2]

As opposed to a picture-frame stage, where the action is on a raised platform, the "stage" or playing area for an arena theatre generally is lower, with the seats at the lowest near the playing area and raked upward toward the rear. In other words, the audience looks down on the action.

Scenery

Because the audience surrounds the action, arena theatre has many requirements of setting not found in proscenium staging. There can be no realistic box sets, although scrims sometimes are used with backlights.

[2]Southern, p. 284.

Although the setting cannot be as realistic as that of the proscenium stage, the properties have to be more realistic. The audience sits closer to the action and can spot substitutes.

Makeup in arena theatre must be more subtle and costumes more realistic. Often on a proscenium stage the costumes, properly dyed and lighted, can look rich and costly from the audience, when actually they are constructed from a relatively inexpensive fabric. For example, monk's cloth can look like brocade. Audiences in an arena theatre would immediately detect such "fakes."

The designer in an arena setting has to be careful to include set pieces and furniture that are low enough for even the audience members seated closest to the action to be able to see over them.

Advantages and Disadvantages

In arena theatre there is a *grid* above the stage, and the lighting instruments always are in view of the audience, whereas in proscenium theatre the lighting instruments can be masked behind the teasers or focused on the stage from points in the ceiling of the auditorium.

There are other problems of concealment. The actors are in view of the audience at all times or have to make long entrances and exits down the aisles. Changes in setting are limited and must occur in full view of the spectators.

Another disadvantage of arena staging is that the director cannot be so concerned with presenting an aesthetically pleasing picture. A bigger concern is to make sure that all of the audience will be able to see at least most of the action. Difficulties arise when bodies must fall from closets, when someone must appear to be dead for a long period in view of the audience, and when someone has to exit quickly. In Chapter 9 we will explore the special demands arena staging makes upon a director.

Still, arena theatre has many advantages. Most importantly, the audience is close to the action; there is not the physical barrier of the proscenium theatre. There can be more intimacy between spectator and performer, and there can be more subtleties of facial expression and movement than in a theatre where the audience is seated a great distance from the playing area. A playwright or performer who wants to communicate directly to the audience can do so much better with arena staging. The audience too can communicate better because the nearness of the actors allows audience members to feel involved.

Another important consideration is that almost any room or space can be adapted for arena staging. The playing area itself can be much smaller, because it is three-dimensional rather than giving the two-dimensional effect of the picture-frame stage. Also, because the audience closely surrounds the action, the seating area covers a smaller space than in a proscenium theatre, where the spectators view the action from only one side and generally sit farther from the stage.

This arena production of *The Lady's Not For Burning* was presented in Montclair State College's Studio Theatre, which can be adapted to both proscenium and arena staging. Director, Dennis McDonald; set designer, W. S. MacConnell. *(Photo courtesy of Montclair State College.)*

The Thrust Stage

Thrust stage a stage that juts into the seating area; the audience sits on three sides.

The third major type of stage in current use is the **thrust stage.** Sometimes the playing area is raised above the level of the audience, but most often the audience looks down on the action, as they do in arena theatre.

Basically, a thrust stage consists of an open playing area similar to that of an arena theatre, with a stagehouse or wall in the background through which the performers enter and exit. The audience area is three-sided. The arrangement probably resembles ancient Greek staging more closely than any of the other major types do.

Because there is a stagehouse at the rear, more scenery can be used than is possible in arena theatre. At least there can be a background for the action if the director and designer want one. There also is a place for the storage of properties and set pieces, which can be changed more quickly than in arena theatre, although the changes still occur in full view of the audience. As in arena theatre, lighting instruments hang in view of the spectators, and there can be no curtains.

The audience can become more involved than is generally possible in a proscenium theatre, because they are closer to the action; but again, realistic properties must be used for a representational production.

Variations of Stages

There are several other types of stages, but they are variations of the three we have just discussed. There are *modified thrust stages,* which are theatres with a proscenium opening and a large apron that projects into

The top two photos show a side and front view of the thrust stage at Porthouse Theatre at Kent State University's Fine and Performing Arts Center, adjacent to Blossom Music Center. The third photo shows the grid where lights can be hung above the thrust stage. *(Photos by Bill Douds.)*

The setting for this thrust-stage production of *A Streetcar Named Desire* was designed by Barry Baughman for Porthouse Theatre at Kent State University's Fine and Performing Arts Center, adjacent to Blossom Music Center. Director, Louis O. Erdmann. *(Photo by C. James Gleason and courtesy of Kent State University Theatre.)*

the audience. There also are platform stages, similar to proscenium stages, but without a framing device. Theatres occasionally have ramps reminiscent of beauty pageants, but most often the ramps are part of a setting for one play rather than a permanent part of the theatre structure. There have been experiments with *wrap-around stages*, which form an arc around part of the audience, similar to the film industry's experiment several decades ago with cinerama. Many theatres also have both a proscenium opening and *side stages*, or small playing areas, in front of and to the sides of the proscenium opening, where intimate scenes with simple settings or few characters can be played.

There is a great deal of difference among structures of a single type. Some proscenium theatres seat only a hundred spectators and have a small stage, whereas others seat several thousand, before a giant stage. The size has varying effects. In a large theatre there is not the intimacy of a small one. The actors have to project their voices more and use broader gestures and movements to convey physical action in larger theatres. They forego the subtleties of facial expression and the nuances of vocal tone that work in small theatres. On the other hand, a small theatre would not be able to handle elaborate productions such as *My Fair Lady*, with its large cast and numerous changes of scenery, as well as a larger theatre could.

Environmental Theatre

The fourth major type of theatre is not a structure but **found space** or **environmental theatre,** a term Richard Schechner introduced. Jerry N. Rojo, who designed for Schechner's Performance Group, says: "The term environmental theatre defines an aesthetic approach to production. It provides highly controlled conditions so that transactions involving performer, space and text may be developed organically."[3]

Environmental theatre or found space means adapting whatever space is available to a theatrical production. Antonin Artaud of France was an advocate of this type of theatre. He believed theatre should affect more people more directly than has been the case throughout much of theatre history. Schechner also was an advocate of drastic change in the audience-actor relationship. With his group he presented plays in an abandoned garage in New York City. He experimented with seating audience members at various places, in various groupings, and even amidst the action. Sometimes the spectators sat on scaffolding and ledges.

Groups experimenting with found space desire to break down all barriers between stage and auditorium for more direct communication between actor and audience.

Rojo explains the experience this way:

> The environmentalist begins with the notion that the production will both develop from and totally inhabit a given space; and that, for the performer and audience, time, space and materials exist as what they are and only for their intrinsic value. All aesthetic problems are solved in terms of actual time, space and materials with little consideration given to solutions that suggest illusion, pretense, or imitation. An environment, for example, never creates an illusion of, say, a forest, although actors and audience may discover danger literally in a precarious arrangement of platforms, or a sense of safety may be achieved where a high place is conquered. In the more traditional

Found space or Environmental theatre any available space, not a formal theatre structure, adapted to a theatrical production.

[3]Jerry Rojo, "Environmental Design" in *Contemporary Scene Design U.S.A.*, Elizabeth B. Burdick, et al., eds. (New York: International Theatre Institute of the United States, Inc., 1974), p. 20. Reprinted with permission.

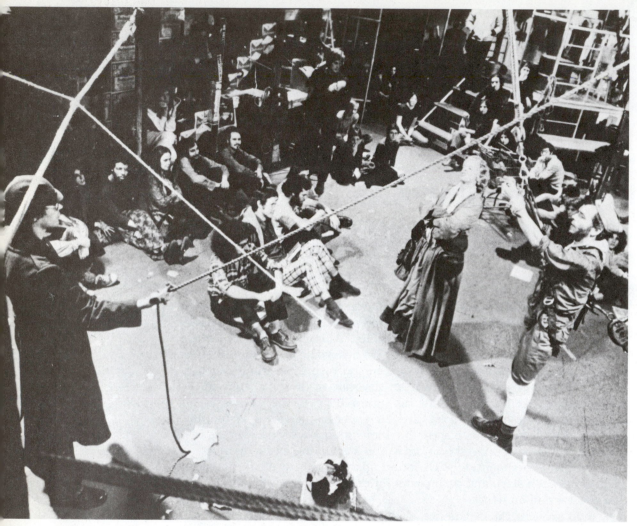

Mother Courage and Her Children presented by Richard Schechner's Performance Group. The group did away with the use of a traditional stage or acting area, and the actors and audience shared the same space, thus providing intimacy and the breaking down of barriers. *(Photo courtesy of the Wooster Group.)*

theatre experience, the production is appreciated from *outside*, in a world especially created for the relatively passive observer. In the environmental experience, on the other hand, appreciation generates from *within* by virtue of shared activity. Each environmental production creates a sense of total involvement.[4]

Found space includes street theatres. Actors perform in the streets

[4]Rojo, p. 20.

to provide cultural experience, to entertain, or to address the concerns of the audience.

Theatre space today is a combination of the old and the new. It looks backward and forward at the same time. It exists in hundred-year-old buildings, and in weeks-old found space. Just as the types of writing and performance in theatre are changing, so are the concepts and manners of production, which makes theatre much more exciting than ever before in history.

QUESTIONS FOR DISCUSSION

1. What are the only physical requirements for theatre space?
2. How does the type of theatre structure affect the type of audience and its expectations?
3. What are the characteristics of the proscenium stage, the arena stage, the thurst stage, and found space?
4. What are the advantages and disadvantages of each type of physical theatre?

SUPPLEMENTARY READING

BOOKS

The American Theatre Planning Board, Inc. *Theatre Check List: A Guide to the Planning and Construction of Proscenium and Open Stage Theatres.* Middletown, Conn.: Wesleyan University Press, 1969.

Boyle, Walden P. *Central and Flexible Staging.* Berkeley: University of California Press, 1956.

Burris-Meyer, Harold, and Cole, Edwin C. *Theatres and Auditoriums,* 2nd ed. New York: Reinhold Publishing Corporation, 1964.

Cogsworth, Margaret, ed. *The Ideal Theatre: Eight Concepts.* New York: The American Federation of Arts, 1962.

Rojo, Jerry. "Environmental Design," *Contemporary Scene Design U.S.A.* Elizabeth Burdick, et al., eds. New York: International Theatre Institute of the United States, Inc., 1974.

Southern, Richard. *The Seven Ages of the Theatre.* New York: Hill and Wang, Inc., 1961.

Tidworth, Simon. *Theatres: An Architectural and Cultural History.* New York: Praeger Publishers, 1973.

CHAPTER 8
The Designers

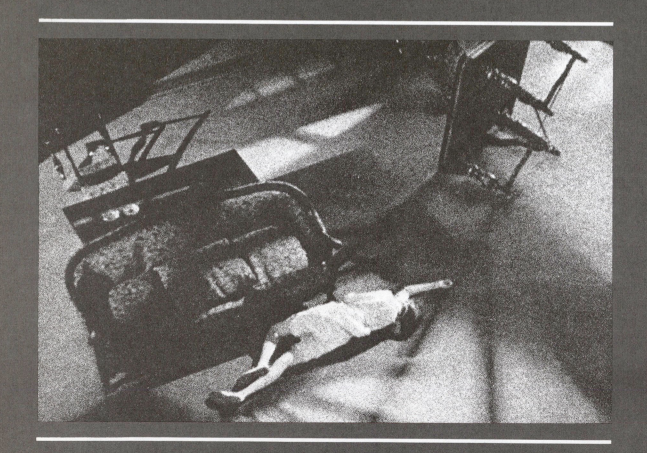

Theatre is a collaborative art. Several designers work with the director, taking into consideration what each of the others is doing. Because of this collaboration, the production is a unified whole whose elements blend together. As Patricia Zipprodt, a costume designer, says:

> I look upon theatrical designers as creative extensions of the director; we are the people who make visible the world in which the piece will *live*. If we are working well together, it is because we are working *closely* together. In these discussions we explore verbally and with rough sketches the many different approaches and ideas that might bring the script into dramatic focus on the stage. The designers supplement the concepts of the director visually; in so doing we sometimes have the joyous experience of inspiring the director to the discovery of new ideas. Contrary to popular opinion, the craft of theatre is a collaborative enterprise, not an 'ego' trip.[1]

The Scene Designer

One of the collaborators is the scene designer, whose work must be as aesthetic as that of a painter and as practical as that of an architect. At the same time the scene designer's work is different because it is not complete in itself. After the setting is constructed, it requires the actors, the costumes, the lights, the makeup, and the properties to complete the picture. Throughout the production, the picture changes continuously as the actors move and the lights come up or fade.

The Scene Designer's Background

To design an effective, practical, aesthetically pleasing set that will match a style or period, the designer needs a great deal of training, experience, and talent. The designer's training may consist of courses and practical experience in the theory of light and color; in draftsmanship, art, and architecture; in costuming, acting, directing, and makeup; and in theatre history and world history. Designers should be familiar with various styles and genres of plays and with all forms of theatre structures. They should be acquainted with the work of the other theatre artists so that their designs fit the others' requirements.

During the Renaissance and even recently, professional artists who painted sets tended to make them works of art in themselves. Now scene designers have come to recognize that they are only one of many artists working on a production. They not only collaborate and sometimes compromise, but at times they have to bow to the wishes of the director. As

[1]Patricia Zipprodt, "Designing Costumes," *Contemporary Stage Design U.S.A.*, Elizabeth Burdick, et al., eds. (New York: International Theatre Institute of the United States, Inc., 1974), p. 29. Reprinted with permission.

The photos show contrasting types of design in two productions at the University of Hawaii. Both were designed by Richard Mason. The director of the first, *Don Juan in Hell,* was Evelyn McQueen, while Bernard Dubere directed *Beelzebub Sonata.* (Photos courtesy of University of Hawaii.)

The set for this out-door drama, Paul Green's *Trumpet in the Land*, includes a large mountain and an asphalt stage. *(Photo courtesy of Trumpet in the Land, New Philadelphia, Ohio.)*

director Harold Clurman comments: "The theatre cannot live through any single organ of its being. The theatre as an art is indivisible."[2]

Because they work with many others and because they design so many different scenes, the designers need a broad background. For instance, there is a big difference between constructing an apartment on stage and constructing an apartment building. Scene designers know both real architecture and how to adapt architectural design to a theatre production. They know enough about stage carpentry to design a set that can be built without major difficulty. They plan so that scenery can shift quickly and quietly.

Scene designers also are acquainted with the principles of lighting and know how light will affect their sets. They know the emotional impact of various colors, textures, and masses. Often, as a matter of fact, the same person who designs a set also designs the lighting.

Besides knowing the principles and practices of lighting, scene designers are acquainted with all the building materials for set construction and know which type is best for any particular effect. They have a good idea of the cost of various materials so they can stay within a budget.

Designers are acquainted with interior decorating. Of course, stage

[2]Harold Clurman, *On Directing* (New York: The Macmillan Company, 1972), p. 3.

living rooms do not look exactly like real ones, but the designers can adapt real decor to the requirements of the stage. Designers are able to visualize what type of furniture belongs in a set and how it will modify the setting. Not only are scene designers familiar with current style, but they know or at least know where to research period furniture and architecture. They know how to use space, line, shape, color, texture, and ornamentation to build an atmosphere and environment that are appropriate.

Although scene design is not considered as old as acting, it dates back at least to classical Greek theatre. If we consider that any space used for a performance is a setting, then scene design—at least in the choice of space for a performance—is as old as any other aspect of theatre, and as important. As designer Donald Oenslager says: "Wherever he works, the designer is an artist and craftsman who translates the world around him into the theatrical terms of the stage."[3]

Functions of Scene Design

Beyond the practical purpose of providing a channel for the playwright's message, the setting helps convey the theme and provides information essential to the understanding of the play. It fulfills the director's interpretation; provides an environment, mood, and playable area for the actor; remains faithful to the playwright's style, and complements the work of all the other designers.

The design provides a framework for the action and a *focal point* for the audience. In the medieval theatre designers used the concept of simultaneous staging. Each scene began at a different location. Each place (or *mansion*) represented a specific area, such as heaven or hell. After the scene began at one of these mansions, the action moved into an unlocalized area or central space. Designers and performers recognized that there had to be a reference point at the beginning of each scene so that the audience would know where each was supposed to take place.

Circuses often use three rings, with acts performing simultaneously in each of the playing areas. In this case the audience members provide their own focal point by watching either what interests them the most or what is nearest them. Their enjoyment need not be marred by missing some of the action. In a well written play each scene is important, so the designer defines and indicates a focal point. For different scenes various areas in turn become focal points. Every member of the audience must have an undistorted view of every point. For example, one scene may take place in a bedroom and another in the kitchen. The focus may be provided in part by lighting, but the designer makes each location interesting and easily seen from any part of the audience.

[3]Donald Oenslager, *Scenery Then and Now* (New York: W. W. Norton & Company, 1936), p. 11.

A setting also is designed for easy use by the actors. For instance, treads on steps in a set usually are wider than those in a house so the actor will not have to look down at them and can concentrate on action and character. Actors do not have to worry whether a platform will support them. Windows open and close easily. Of course, these matters depend upon the stage crew's skill, but the designer helps by fully explaining how the set should be built.

The setting presents an aesthetically pleasing image, although, of course, the image will alter each time an actor moves. It cannot be so elaborate that it will call attention to itself to the exclusion of the other elements of the production. It should not have so many special effects that the audience rivets its attention on the magic appearance of flying objects or on wagons running in and out or twirling in grooves on the floor. The scenery should be "beautiful" in adding a new dimension to the production, but it should not be distracting.

Balance and Harmony

Symmetrical balance giving either side of a setting exactly the same elements in the same relationship to each other.

The set should be balanced, either symmetrically or asymmetrically. **Symmetrical balance** means that the left half of the set contains exactly the same elements as the right half. Scene designers often use symmetry for staging Greek plays, because it can appear crisp and unadorned. This type of setting can be effective, but it can bore the audience through sameness and a lack of interesting detail.

Symmetrical balance was used for this setting of *Midsummer Night's Dream* at San Diego State University. Director, C. E. Stephenson; scene designer, Don Powell. (*Photo courtesy of San Diego State University—Dramatic Arts Department.*)

Asymmetrical balance was used by designer Michael Smanko for Montclair State College's production of *Scapino*. *(Photo courtesy of Montclair State College, Summerfun Summer Theater.)*

Asymmetrical balance is achieved through mass, color, and shape that differ from one side of the stage to the other. If, for instance, a huge, grey brick wall were facing front, at Stage Left, another object or combination of objects should go at stage right to counterbalance the feeling of heaviness. The designer might use dark colors, a grouping of heavy furniture, or platforms.

A well-designed setting has harmony as well as balance. Each element appears to "belong" or to be consistent. In some plays there is a mingling of styles of furniture and of other elements in the set. They still provide a harmony if they enhance the theme of the play. In *You Can't Take It with You* each member of the household has a separate interest, such as writing or dancing or making firecrackers, and these interests show up in a diversity of elements in the set. This mixture contributes to the theme of nonconformity, which provides harmony to the production as a whole. On the other hand, if a person were to design a setting for *Our Town*, using the bare stage with only a ladder to represent the second story of the Gibb's house and sawhorses and a plank to represent a soda fountain, but then constructed a box set and placed actual furniture in the Webb household, the set would not have harmony.

Asymmetrical balance making mass, shape, and color differ from one side of the stage to the other, but keeping the total weight or mass the same so that there is a feeling of balance.

Although current theatre is eclectic, scene designers must be artistic enough to recognize what styles can mingle. They must have a feeling for style.

What Setting Conveys

A setting, when first viewed, prepares the spectator for the production. The colors and shapes help convey the style and genre. For instance, curved lines and shapes often convey lightness or gracefulness, whereas straight, angular shapes convey austerity or somberness. An audience is able to tell immediately whether the set is meant to be realistic or non-realistic. If it is nonrealistic, the shapes and colors help create mood and feeling.

A designer often may exaggerate an element of the setting to show that an aspect of the play is exaggerated. For instance, some of the set pieces may be two-dimensional to show that the action is farcical.

From the set, we should be able to recognize the environment of the play, if the environment is important to the action. The set may locate time and place. The style of architecture and the furnishings can indicate the historical period. We should know immediately if the play takes place in the home of a well-to-do person, in an office, or in a fairy-tale forest. The setting tells us about characters' tastes, interests, hobbies, and financial status. It becomes almost a character in itself.

Of course, for some plays it is important *not* to establish time and place exactly. We know that *Our Town* takes place in Grover's Corners, New Hampshire, but we are free to imagine what Grover's Corners is like and to relate it to our own backgrounds. If the setting were too specific, we would not identify with the characters so strongly.

Often, too, establishing a specific location weakens a play's impact. *Waiting for Godot* relies heavily on audience interpretation. For instance, when prisoners at San Quentin saw the play, they interpreted Godot as the warden. Tying the play to specifics could confuse the spectator. The designer should be able to interpret the playwright's message well enough to know instinctively what form of scenery to use.

A setting should provide a visual image that conveys the specific message of each play. It must be "aesthetically right" for each production.

Planning a Setting

The scene designer's actual work on a production begins with a study and analysis of the script. The designer tries to determine the mood and theme of the play. Then come practical questions: Where does the play take place? How many doorways are needed? Where do they lead? Are windows, fireplaces, or levels needed? How can the set add to the effectiveness of the action?

Once they have ideas in mind, designers prepare sketches for the

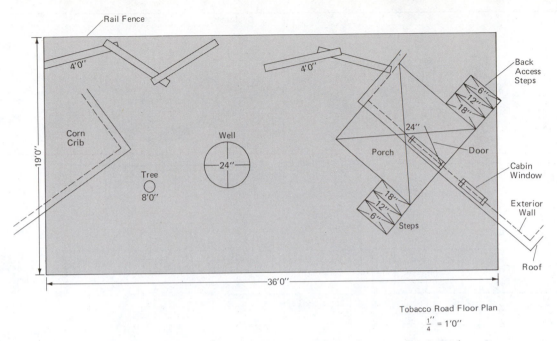

Tobacco Road Floor Plan
$\frac{1''}{4} = 1'0''$

This floor plan shows a scale drawing of the exterior setting for a production of *Tobacco Road*.

director. Sometimes directors have definite ideas about the setting; at other times they give the designer a free hand. In either case the director sees to it that the proposed design meshes with the work of the other theatre artists.

> The well-known loneliness that attends the painter working in isolation in his studio for long periods is not known to the stage designer, the very nature of whose work guarantees that he is in constant touch with others involved in the project. This proves a stimulating and even necessary experience for artists of a certain temperament.[3]

After the director approves the preliminary sketches, the designer prepares more exactly plans for the construction of the set. A **floor plan** or the setting as viewed from above shows how the set fits the stage. Sometimes the designer draws several floor plans, showing a shifting of furniture, so that the director can visualize where to place the actors. Often the designer constructs a model of the set, so the director can see what it will be like. The plans and model are on a scale of one-fourth inch (or occasionally one-half inch) to the foot. Then the designer may draft elevations, showing the height of platforms, steps, other three-dimen-

Floor plan a drawing of the setting as seen from above.

[3]Kenneth Rowell, *Stage Design* (New York: Van Nostrand Reinhold Co., 1969), p. 82.

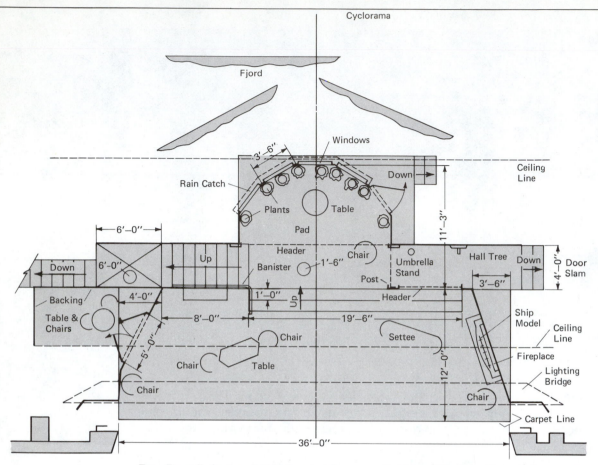

Don Powell designed this box set for a production of Ibsen's *Ghosts*, directed by Kjell Amble. *(Photo courtesy of San Diego State University—Dramatic Arts Department. See Color Plate 8 for a view of the set.)*

sional shapes, and flats. Often the designer prepares a sectional view of objects to show the method of construction, or isometric views that show an object from the corner and slightly above to give the builders a clear understanding of the platform or figure. Copies of the drawings and plans go to the director, the technical director, the stage manager, and the head of the construction crew.

After the planning, the scene designer's duties differ in various types of theatres. Often the designer chooses the furniture and set dressings and supervises the painting. According to designer Howard Bay:

> What differentiates the Broadway artist-craftsman from others of the species is the breakneck speed of the operation; the balancing of the widely disparate backstages that have been booked; the iron necessity of holding the operational crews to the minimum by devising

clever mechanisms; the hectic and simultaneous production of ren-
derings, working drawings, scenic elevations, prop drawings, light
plots; the search for drapery and upholstery fabrics, furniture,
dressing, foliage, carpeting; plus the daily visits to the widely separated shops that are turning out the artwork.[4]

In educational and community theatre the designer often supervises or
carries out much of the construction.

The Lighting Designer

When electric lights first came into use in the theatre, they simply illu-
minated the stage to enable the spectators to see the action. Modern lighting has many other purposes. Like scenery, it enhances the total production.

There are two categories of stage lighting: **general** and **specific.** General lighting provides a well-lighted performance area. Specific lighting
provides special effects. It enhances the playwright's message through
intensity and color. A dimly lighted stage can suggest a foreboding, mysterious atmosphere, whereas a brightly lighted stage often means "lightness" in treatment of subject matter. There are exceptions. In *Motel* glar-
ing lights focus on the audience in almost blinding intensity to make the
spectators uncomfortable.

General lighting lighting that provides visibility on the whole stage.

Specific lighting lighting for special effects, such as to suggest sunlight or to set the mood.

Functions of Lighting

Lighting complements the other areas of design and helps to convey the
mood and message of the play. It provides **selective visibility.** Often only
certain areas of the set are important to the action. In such cases the lights
can provide a point of focus by fading to black on the areas to be deemphasized and coming up on the important areas. Large follow spots
sometimes are used in musicals to focus on the star performer.

Lighting can provide exposition by showing time and place. A
bright light could indicate midday in a warm climate. Softer light could
portray moonlight. Blazing chandeliers can indicate nighttime in a
wealthy home.

Of course, lighting, like scenery, is a symbol. It cannot exactly duplicate sunlight or moonlight. It suggests; then it is up to the audience to
use imagination. Even a practical table lamp on stage would not provide
enough illumination. Its light must be intensified, usually by focusing
additional overhead lighting on the lamp.

Selective visibility providing focus through lighting.

[4]Howard Bay, "The Designer and the Broadway Scene" from *Contemporary
Stage Design U.S.A.* (New York: International Theatre Institute of the United
States, Inc., 1974), pp. 18–19. Reprinted with permission.

A technician hangs fresnels at the Little Theatre of Tuscarawas County, Ohio. *(Photo by Bill Douds.)*

Another function of lighting is to reveal or define mass and form. For instance, properly lighted, a papier-mâché rock can become "real" for the audience.

Lighting Components

Floodlights nonfocusable lighting instruments used for general illumination.

Spotlights focusable lighting instruments customarily used for specific illumination.

Fresnel a type of spotlight that provides a circle or oval of light with a softened edge.

Lighting consists of two components: a *source* and a *system of control*. By *source* we mean the lighting instruments. The two major kinds are **floodlights,** which are nonfocusable and have no lens, and **spotlights,** which can be focused and usually do have a lens. Floodlights usually are for general illumination, whereas the various types of spots are for specific illumination.

Spots come in various sizes and can focus from a very small area to a large one. Most have a metal frame into which gelatins (color transparencies) can be fitted for emotional effects.

One of the most common spots is a **fresnel,** which provides a circular or oval area of light. The lens that covers the lamp (bulb) softens the edge of light so that it's difficult to define exactly where the lighted area ends. The other most common spot is the **ellipsoidal reflector,** which is brighter than a fresnel and more controllable. It has a framing device that allows the area the light strikes to be specific. The edge, un-

A view of the lighting control board at Kent State University. The operator is working one of the dimmers. *(Photo courtesy of Kent State University Theatre.)*

like that of the fresnel, is exact. It can provide a contrast from intense brightness to total darkness with no "spill" into the unlighted area. Ellipsoidal reflectors can be used at almost any distance from the stage; fresnels generally are placed within forty feet.

Another common source of illumination is the **striplight,** a long, troughlike instrument with lights a few inches apart along the length of the trough. The lights are covered with colored lenses, alternately consisting of the primary colors. Often strips light the cyclorama or circular curtain surrounding the sides and rear of the acting area in exterior scenes, providing the illusion of distance. There are a variety of other instruments, but they aren't used so often.

The control system is the board or panel from which the lights are operated. It allows the lighting technician to dim from one area to another and to control both the intensity and direction from which the light originates. It also can provide control over color. For example, if a play were to progress from noon to evening, the lighting technician could change the direction of the light by switching to other instruments, indicating that the sun was setting. Various colors of gelatins could indicate increasing darkness.

Planning the Lighting

People often think of the lighting designer as an expert electrician rather than as an artist. Certainly designers know a great deal about electricity, and many of them do have an electrician's license; but they are as creative

Ellipsoidal relector a type of spotlight that has a framing device and is quite controllable. It allows no spill of light from one area to another.

Striplight a troughlike lighting instrument with lights a few inches apart, covered with lenses in the primary colors.

and imaginative as the other theatre artists, and they possess a general knowledge of all areas of theatre production.

Lighting designers work closely with the director and the other designers to provide a cohesive image for the audience and to convey the mood of the play. They analyze the script to determine the source of light for each scene, and plan how to indicate time, place, and even season. At the same time they make certain that the lighting does not call attention to itself.

Lighting designers understand where to hang lights for the best effect. They know that an actor or a set piece is lighted from various angles to appear three-dimensional. They know the psychological effects of lighting. For instance, people are more alert in high intensity lighting, which the designer could use for a fast-moving comedy. At the same time the designers recognize that many quick changes in lighting tire an audience.

The designer plans to control three aspects of lighting: *color, intensity,* and *distribution.* Warmer colors, or yellow to amber shades, generally are used in comedies, cooler colors in serious plays. For maximum visibility yellow is best, whereas orange and red tend to inhibit visibility, as do blue and green. Colored light most often is used because white light glares and hurts the eyes.

The designer can plan color in lighting symbolically; but always in conjunction with the other elements of design. For example, focusing a red hue on an actor could indicate a state of health, or it could be associated with shame, embarrassment, or passion. The color in lighting is directly related to the color of the other scenic elements. Most often a designer

Mood is established through lighting for this production of *The Physicists.* Scene and lighting design was by Louis O. Erdmann. *(Photo by C. James Gleason and courtesy of Kent State University Theatre.)*

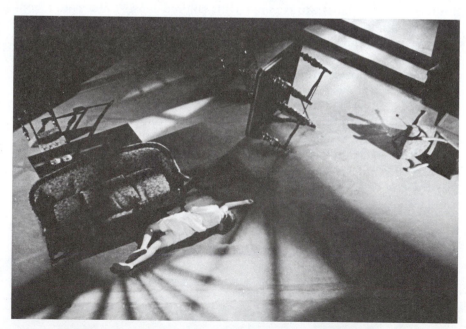

avoids green light, except for an eerie effect, because it suggests an unearthly or ghostlike quality. Mixtures of color in makeup, costuming, and lighting also can produce undesirable effects. When you color a surface with a yellow crayon and then cover the yellow with blue, you end up with green. The same kind of overlap can happen if the lighting designer does not take the other visual elements into consideration.

Lighting does not remain static but becomes a new design with each movement of the actor or each change in intensity or focus, much the way the image in a kaleidoscope changes as it turns.

Once lighting designers determine the lighting requirements, they make a lighting plot, which is a mixture of general and specific lighting for illumination and shadow. They make an instrument schedule, which includes such information as the instruments to use, where to hang them, and where to focus them. They take a floor plan of the set and draw in the location of each instrument and the area the light will hit. Most often in a proscenium theatre the acting area is lighted from overhead, from the back, and from instruments placed somewhere in the auditorium.

The designer divides the stage into areas, using a minimum of two instruments for specific illumination in each area. At least two are needed to eliminate long shadows and to light each side of the actor or set piece. The walls of a set are not well lighted, because the reflected glare would distract the audience. The designer also prepares a list of the lighting cues, so the technician knows exactly what to change and when.

The Costume Designer

What Costume Conveys

Costuming in a play, like clothing in real life, conveys a great deal. It can symbolize occupations. For instance, an actor playing a businessman wears a different outfit than does an actor playing a Roman Catholic priest. What we wear also can reveal our characters and personalities. A formal person wears different clothing than a relaxed, easygoing person. Costuming can indicate how a character feels. In everyday life, for instance, many people wear colorful clothing when they are happy. When they aren't feeling well, are unhappy, or just don't care, they tend to dress in darker colors. Usually, this choice is unconscious. Nevertheless, costume color is a clue to a character's feelings. Each person develops an individual style of dress. One person may prefer to wear jeans and a T shirt for relaxed occasions, while another feels comfortable only in dress slacks and a shirt or blouse that buttons. Each of these styles is acceptable, but we associate them with different lifestyles and personalities.

We also want to be recognized as standing apart. Maybe we want others to think we have good taste in clothing, or we may accentuate aspects of our personalities through what we wear. A woman with dangly bracelets probably would be more outgoing than one with little or

An audience should be able to recognize differences in the personalities of the two characters shown here in *Oklahoma*, presented by the Footlight Players of Coshocton, Ohio. Steve Mitchell on the left played Will Parker and Phil Huffman played Ali Hakim. *(Photo by Gary Anderson of the The Coshocton Tribune.)*

no jewelry. There is the old cliché of wearing a red carnation to be recognized. Most people don't wear red carnations, but many people do choose a distinctive touch—bowties, big earrings, or a cowboy hat, for example. Such features in a costume tell us about the character's self-image.

Sometimes people are total nonconformists in what they wear. Often as a kind of protest people embrace current styles or fads and take them even further than the average person. A character who appears in unconventional clothing probably will turn out to be a rebel.

Costumes can also tell the audience many things about a character's situation. We dress according to the occasion. For instance, if an actor entered wearing a tennis outfit, we might assume several things: the character plans to play tennis or has just finished playing tennis; he is athletic and competitive; he has free time, and he wants exercise. We infer many ideas at once, usually without conscious thought.

Basically, costuming for the stage conveys the same messages as everyday clothing, but the effect is heightened. Of all the scenic elements, costuming and makeup provide the strongest clues to character. They are the most personal elements of design, and the audience perceives the character and costume and makeup as a unity.

Planning the Costumes

The costume designer has to have a specialized background and a flair for style, not only the style of the character but the style of the actor playing the part. What one actor feels comfortable wearing could inhibit another. The actor should feel at ease with the costume, both in characterization and in appearance. The designer keeps in mind what actions the actor will be performing, and whether a particular design will aid or hinder these movements. A gown that is appropriate for the straight play *The Importance of Being Earnest,* might not work for the musical version, *Earnest in Love;* yet both costumes must fit the historical period and the status of the character.

The costumer keeps in mind the character's motives and personality. When we watch old Hollywood westerns, we can tell immediately who is the "good guy" and the "bad guy" by the color of their hats and horses. Stage costuming usually is not so blatant in its symbolism but tries subtly to convey mood and personality. Often the audience is not even conscious of the design.

Like the other elements, costuming must fit the overall concept of the play. There should be no incongruity of character, as happens, for instance, when a married actress forgets to remove a wedding ring when she plays a single woman.

No costume will appeal to every member of the audience. Often we form wrong impressions of people through their appearance. We may not

Joe Bella, who has designed for various professional and college productions, did the costume designs for Georges Feydeau's *The Happy Hunter. (Photos courtesy of Joe Bella.)*

like a particular color, and when we see it on anyone, it tends to bring out negative feelings. Nonetheless the designer has to be aware of what a color usually signifies. Just as red light tells us any number of things, so can red in costuming.

Color also serves as a point of focus. Although all the dancers in a musical are performing the same step, the lead dancer is emphasized through costuming that differs in color or style from that of the chorus. Color and style help identify groups as well as individuals. Just as opposing football teams wear different-colored jerseys, so do opposing sides in a play. In *West Side Story* the Sharks dress differently from the Jets for easy identification.

A costumer may be required to design any type of clothing from any historical period. The costumer is acquainted with various styles of dress, both modern and past, even though many times it is impossible to duplicate period clothing exactly. For instance, in many past periods women's costumes were cumbersome to wear and difficult to put on and take off. In the theatre quick changes often are required, so tear-away seams, snaps, and zippers are used. Fake furs take the place of hot, heavy, real furs. The designer has to have a thorough knowledge of historical styles

Unusual costuming was used for this production of *The Firebird. (Photo courtesy of Pick-A-Pack Players.)*

to know how to adapt a costume without inconsistency or distraction. Patricia Zipprodt describes her research:

> During the preparation phase, I research in all pertinent ways the period, its people and places, its history and whatever else might relate to the look and mood of the costumes. For *Fiddler* I spent months learning about the clothes and a way of life which had been totally unknown to me. By the time I was ready to sketch I could call with ease upon a vast amount of deeply absorbed knowledge. I found that I knew almost instinctively what each character should look like.[5]

The costumer meets with the director before designing a show. They work out an overall concept to avoid a clash of colors and styles from one type of design to another. Zipprodt discusses this stage of designing:

> A thorough analysis of the script is the first essential step. And because the costume designer is a part of a team, there follow conferences between the director and his designers. Actually, I find one of the most satisfying times in the preparation of a new production to be these preliminary meetings, for it is at this time that the overall concept of the work is hammered out.[6]

Costuming complements the other areas of design but also provides contrast. If an actress wore a light blue dress against a light blue wall, she would fade into the background or appear to be a bodiless apparition.

The designer has a knowledge of texture and fabric. From a distance and under light, inexpensive fabric sometimes appears costly. The costumer also recognizes that different fabrics or textures drape or hang differently. Stiff fabric tends to be more angular and severe and possibly would be better suited for a serious play or a formal character than would a clinging fabric.

The costumer knows how a fabric will flow or cling as the performer moves. Properly designed costumes can help an actor move in character. In *Sugar* Joe and Jerry dress as women and join an all-girl band to escape pursuing gangsters. Because the play takes place in the thirties, the two "girls" wear spiked heels. The heels help them take shorter, mincing steps. Many times actors begin really to feel the part once they have their costumes and accessories.

The Makeup Designer

Like costuming, makeup aids the actors in their portrayal of character and helps them "feel" the part. It also helps identify the actors for an audience. There are two types or categories of makeup: straight and character.

[5]Zipprodt, p. 29. Reprinted with permission.
[6]*Ibid.*

Straight Makeup

Straight makeup enhances or projects an actor's natural features. Under theatrical lighting a person's face tends to "wash out," leaving few distinguishing features. By using straight makeup, actors bring out their features more clearly. Generally, actors wear heavier makeup in larger theatres than in intimate structures. Still they must take care, or they will appear heavily made up from the front rows and natural only from the rear of the seating area.

Straight makeup begins with the application of a *base* or foundation, often redder in hue than normal skin color to compensate for the bright lights. The only considerations are that the makeup should be consistent with the actor's natural complexion and coloring and with the character.

After the base is applied, features of the actor's face may be highlighted. Eyebrows usually are darkened, as are the eyelashes and rims of the eyes. Straight makeup is completed with a touch of rouge to the cheeks and lips.

Character Makeup

Actors often choose and apply their own straight makeup, but often they need a designer for **character makeup,** when they have to change their appearance. An example would be a college actor who plays a middle-aged or old person. Then there are additional steps after a base is applied. One step could be to paint wrinkles on the face, for instance. Character makeup also could include a fake scar or "beauty mark," or in *Cyrano de Bergerac,* a longer nose made of putty. Often crepe hair is glued to the face to represent beards or moustaches.

Planning the Makeup

Makeup designers, like the other designers, are acquainted with the theory of color and its symbolism. They know how each type of makeup will look under lights of a certain color. For example, blue light will make rouge or lipstick appear black.

For any special needs, designers prepare **schematics,** outlines of the head with the face divided into areas and planes. Upon them they indicate the color and special features to apply to each area. Also, it may be necessary to change a character's makeup during the course of the play to correspond with different physical and emotional states.

The Property Master

Another theatrical artist is the property master, who works with three types of props: set props, set dressing or ornamentation, and hand props. **Set props** include anything that stands within the set, such as furniture, trees, rocks, or depending on the technical director's interpretation, even small platforms. In some cases the scene designer indicates the type and

Kathryn Drury uses straight makeup for Agatha Christie's *The Mousetrap. (Photo courtesy of Old Creamery Theatre of Garrison, Iowa.)* Character makeup was used for the character of James Tyrone in *Long Day's Journey into Night.* Jacque de Cosmo designed stylized makeup for the characters in *Once Upon a Mattress. (Both photos by C. James Gleason and courtesy of Kent State University Theatre.)*

A variety of props and set decorations were used for *Macbett,* produced by the Old Globe Theatre and presented at the Cassius Carter Centre Stage, San Diego. Director, Floyd Gaffney; setting and costume design, Peggy Kellner. *(Photo by Bill Reid and courtesy of the Old Globe Theatre.)*

Set dressing articles such as draperies or paintings that are attached to the walls of the set.

Hand props articles that are handled or carried by the actors.

even chooses the actual furniture or standing props to be used. At other times it's up to the property master to choose or design them. **Set dressing** includes wall fixtures, paintings, plaques, vases, and figurines. **Hand properties** are those objects an actor either carries onstage or handles while there.

Some productions require little in the way of props: some have properties that run into hundreds of items. For many shows the property master has to research historical items and build substitutes that appear accurate. More often it's simply a matter of deciding what is needed and buying or borrowing it. Items can be anything from a wrought iron bench to a stuffed elephant head.

The job of property master is demanding. It can be frustrating trying to round up everything, but it can be satisfying to use imagination and creativity.

The Audio Designer

Still another theatrical artist is the audio designer, the person who designs the sound effects. Such effects serve many functions. They can help create mood, as does the playing of the flute at the beginning of *Death of a Salesman*. They can provide exposition through traffic sounds or a steamboat whistle. They can combine the two in showing the style of the production. For instance, a gay Mozart sonata might set the tone for a light, eighteenth-century comedy. Sound can include anything from instrumental music to cars crashing, dishes breaking, horses galloping, or guns firing. Recordings can be bought containing almost any kind of sound effect. A train whistle, for example, can sound either comforting or eerie.

Although all the designers work with the director in planning a production, most often after the actual work has begun, they are responsible to the technical director. This person has the responsibility of seeing that all the designs are carried out as planned.

QUESTIONS FOR DISCUSSION

1. What sort of background should a scene designer have?
2. What are the functions of scene design?
3. What are the requirements of scene design?
4. What kinds of information can an audience learn from a setting?
5. What are the functions of lighting, and how might they be achieved?
6. What are the major types of lighting instruments? How do they differ from each other? What are their purposes?
7. What kinds of messages can costuming reveal to an audience?
8. What do the two different types of makeup—character and straight—involve?

SUPPLEMENTARY READING

BOOKS

Burdick, Elizabeth, et al., eds. *Contemporary Scene Design U.S.A.* New York: International Theatre Institute of the United States, Inc., 1974.

Gassner, John. *Producing the Play*, 2nd ed. New York: Holt, Rinehart and Winston, 1953.

Gillette, A. S. *Stage Scenery: Its Construction and Rigging.* New York: Harper & Row, Publishers, 1959.

Larson, Orville K., ed. *Scene Design for Stage and Screen: Readings on the Aesthetics and Methodology of Scene Design for Drama, Opera, Musical Comedy, Ballet, Motion Pictures, Television and Arena Theatre.* East Lansing: Michigan State University Press, 1961.

Oenslager, Donald. *Scenery Then and Now.* New York: W. W. Norton & Company, 1936.

Rowell, Kenneth. *Stage Design.* New York: Van Nostrand Reinhold Company, 1969.

CHAPTER 9
The Director

The director has the ultimate responsibility for the success or failure of any production. *(Photo of Earl Curtis, courtesy of Kent State University Theatre.)*

The director usually is the first theatre artist to be involved in the creative process of bringing a script to life before an audience. A myriad of responsibilities make the director's job one of the most exciting and satisfying of theatrical endeavors. As Stanislavski puts it, "The true director comprises within his own person a director-teacher, a director-writer, a director-administrator."[1] According to director Harold Clurman: "Direction is a job, a craft, a profession, and at best, an art. The director must be an organizer, a teacher, a politician, a psychic detective, a lay analyst, a technician, a creative being. Ideally, he would know literature (drama), acting, the psychology of the actor, the visual arts, music, history, and above all, he must understand people. He must inspire confidence."[2]

Directors usually are responsible for choosing a play, so they must be able to judge what will be acceptable to their potential audience. After they analyze the script, they decide upon their interpretation, then meet with the designers to coordinate an overall concept of production. They hold auditions, cast the play, approve the basic floor plan, and work with

[1]K. S. Stanislavsky, *Stati, Rechi, Besedi, Pisma* (Moscow: Iskusstvo, 1963), from *Directors on Directing,* Toby Cole and Helen Krich, eds. Chinoy (Indianapolis: The Bobbs-Merrill Co., Inc., 1963), p. 109.

[2]Harold Clurman, *On Directing* (New York: The Macmillan Company, 1972), p. 14.

the cast in providing a style of performance that is agreeable to and comfortable for everyone.

The rehearsal period begins with read-throughs and discussion. Then the director blocks the play and helps the actors to establish characters. Finally, all the elements of the production are unified, and the director is responsible for the ultimate success or failure.

Prerequisites

Directors usually acquire quite a bit of training or experience in the theatre before attempting to direct their first play. They become able to put themselves in the place of the actors, which means at least becoming acquainted with the various aspects of actor training, and they also learn to identify with the other theatre artists. They need a working knowledge of the principles of scene and lighting design and of costuming and makeup. They must learn how to manage the finances of a production and how to stay within a budget.

Directors each approach the task differently. Each has individual working methods. Some appear to be understanding of designers' and actors' problems, whereas others are brusque and demanding. The most important consideration is how well the director's personality fosters success.

No matter how they approach their work, directors know that their job is a huge undertaking, involving an almost staggering amount of work and dedication. "Directing is the sum-total of artistic and technical operations which enables the play as conceived by the author to pass from the abstract, latent state, that of the written script, to concrete and actual life on the stage."[3]

Selecting the Script

One of the first tasks for directors is to choose a script they like. They believe in the playwright's message and approve of the style of writing. They look forward to their jobs. In professional theatre, where they often have no choice in the script, directors have an easier job if they find aspects of the script they can admire.

In nonprofessional theatre directors may have several plays they want to direct. They decide whether these plays are suitable to their theatre, its purpose, its audience, and its goals. If they are working with an established organization, they choose a play that fits into the total season. If a college presents four productions a year, the director will not want to

[3]Jacques Copeau, "La Mise en Scéne," *Encyclopédie Francaise*, December 1955, from *Directors on Directing*, p. 214.

Community theatre director Delbert Walker gives instructions to his actors. *(Photo by Bill Douds.)*

choose a melodrama when another is planned. Directors also have to consider plays done in past seasons. If *The Glass Menagerie* was given three years ago, it probably will not draw well in the upcoming season. Directors also consider what plays have been given recently by other theatres in the area and what plays are planned. There should be a degree of balance in the styles and genres of the productions.

How do directors know what will be successful? They can only guess. Even the type of play that was a success in one season is not a guaranteed success in another. By studying trends and box office receipts directors can make fairly accurate "guesses" about the kind of scripts to choose.

Before making their choices, directors become acquainted with a wide range of plays. There are aids for play selection, such as play catalogs, which give a short synopsis of each script. Many books offer plot outlines and sometimes snatches of dialogue to give a feeling for style. Directors should go on to read the entire scripts before they make a final choice.

Directors have to take still other matters into consideration in choosing a play. A practical consideration is finances. When money is limited, a director should not choose an elaborate spectacle. Although they probably will not be doing the promotion for their productions, directors know about budgets and projected attendance. They realize how much money is involved, from box office expenses to royalties. In nonprofessional theatre, a director usually prepares the production budget.

Finally, directors consider the elements of available talent and theatre structure. A small theatre group will have a difficult time presenting O'Neill's *Lazarus Laughed*, because there are fourteen individual characters besides various "choruses," "citizens," and "crowds." A small stage would not be adequate for such a large cast, even if the director could round up enough people to appear in the play.

Analyzing the Script

After a play is chosen, approved, and scheduled for production, the director's work is just beginning. Next the director analyzes the script to try to understand the writer's meaning. When the play is to be a premiere production, the director probably will work with the playwright, but in other instances the chance probably will not arise. Even if it does, according to Tyrone Guthrie, it may not help the director to understand the play:

> With regard to what the script is about, the last person, who, in my opinion should be consulted, even if he is alive or around, is the author. If the author is a wise man, he will admit straight away that he does not know what it is about. . . . The more important the work of art, the less the author will know what he has written.[4]

Often directors spend hours working on the analysis and interpretation because, as play and film director José Quintero says: "I've always thought that the main function of the director is to translate something from the literary form into an active dramatic life—to translate rather than to dictate or to inspire. Of course, you have to inspire your actors as the script inspires you. But I think it is mainly a question of translating."[5]

Finding an Overall Concept

As they work with the script and later the actors and designers, directors may change some of their concepts. Still, the director works out the largest portion of the analysis before meeting with them. The director usually reads the script through a few times just for a general impression or feeling. Then an overall concept begins to emerge.

Some directors look for a central idea. In Neil Simon's *Barefoot in the Park* the central idea might be that each person has to learn to give a little or to become flexible. The two major characters, Corie and Paul, are in

---

[4]Tyrone Guthrie, Transcript of a talk delivered before the Royal Society of Arts, London, March 10, 1952. From *Directors on Directing*, pg. 214.

[5]José Quintero, interviewed by Jean-Claude van Itallie, in Joseph F. McCrindle, ed., *Behind the Scenes: Theatre and Film Reviews from the Transatlantic Review* (New York: Holt, Rinehart and Winston, 1971), p. 256.

love but refuse to adjust to changes in lifestyle after their marriage. The play is the story of how they learn to adjust to new situations and to each other.

Directors often try to develop a metaphor which is carried out in the design and acting. Archibald Macleish's *J.B.*, which uses the book of Job from the Bible as its starting point, traditionally has been done with a circus metaphor. The highest platform in the circus tent represents heaven and the lower levels earth and hell. In the original design for *Cat on a Hot Tin Roof* Maggie and Brick's bedroom resembled a boxing ring, because they were always fighting.

Each production of a play is different from any other, and much of the difference lies in the directors' interpretations. They bring their personalities and backgrounds to the script. Often, too, for a better understanding of the play and the writer they research the historical period, the locale, and the writer's life.

Interpreting More Closely

After deciding upon the overall concept, directors become more specific in their analysis. They figure out which elements of the play are the most important for the audience's understanding, and which can be deemphasized. Often directors will add elements, both in design and movement, to bring out characterization, setting, or circumstances. For instance, "hokey" business sometimes is added to farce to accentuate the silliness of the character or situation.

The director tries to determine the basic action or the areas of conflict in the play as a whole and in each scene. Where does the major climax occur, and how can it be pointed up? Where do the minor climaxes occur in each scene, and how can they be presented?

Betty McCreary directs a scene from a production of the Children's Wing of Trumpet in the Land. *(Photo by Isabel Kopp.)*

The director determines the prevailing mood or atmosphere. Is it basically nostalgic or comic, tragic or sentimental? There are subtle or abrupt changes in mood throughout a play; but there is a prevailing atmosphere or feeling that is most important to the script's message.

Directors determine how each character relates to the play as a whole and how the characters relate to each other. Director Alan Schneider states: "To me a play is a series of relationships. A dramatic action, to me, means a change in relationship."[6] Directors determine why each character is included and how each advances the theme. What struggle is the most important in providing the play's dramatic movement? What needs or desires do the characters symbolize? How is each character unique?

Anticipating Design

During the analysis a director also thinks in terms of setting and technical elements. What type of environment will best portray the atmosphere, mood, actions, and circumstances? What elements of design are necessary? At some point in the planning the director meets with the designers to present these ideas. Some directors prefer to work out the total design concept themselves, whereas others are open to suggestion.

Anticipating Blocking

After approving the set design, the director considers how much blocking to plan before the show is cast and rehearsals begin. As a general rule, directors plan the broad movements but leave the subtleties of gesture and characterization up to the actor. Experienced actors are likely to have a sense of what is right for any situation, and directors may prefer to give them more freedom than they give beginning actors. Alan Schneider, in discussing this issue, remarks:

> Helen Hayes used to say to me: "Edit me, Alan. Don't direct me." I understand exactly what she meant. She wanted me to tell her when she was doing too much or too little. The director is a kind of editor. As a matter of fact I think there's a real analogy between an editor and a director, and I certainly don't figure an editor as important as the guy who wrote the original sentence. I'm not saying that in any modesty; I simply believe the director is a kind of necessary evil, rather than the fountainhead of the theatre or anything like that. I'm delighted when I don't have to direct, when the actors have it all there, and when the playwright has got it very clearly established. Normally speaking an actor can't watch himself from the outside; he hasn't got a sense of perspective. And that's when the director is valuable.[7]

[6] Alan Schneider, interviewed by van Itallie, in McCrindle, p. 279.
[7] McCrindle, Schneider interview, p. 280.

If the blocking has been planned in detail, rehearsals probably will proceed more smoothly, but there is a chance the physical action will appear too rigid and controlled. If there is too little planning, the director risks wasting time.

Casting the Play

The director has to be a good judge of human behavior, particularly in educational and community theatre. Because actors in these situations receive no financial compensation for their work, they must have other incentives for auditioning. The director tries to judge the actors' sincerity and reliability, as well as their talent.

Another consideration is how well the actors and the director can work together and whether a good rapport can be established among the actors.

> Dealing with actors is a very personal relationship, and no two can be treated in the same way. Actors are notoriously sensitive, and during rehearsal, particularly as the opening night approaches, they are as fretful as thoroughbreds at the starting gate. Their nervous insecurity betrays itself in diverse ways; the director becomes a father figure, who, by his very being, is loved by some and hated by others, and often loved and hated by the same person at the same time. He must build up the confidence of some and puncture the cocky and limiting self-assurance of others. He must have a word for everybody . . . . The company is a tightly knit family engaged on the same adventure, and it experiences all the joys and tribulations of family life . . . .[8]

Although they have in mind the type of actor they want for each role, directors usually do not precast their shows. Often they do visualize a certain build, type of voice, or age, but they should keep an open mind.

Typecasting

There always is a certain degree of typecasting in theatre, but it is not the general practice. Typecasting means casting actors in roles that are similar to them in real life. In terms of physical attributes, of course, most directors do typecast. Some go beyond that to cast a boisterous, quarrelsome person in the role of a boisterous, quarrelsome character.

This sort of casting sometimes makes for a good performance, but many times people fail to see themselves as others do. Actors may have

[8]Philip Burton, *Early Doors: My Life and the Theatre* (New York: The Dial Press, Inc., 1969), p. 202.

Professional director Charles Kray explains how the actor should play a scene in Paul Green's *Trumpet in the Land.* *(Photo by Isabel Kopp.)*

trouble portraying characters similar to themselves. They may feel that they are not really acting.

Auditions

"Choose a good script," I sometimes advise students, "cast good actors—and you'll all be good directors!" There is more than a little truth in the jest. Casting constitutes the first step in the practical interpretation of a play.[9]

The most common type of audition is *open tryouts.* The actors all appear at a certain time and audition in front of everyone there. Often the director makes scripts available ahead of time and takes time at the beginning to summarize the action and explain the script. Sometimes directors allow the actors to audition for specific parts of their choice; at other times directors ask them to read certain sections of the script. Some directors prefer that the actors present a pantomime or an impromptu scene.

The open tryout method has several advantages. The director is able to judge how the actors will appear with each other, so there is little danger, for instance, of casting a father who is shorter than his thirteen-year-old son. Also the director can see how well the actors relate to each other and how well their voices blend. An advantage for the actors is that they are able to judge the competition.

There are several disadvantages. One is that certain actors may have adverse reactions to the auditions of other actors, which affect the way they read. Auditioning first, last, or in the middle may also affect how well an actor does. If the auditions last a long time, the director may tire and stop concentrating.

[9]Clurman, p. 64.

Two students audition for a university production. *(Photo by James D. Kitchen.)*

A second type of audition is the *interview*. The actor and the director see each other without anyone else present. Sometimes directors just talk with the actors: sometimes they have the actors read from the script or perform an impromptu scene. One advantage is that the director can concentrate on one actor at a time. An advantage for certain actors is that they don't experience the pressure of having to compete openly with others and are not so nervous. A disadvantage is that the director cannot see the way actors look together nor how well they work with each other. Sometimes too the director has to read a part to cue the actor and loses concentration. Because this type of auditon often is held in an office or small room, the director is unable to consider the vocal projection of the actor.

There are various other methods of auditioning. At times actors are asked to prepare a short scene of their choice to present either at open auditions or at interviews. Sometimes a director will interview actors and then have them come to open tryouts. In professional theatre, auditions with experienced actors often are handled through interviews, while the majority of those auditioning go to open auditions, or as they are termed, "cattle calls," where they may be eliminated on the basis of physical appearance even before seeing the director.

At any type of audition the director has many questions to consider: how easily the actors move; their emotional depth and range; the quality, range, and projection of their voices; and their overall potential for a role. Some actors do not read well but have the potential for growth and development in a role. Others read well at first but fail to develop characters much further.

Often actors will need special abilities. For a musical they may be asked to come to auditions with a prepared song to sing. They may perform their own dance steps, or they may be given several steps to learn and execute.

Rehearsing the Play

After the cast is chosen and the technical elements are planned, directors devote most of their time to the actors. The rehearsal period can vary from a usual four weeks in professional theatre to six weeks in educational and community theatre. A shorter period is needed in professional theatre because the actors can spend an entire work day rehearsing, whereas in other theatres they have school or a job.

There are six stages of rehearsal: *reading rehearsals,* in which the purpose is to come to a clear understanding and interpretation of the play; *blocking rehearsals,* in which the action, movement, and business are worked out; *character and line rehearsals,* in which the performers develop and build their characters and try to discover the most effective method of delivering their speeches; *finishing rehearsals,* in which all the elements of acting are developed and unified; *technical rehearsals,* devoted to coordinating the visual and sound elements with the total production; and *dress rehearsals,* in which the play ideally is given just as it will be in performance.

The length of the entire rehearsal period depends upon several factors. One is the background and experience of the actors. In educational theatre the director often has to serve as a teacher. Also, some plays are easier to perform than others. It will probably take a shorter time to ready

This scene shows how mood and atmosphere can be achieved through placement of characters, in Seton Hall University's production of *The Playboy of the Western World.* Director, James McGlone. *(Photo courtesy of Seton Hall University.)*

a simple comedy for production than it will a musical in which the actors must learn songs and dances as well as learning lines and building characters. The theatre schedule affects the rehearsal period, too. Often summer stock theatres change the bill each week. In educational theatre plays sometimes are presented every two or three weeks during the summer. Then there are some theatres that rehearse for months, as Stanislavski did at the Moscow Art Theatre.

The length of time for each type of rehearsal varies. When the business and blocking are intricate, blocking rehearsals have to be prolonged. This happens in a highly stylized production where every movement down to the smallest gesture or facial expression is planned. Character and line rehearsals take longer if the speeches are difficult and the characterizations unusually involved. Often, if there are many special effects, additional technical rehearsals will be needed.

No matter how long the rehearsal period, directors do their best to maintain interest for the actors, who, in turn, try to continue to build their roles. In nonprofessional theatre the director usually schedules rehearsals of no longer than two or three hours. Otherwise the actors will tire, and the rehearsal will be of little value. There is little advantage in holding rehearsals of less than an hour, except, perhaps, to work with individuals.

Reading Rehearsals

For the first few rehearsals it is not necessary to have a stage or rehearsal hall. In fact, the director often prefers to have a relaxed atmosphere where the actors feel free to discuss the script. Reading rehearsals are somewhat misnamed, in that the major purpose is to agree on a script's interpretation. At the first rehearsal the director may have the actors read through the play to grasp the overall concept, without attempting to develop character. The director may then assign the actors to do an analysis on their own, paying particular attention to their own character's needs, drives, relationships, and place in the script.

There is no pattern that all directors follow for reading rehearsals. At some point the director may show sketches and floor plans to the actors so they can better visualize the action. Most importantly, the director discusses interpretation with the actors and listens to their ideas. Often the director tells the cast to go ahead and bring out new ideas or to experiment. If what the actors do seems appropriate, it can be retained. Otherwise the director can change it.

At the reading rehearsals directors explain the effects they hope to achieve and their interpretation of the play's central idea. The play is torn apart and put together again. The actors and the director should come to understand the basic action and motivation, why the characters act as they do, and what the goals of each are. The actors have to understand what their characters are trying to achieve at every second in the play.

   It is only after this work that the director and cast are ready to move to the stage or rehearsal hall, where they work out the movement and business.

Blocking Rehearsals

Most obviously, movement and business keep the play from appearing static and give it life and activity. Another purpose is to present an aesthetically pleasing picture both in the placement and movement of the actors. The director remembers that the stage picture is constantly changing and is perceived differently from each section of the audience.

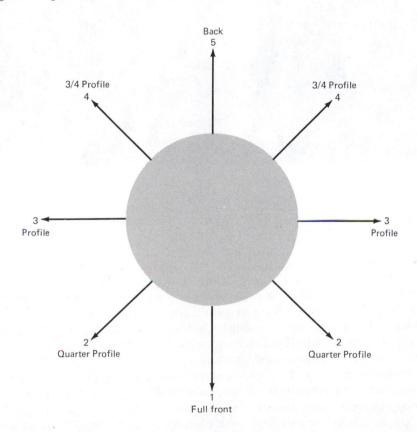

The full front body position is the strongest for an actor onstage, while the quarter profile often is used when actors talk with each other. The further upstage an actor turns, the weaker the positioning usually becomes. Three-quarter profile may be used to focus attention on another actor. The back position is rarely used.

   Because blocking does involve placement and movement, the director always considers sightlines and knows which stage areas are the strongest for emphasis. Body position, focus, and levels all are used to emphasize specific characters, speeches, and scenes.

   Movement has to be motivated by the script, or at least appear to be motivated. The director cannot just move actors to balance the stage. It takes a great deal of thought to make the blocking fit the situation and

It's easy to see where the center of focus should be in this production of *Something's Afoot* at the University of Kentucky. *(Photo courtesy of University of Kentucky, Department of Theatre.)*

the type of play. In a funeral scene, for instance, the movement should be slower and more stately than in a party scene. Different types of characters move differently, and their movements provide variety and contrast.

There are two categories of movement and business: inherent and supplementary. The first is any action that advances the story or is an integral part of the plot. It includes exits and entrances, fights, and phone calls. Supplementary business is added for effect, either to enhance the message of the play or to establish character. It includes how the actor stands, sits, or walks. This business helps to establish the mood of each scene and the emotions of the characters.

Both inherent and supplementary business are used for focus. A moving actor, whether walking from one spot to another or fiddling with a prop, attracts more attention than does a stationary one. Focus also applies to the characters' use and placement of furniture; it can provide psychological groupings, as when a family is united around a table.

Physical closeness sometimes implies emotional closeness, whereas distance often implies disagreement. A tendency to stay in certain areas of the stage can show much about the psychological aspects of a character. A character who stays toward the back of the set probably seems timid, whereas another who is downstage appears more extroverted or confident. A scene appears weak if the characters constantly move behind

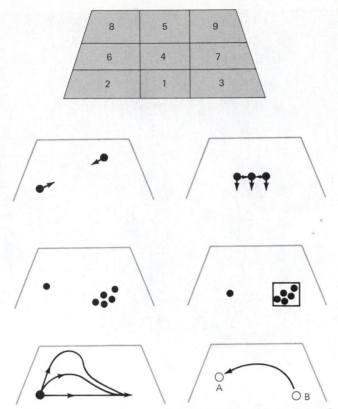

The #1 area of the stage is strongest and the areas decrease in strength the higher the number. Of course, other things affect the relative strength or weakness of an area. In the second drawing the person in the #2 area actually is weaker than the one in #9 because he's facing upstage. In the drawing on the right, all three actors can be of equal strength when they face front. But when the two on the ends face inward, the middle one becomes a strong focal point. The drawing on the middle left shows that the isolated individual receives the emphasis, but on the right the emphasis is nearly equalized when the group stands on a platform. The strongest movement, bottom left, is straight across the stage. The other moves show decreasing strength or uncertainty. The bottom right drawing, however, shows that it is stronger to move in a curved line than a straight one because of final positioning. If the actor walked straight upstage, he would be facing upstage, which is a weak position.

the furniture rather than in front. A dominant character usually will not stand looking up at a platform while browbeating a weaker character.

The director constantly is aware of providing unity and variety in picturization, as well as showing conflict, focus, emphasis, and characterization. Movement can complement or even replace lines. It can show the progression of the play or prepare the audience for future events.

Although movement is planned just after the reading rehearsals, it continues to build and change throughout the rehearsal period.

The actress is the point of focus in Colgate University Theater's production of *The Hound of the Baskervilles.* Usually, a point further downstage is stronger. Here, however, the actress is stronger for three reasons. She is on a platform, her body is in a more open position to the audience, and the actor is looking upstage. Director, Atlee Sproul. *(Photo courtesy of the Colgate University/Summer Theater, Hamilton, N.Y.)*

Character and Line Rehearsals

In the script analysis and the first rehearsals the actor will begin working out a character interpretation and delivery of lines. After the blocking rehearsals the actor begins to concentrate fully on the development of the role. The director tries to free the actor from inhibitions about establishing a character or experimenting with the character's development.

Throughout this stage of rehearsal the character begins to come to life. Occasionally, the director has to provide more guidance than usual for the actor who has failed to understand the style of the play or the intricacies of the character. Line and character interpretation usually go hand in hand. Once established, a character has a certain way of speaking. The director makes certain that the actor understands the significance of each line. A great deal depends on how the dialogue is delivered rather than just on content. It is ultimately the director's responsibility to see that the lines are delivered in character and in accordance with the play's mood and style. The director sees that the actor properly identifies with the role.

The director also is concerned with the technical aspects of projecting lines and character. For instance, a good rendering of character for television will not be suitable for a proscenium stage. Many of the subtleties of movement and facial expression will be lost, and the lines will not be heard.

Finishing Rehearsals

Action, interaction, delivery, and interpretation are refined and polished during the last few weeks of rehearsal. Up to this point the director has stopped scenes when necessary and corrected blocking or line delivery. Now, unless something is really wrong, the rehearsals proceed without stopping. This way the actors gain a better sense of the play's meaning. Often it is not until the finishing rehearsals that an actor can fully appreciate the impact of a role. The director usually takes notes and discusses inconsistencies between the running of the acts.

Until the finishing rehearsals it has been difficult to concentrate on the show's overall movement, because there have been so many stops and starts. Now the director concentrates on the three broad aspects of movement: **pace, timing,** and **rhythm.**

Pace refers to the fastness or slowness in handling business and speaking lines. The pace will be faster in scenes of excitement or tension and slower in a relaxed atmosphere. All plays, even tragedies, lose effectiveness if they drag. Plays also suffer if the scenes are presented too quickly, but slowness is much more usual.

Timing refers to the use of pauses within or between speeches. It is important both in pointing up specific lines and actions and in emphasizing reactions. In a serious scene a pause can show that something of importance is about to occur. In a comedy it is important to pause just the right length of time before delivering a punch line or a humorous action. For serious scenes the timing of reactions is important. When somebody hears of the death of a special person, it takes time to absorb the shock. Therefore the actor pauses before reacting. Pauses also are effective in drawing attention to a character.

Rhythm refers both to the flow of the language and to the matter of picking up cues and changing scenes. Every piece of literature, largely through the author's style, has a certain rhythm. Maxwell Anderson's blank verse drama *Winterset* has a very different rhythm than does Ibsen's *Ghosts,* although both deal with serious subjects. Rhythm can be altered by actors who pick up cues too slowly or too quickly.

It is the director's responsibility to establish the pace, timing, and rhythm to suit the production. All three are tied closely to mood and emotional pitch.

Pace the overall rate of speed in handling lines and business.

Timing the use of pauses in delivering lines.

Rhythm the flow of the lines; the speed with which the actors pick up cues.

Technical Rehearsals

By the time the finishing rehearsals end, the performance aspects of the production should look as they will be during the show's run. Out of necessity, during the usual two or three technical rehearsals, the director will devote attention to the technical aspects of the production and neglect the actors. If the director has planned well and worked closely with the designers, there will not be much to do except for helping to correct minor details. As a matter of fact, the stage manager often takes care of the run-throughs from this point through the production of the play. The stage manager sees that the scenery is shifted, that the set is properly dressed, and that offstage effects are carried out.

Dress Rehearsals

An old saying states: A bad dress rehearsal means a good opening. Nothing could be further from the truth. Sometimes there can be a successful opening night despite a poor dress rehearsal, but never because of it. The dress rehearsal is a tryout of the production, much as a Broadway theatre tries out the production either in the theatre where it will be presented or out of town.

Usually there are two rehearsals in full costume with all the technical elements. Directors sometimes invite people so that the actors can become accustomed to playing to an audience. From now on the director's only responsiblity is to take notes on the performance and give them to the actors some time before each succeeding night of the play's run. The job is finished unless the play has a long run. Then the director may call rehearsals to correct inconsistencies that have crept into the performance. During long runs, additional rehearsals may be necessary when actors replace one another. Sometimes the entire cast rehearses with the new actors. At other times, the director, an assistant, or a production stage manager may rehearse the replacements by themselves with only certain members of the cast.

Directing in Arena Theatre

As we learned in Chapter 7, many schools and professional companies use arena staging. Many of the principles of directing are the same as in a proscenium theatre, but there are some differences. The director has to pay more attention to small details and subtleties of characterization, because the audience is closer to the action. The director also loses some control over picturization, because the groupings of characters will be viewed from all sides.

Although furniture can be placed in closer approximation of real life on an arena stage than on a proscenium stage, it is ineffective and monotonous to line the edges of the stage as in a real living room. Furniture can be centrally placed, and then the actor can play toward the audience rather than toward the center of the playing area. Some directors place the furniture at the corners of the arena so that each section of the audience will have a good view of each actor at least part of the time.

Focus is similar in arena theatre to that in proscenium theatre. The actor who is standing is more dominant than the one who is sitting, and the audience plays more attention to the moving actor than to the one who is still. There is an advantage in that there are no weak areas except

In arena theatre the director has different considerations in regard to the audience than he or she does in proscenium theatre. (*Photo courtesy of Pick-A-Pack Theatre.*)

possibly center stage, because only half the audience can see the face of an actor who stands there. The actor who plays off center but faces center is facing more than half the audience. An actor in an aisleway or corner can, just by a turn of the head, face all of the audience. There is more variety in playing area because the groupings are more plastic and moveable. There is a loss in emphasis through grouping, but the director makes better use of depth in movement.

Body position is of little value in arena staging, because an actor who is open to one part of the audience is closed to another. Similarly, upstage for some viewers is downstage for others. Often the director will designate areas of the stage to correspond to the dial of a clock. One area is the twelve o'clock position, one the three o'clock, and so on. The positions remain constant and are referred to in terms of the clock rather than as Down Right or Down Left.

Spacing is unimportant; an actor separated from the group at one angle appears to be part of it at another. Body positions relate to the other actors and not to the audience, but the actor can move away from or come closer to the other actors and give a sense of psychological closeness or separation through the movement. Often the movement is curved, so that the actor making a cross is open to several areas of the audience. In proscenium theatres such curved movements could denote weakness or indecision, but in arena theatre they are not so likely to carry these connotations unless the actor moves slowly or hesitantly. Weakness or strength depends on how the actor executes a movement.

If the actors keep at least four feet of space between each other, the scenes will be opened for all parts of the audience. If two actors face each other directly at close range, each one's back is to part of the house, meanwhile blocking the other actor from the same part. It is better if each stands slightly sideways in relation to the other. Most positions are not bad if they are held only briefly. It is best not to hold any position for long. Even subtle changes in movement give the audience the impression of having a better view.

In two-character scenes the director can place one or both actors near an aisleway, providing better sightlines. Often, since the actor speaking cannot be the center of attention for the entire audience, reactions through facial expression and movement become more important in arena theatre.

It is easier to block three characters, because there can be a triangular arrangement. Now most of the viewers will be able to see one actor full front and another in profile. Large groups can be divided into several triangles.

Movement can be less restrained and more natural in an arena, but it should have meaning. Any placement of actors should be aesthetically pleasing to as much of the audience as possible. Tempo usually is faster because the lines and characterization do not have to be projected so far. One aspect of tempo that requires more rehearsal is entrances. The actor has to walk down an aisleway and must not arrive too early or too late. The director makes sure that the audience knows early in the action just where each of the aisleways is supposed to lead.

In casting for the arena stage, the director takes more care in choosing the right physical type, because makeup and costuming are more subtle. The director also must take care in choosing the play. Although most plays can be adapted for arena staging, it may be difficult to present extravagant musicals. Plays with many changes of locale also will be difficult to stage with realistic settings.

With common sense and imagination, a director will succeed in any type of staging.

QUESTIONS FOR DISCUSSION

1. In trying to judge what play will draw a good audience, what should a director take into consideration?
2. Besides the audience, what else should the director take into consideration when selecting a play?
3. What is involved in the director's analysis of a script?
4. What are the advantages and disadvantages of the two common types of auditions?
5. What are the goals of the six types of rehearsals?

6. How is directing in arena theatre similar to directing in proscenium theatre? How is it different?

SUPPLEMENTARY READING

BOOKS

Clurman, Harold. *On Directing*. New York: The Macmillan Company, 1972.

Cole, Toby, and Chinoy, Helen Krich, eds. *Directors on Directing*. Indianapolis: The Bobbs-Merrill Company, Inc., 1963.

Jones, Margo. *Theatre-in-the-Round*. New York: Holt, Rinehart and Winston, Inc., 1951.

McCrindle, Joseph F., ed. *Behind the Scenes: Theatre and Film Reviews from the Transatlantic Review*. New York: Holt, Rinehart and Winston, 1971.

CHAPTER 10
Approaches to Theatre

For years Broadway has been considered the mainstay of theatrical performances; but Broadway makes up only a small segment of the total theatre in the United States. In recent years there has been a move toward off-Broadway theatre in New York City and toward decentralization of professional performance by the establishment of regional theatres. Moreover, theatre, both in New York and across the country, takes many forms.

We can categorize theatre as professional, community, and educational, which provides a starting point; but the division is arbitrary, and there is overlapping among the three. Even in strictly professional theatre there are many subdivisions, as there are in community and educational theatre.

Each type of theatre exists for somewhat different purposes, and even similar types differ from place to place. It is basically true, but an oversimplification, to say that the purpose of educational theatre is to train or teach; of community theatre, to provide enjoyment; and of professional theatre, to make money.

Educational Theatre

Basically, educational theatre is a training ground for both theatre artists and audience members. The degree of training and experience depends on the type and size of the school. There are four levels of educational theatre: elementary, high school, college or university, and graduate school. Other theatres also provide a training ground for the theatre student. Resident companies, for instance, take on apprentices, and some communities have cultural arts programs every summer.

Elementary School Theatre

Theatre in the elementary school usually is simple. Often children present short plays for P.T.A. meetings or for holidays. Some schools regularly present a major production each year, involving children in all grades. Such presentations are extracurricular and are staged for the enjoyment of both the children and the audience. This type of program can awaken an interest in theatre.

Often the teacher who directs plays in the elementary school has had little training in theatre. Fortunately, more colleges and universities are adding courses in children's theatre to their curriculum.

Because children often play games of "pretend" during their early years, it is easy for the younger child to learn to appreciate theatre. In so doing a child becomes more self-confident and learns to channel the mimetic instinct, rather than to suppress it.

Creative Dramatics   An important area of theatre for the young child is creative dramatics, now becoming more common as a course of study in colleges. The goal of creative dramatics is not production. Rather it is closer to improvisational theatre. Children are encouraged to dramatize stories, fairy tales, situations, or events they are studying. For instance, they may dramatize the hardships George Washington and his troops suffered at Valley Forge. Often, when children enact historical events, they understand and remember them more clearly. They also practice co-operation and other social amenities by sharing in a dramatization, even of simple stories.

Creative dramatics also can teach practical skills, such as math. Children in kindergarten or first grade often have difficulty in grasping the concept of numbers. When two children at each end of a classroom walk toward the center of the room, then the children walking and watching can easily see that two children and two children add up to four children.

Creative dramatics offers the fun of performing or doing something, teaches the child important concepts, instills confidence, and develops the mimetic instinct. Just as children should be encouraged to take freedom in their drawing or painting, so should they have freedom to pretend.

Usually, creative dramatics is not for an invited audience but for the children involved. Most often there are no theatrical settings, no costumes, no lights, and limited properties. This simplicity can make the event even more real. Children like to use their imaginations, and when things are spelled out in detail, the imagination is inhibited. That is one reason "story hours" at libraries are popular. As children hear a story read, they can visualize the setting as they wish it to be.

Cultural Opportunities   In conjunction with a school district a number of communities have instigated summer cultural programs where the child from the age of five through high school may choose to study an art. Often for the younger child enrolled in theatre classes, this program means spending three or four hours each day in creative dramatics and improvisational theatre. The children may even participate in simple plays. As the age group goes up, so does the complexity of the training. From creative dramatics the older child may move on to training in acting or set construction.

Similar to the community cultural programs are courses for children taught in conjunction with colleges. The classes are held on Saturdays during the school year and on weekdays during the summer. Often a college professor of creative dramatics or children's theatre courses is in charge.

Training for children also is available in many of the larger community theatres across the country. The variety of theatrical experiences for

A member of the Theatre of Youth Company leads elementary school children in creative dramatics. *(Photo courtesy of the Theatre of Youth Company.)*

the elementary school student seems to be increasing. Professional touring groups give shows in the schools and community theatre presents shows by and for children.

High School Theatre

Even a decade ago, only a small percentage of the high schools in the United States offered any type of theatre education or training. Now the number offering courses in acting, dramatic production, playwriting, and technical theatre is increasing. Many of the schools that do offer theatre courses of any sort deal largely with studying dramatic literature; but other courses are rapidly increasing in number.

During a random sampling of high schools in the New York-New Jersey area in the late seventies, all those queried presented at least one production each year, and nineteen out of twenty offered at least one course in theatre. Many had several courses. Admittedly, the East is considered the theatre capital of the United States, and more secondary schools in that part of the country might offer training in theatre, but schools in other areas also are beginnning to add more practical training.

Secondary education has a long way to go in adding theatre courses and training for students, but it is well on its way. It is rare to find a high school in any area of the country that does not present at least one major production a year, and many schools have two or three, in addition to

The Diary of Anne Frank was presented at New Philadelphia, Ohio, High School under the direction of Lynne Tschudy. (Photo by Art Mitchell and courtesy of Lynne Tschudy.)

participating in local and state one-act play competitions.

High school plays often are staged to make money for a class or organization, but at least they are being presented. There is a trend in many schools to do away with the junior or senior class plays and move toward "all-school" plays, although the profits still often go to a specific group. This trend is advantageous for freshmen and sophomores; now they can participate in several full-scale productions, and if they are truly interested in theatre, can gain experience in all phases by the time they receive a diploma.

It still is sometimes the case that the director of high school plays has limited training in theatre; but as there is a trend toward more theatre coursework, there seems to be a trend toward more qualified directors. It is not at all unusual to find several teachers in a secondary school system who have at least a college minor in speech/theatre or in theatre.

Because high school theatre often exists largely to make money for a class or organization, production may be confined to recent Broadway shows or popular musicals, limiting the type of training a student can

M*A*S*H was pre-sented at Troy, Ohio, High School, under the direction of Sandy Zimmerle. (Photo by Drew Foster and courtesy of Troy High School.)

gain. However, most larger high schools no longer seem to be presenting obscure, nonroyalty plays, nor slapstick plays with inane dialogue and even sillier plots. Many schools, particularly those with an active program, are presenting a large variety of shows.

Besides raising money, high school theatre serves many purposes. It can awaken interest and develop talent in various areas of theatre. Properly handled, it can broaden cultural horizons, not only for the students participating in productions, but for the general student body that sees the plays. It can train students in the areas of lighting, makeup, costuming, and set construction. Many schools have an annual evening of one-acts, which are entirely in student hands.

Often, of course, secondary schools have limited facilities and small budgets for the production of plays. In a way this constraint is good, because the student who is interested in theatre learns to improvise. The student learns that an ordinary bulb in a large tin can can provide general lighting, or that large cardboard boxes can be cut and fitted to take the place of flats. If students work under less than ideal conditions, they will have a much easier time when and if they ever work in a better theatre facility.

College and University Theatre

Educational theatre in colleges and universities has as its major purpose the training of students. Because the department of the school is the producer, there need not be the concern about making money that there often is in other theatres. The school tries to break even each season, but money is not usually the primary concern. Acquainting the student, both as theatre worker and as audience member, with as many styles, genres, and historical periods of theatre as possible is more important. Most schools try to teach at least the fundamentals of the various phases of theatre.

Even so, schools differ somewhat in their philosophies as to what a theatre program should accomplish. Some hope to train the student major for a career in theatre, whereas others want only to acquaint the student with as much theatre as possible. Still other schools, which offer limited work in theatre, define their goal as developing an appreciation of theatre or broadening the students' horizons. Regardless of the school's philosophy, college students usually have the opportunity to experience theatre. It is up to them to decide to what degree they want to pursue it and with what goals.

The amount of theatre training varies greatly from one school to the next. In some, the theatre division is under the English department, whereas in other schools there is a large theatre department with specialization available in the areas of design, acting/directing, or theatre history and criticism. At some schools the students can obtain only a general speech major, which includes a few courses in theatre. At others they can major in theatre education. At a number of schools they can work toward a bachelor of fine arts degree with a high concentration in practical training.

The size of a department offering a program in theatre ranges from one part-time theatre professor covering the whole field to several instructors in each area. There are some colleges that present plays only as an extracurricular activity; but more than half the colleges and universities in the United States offer majors in theatre. Of the remaining schools, at least half offer a limited number of theatre and drama courses.

The range of experience often is a wide one. In addition to presenting three or four major productions during the academic year, many schools have studio theatres. Here the student can experiment without close faculty guidance. Productions are student-directed and often student-written. Studio theatres also allow the presentation of plays that have limited audience appeal. Larger schools may have as many as four or five theatre facilities, from proscenium to thrust to arena.

Many schools have summer programs in which a different play is presented every few weeks. Often these programs are operated under the resident company concept. The same students are members for the entire

Orestes was pre-
sented at San Diego
State University. Di-
rector, Mack Owen.
*(Photo courtesy of San
Diego State Univer-
sity—Dramatic Arts
Department.)*

season. In one play the student may have a small part and in the following production a leading role. Often, much like professional resident or
summer stock theatres, the college summer theatres provide the opportunity for students to study a variety of roles or to work on all phases of
a production. In many cases students from a number of schools or areas
will audition for the summer company.

Often the student in a college theatre program will have the chance
to work with professionals who guest star in a production. Other schools
hire visiting lecturers, who make their living in a professional theatre, but
teach part-time for a year or more at a particular school. Some schools
have professionals in residence. The school may employ a playwright, an
actor, or a director at full salary. Such artists then pursue their profes-
sions as part of the school's program. They are hired only to work on
university productions, or they also teach a limited number of courses.
Some schools have professional companies in residence. One of the most
widely known is the Minneapolis Theatre Company at the Tyrone Guthrie Theatre, where students from the University of Minnesota are offered
internships and can earn credit.

Similarly, a number of schools offer the student an opportunity to leave for a quarter or a semester and work for credit with an established professional theatre. There is not a close association of any one professional theatre with the school, but the school has a limited arrangement with a number of theatres.

Because the purpose of educational theatre is to train audiences and students, colleges usually present a larger variety of plays than community or professional theatres. A college theatre may present a musical, a Shakespearean play, a Greek play, and a French farce all in the same season. Some schools devote one season in every four to a particular type of production. For instance, they devote one season to American writers, another to plays by continental European writers.

In any case the training in theatre for a college student is broad and meets any number of goals. Students who are interested should investigate which schools fit their particular needs.

Graduate School Theatre

Theatre students usually study a variety of areas as undergraduates, but in graduate school they specialize. In some graduate schools the students will be required to take courses in all areas of theatre, with specialization in a particular area.

Students who enroll in a graduate program usually have decided that they want to spend their lives working in theatre. They prepare to teach or to pursue a career in some aspect of professional theatre. They can take courses in performance-related areas, or they can concentrate on theatre history or dramatic theory and criticism.

There are a variety of degrees they can work toward. On the masters level there are the M.Ed., the M.A., and the M.F.A. The last is more performance-oriented than the others and sometimes is considered a terminal degree. Students also may pursue a variety of doctorates. The choice they make depends on their goals.

Community Theatre

There is almost as much diversity in community theatre as there is in college theatre. Often the community theatre is associated with a city's division of parks and recreation. At other times it is established entirely by area residents interested in theatre. It is not unusual for "community" or nonprofessional theatres to crop up just for the production of a specific play and then to disband when the production ends. Maybe the play is presented to raise money for a fund drive or project, to show the work of a new playwright, or to let people who have no theatre group participate in a production. Often communities present a play once a year or once a decade to commemorate a special event.

A community the-
atre, Footlight Play-
ers, presented this
production of *Apple
Tree.* (*Photo by Gary
Anderson of* The
Coshocton Tribune
*and courtesy of Foot-
light Players.*)

The facilities for community theatre vary from rented space to a fully
equipped theatre that offers workshops and classes. Like the educational
theatre, the community theatre does not have to be so concerned about
making money as professional theatre. For the most part the organization, unless it is paying off the mortgage on a building, need worry only
about money to meet expenses. These costs include building materials,
lighting equipment, royalties, script purchases or rentals, promotion, tickets, and space.

Because it is not so concerned with money, the community theatre
is not under so great a strain to attract audiences, although nobody likes
to play to an empty house. The theatre exists for the enjoyment of the
participants and the audience members, so community theatres most often present well-known musicals, recent Broadway hits, or older plays
that continue in popularity. For instance, at any given time a community
theatre somewhere in every state probably is presenting *Our Town* or
South Pacific. Of course, the well established theatre often is able to present a variety of other plays members feel they can "get their teeth into"
and which provide more complete artistic outlets. Although these shows
may not draw well, they can provide satisfaction for the group.

Most of the people associated with a community theatre are volunteers who have other jobs. Sometimes the directors are volunteers, although established theatres usually have a full-time, salaried director
and, less frequently, a technical director. These persons may be respon-

sible for developing a full program of workshops, experimental theatre, creative dramatics, and children's theatre. Even those community theatres that have no full-time director often present children's shows, either plays by adults for children or plays in which the children appear.

Most community theatres do additional presentations. Many have programs in city parks during the summer, participate in one-act play competitions, and present a wide range of programs for clubs and organizations. The community theatre participant has a wide choice of activities.

Good community theatre strives for professional quality in production. Community theatre also is one of the few places where the novice has a chance to learn. All in all these groups serve an important need for the members and for the community.

Professional Theatre

Although the commercial theatre in the United States still centers in New York City, it has become highly diversified even there. Both in the East and in other areas of the country are a number of professional theatres that range from repertory companies to various types of resident and nonresident stock companies. There are dinner theatres, cafe theatres, road companies of Broadway shows, outdoor dramas, and children's theatre.

No matter what form professional theatre takes, its goal is largely to make money. Whereas European countries subsidize theatre through government funding, the theatre in the United States remains independent of government control. This arrangement theoretically allows more freedom, but it has had an adverse effect on the overall quality of drama. Fewer serious and experimental plays are produced. Most new playwrights are forced to open somewhere else than Broadway.

Broadway Theatre

Broadway has come to symbolize the epitome of dramatic production in the United States. When the booking of shows for a season and the casting for touring shows became centralized in the United States, the location was New York City. Consequently, more and more plays began to be produced in a small section of Manhattan on and around Broadway.

Within the last few decades rising costs have made Broadway a risky venture, even for the most courageous producer. Most shows are presented to appeal to a mass audience, and untried playwrights have little hope of production. The Broadway producer is concerned, and rightly so, with staging a show that will be a hit. Even at that, the majority of shows never regain their initial investment.

A scene from the off-Broadway production of *Dispatches*, presented by the New York Shakespeare Festival. *(Photo courtesy of Martha Swope.)*

This fact makes it difficult for any inexperienced person to gain a foothold. There are rigid examinations for designers. Although there are no special requirements for joining the professional actors' union, Actors' Equity Association, the actor has difficulty getting a job without belonging, and can not join without having a job. Obviously, the circle is sometimes broken, but it is not easy to do. Even when actors are hired, they may be employed only for a few weeks before their show closes. Then they are forced to look for a job again.

For young theatre artists trying to make a go of it in their profession, it is difficult to realize that Broadway theatre to a large extent is controlled by business people whose goal is to make money. Hence Broadway is subject to the same criticism as community theatre: it has too little substance, and too many plays are light comedies or musicals.

Off-Broadway Theatre

Although location has something to do with calling a theatre off-Broadway, the main factor is size. According to Equity standards, an off-Broadway theatre can seat no more than 299 spectators. There are advantages in being in this category: union rules are somewhat relaxed, and productions can be done less expensively. For this reason many more actors and

A scene from the Broadway production of *Fifth of July,* with Christopher Reeve and Swoosie Kurtz. *(Photo courtesy of Martha Swope.)*

other theatre artists can be employed, but they do not receive either the salary or the recognition of a Broadway actor.

There are compensations. First, off-Broadway theatre does provide the artist with experience. Second, a larger variety of productions can be staged. Whereas Broadway appeals to the mass audience to make money, off-Broadway producers, if they choose, can present plays that have limited appeal. There is the occasional show that becomes so successful it moves to a larger theater.

Even with the movement to more intimate theatres, often located in churches, warehouses, and lofts, only a small percent of actors or designers who seek professional careers ever work with New York productions.

Stock Companies

There are many stock companies throughout the United States. They differ greatly in the way they operate and in the type of performances they give.

Summer stock theatres usually run from late June until early September, presenting a different play each week. There is little time for re-

Twigs was presented by the Old Creamery Theatre Company. A year-round professional theatre company, the organization combines with the Old Creamery Young People's Company to present a twenty-five-week summer stock season. *(Photo courtesy of Old Creamery Theatre.)*

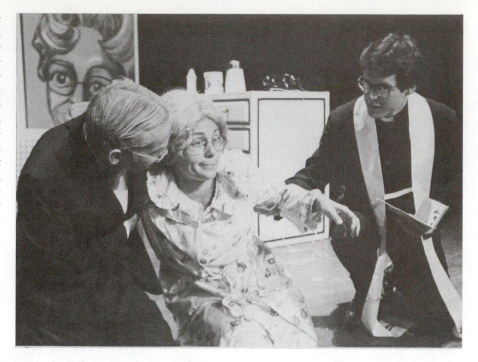

hearsing and polishing; while one show is running, one or more are in rehearsal. Summer stock theatres usually present popular plays, although some do provide an opportunity for untried playwrights to see their work produced. Some summer stock theatres are staffed entirely by professionals; others offer apprenticeship programs.

There are summer theatres that operate under the repertory system. Before the season opens, they prepare and rehearse a number of plays that rotate throughout the season. Some specialize in presenting a particular type of drama, such as Shakespearean plays.

Some stock theatres use the same group of actors for an entire season, but others rely on the star system. The latter type brings in a well-known performer from the Broadway stage, film, or television to play a leading role. Usually the resident company rehearses the play for a week, but the star rehearses for only a day. This system is not as bad as it sounds. The star plays the same role for an entire summer, and rehearsal is largely a matter of adjusting to new people in supporting roles and to different facilities.

A variation of the resident company is the outdoor drama under the guidance of the Institute of Outdoor Drama at the University of North Carolina. Usually, each play deals with some aspect of local history and has a season similar to that of summer stock. There are approximately thirty-five such dramas running yearly, with staff members and perform-

The Theatre of Youth Company of Buffalo, N.Y., a professional group, presents children's shows. This production of *Hansel and Gretel* was directed by the group's founder, Rosalind Cramer. Scene designer, Tim Miller. *(Photo courtesy of Theatre of Youth Company.)*

ers hired for an entire season. Special amphitheatres are constructed for the performances, and the productions often are aided by grants and donations.

Performers in stock theatre sometimes are Equity members and sometimes not. Generally, apprenticeships are offered to students. The designers and directors sometimes belong to theatrical unions.

Other Professional Theatres

There are many other forms of professional theatre, both in New York City and across the country. One is the touring company or road show of a Broadway production. It tours the country as a near duplicate of the show presented in New York.

Touring children's shows are presented for elementary and junior high students. A number of these shows originate in New York, but others come from different areas. (Even some colleges will tour with a production, either of children's theatre or a classic. The latter is presented in high schools where advanced or graduate students then hold workshops.) Sometimes a single show is sent on tour; sometimes touring companies have a repertoire of several plays.

Another type is the dinner theatre, similar to cabaret or cafe theatre. A company presents a production in a restaurant or nightclub atmosphere. Usually the cast is made up of professionals, with a limited number of nonequity performers in some of the smaller roles.

Across the United States various resident companies present a yearly season of plays, rather than confining themselves to a summer season. Some operate independently; others are affiliated with universities. Most of the plays are presented for a limited run, and there is more variety than is likely in summer stock. Although most of these companies keep the same staff for a season, some use guest directors or hire some new people for each production. Often they also accept apprentices.

Showcase productions often are presented in New York with the purpose of showing the talents of a playwright or actor. For these productions union rules are relaxed, and the audience is made up of invited members, including producers and directors. Often the presentations are reviewed by critics.

At the beginning of this century every play west of the Hudson River was considered unworthy of notice. Gradually, however, professional and nonprofessional theatres grew up across the United States. Now many excellent playwrights, directors, and designers have no desire to work in New York. For many years people have been saying that live theatre is in its death throes in the United States, but it is only evolving and changing. New York producers cannot afford to take risky theatrical ventures because of the tremendous cost of presenting a Broadway show, so many of the advances and experiments in theatre are taking place in other areas of the country.

Live theatre flourishes in many forms and in many environments. A share in it is available, at least on a nonpaying basis, to almost anyone with interest and talent.

QUESTIONS FOR DISCUSSION

1. Generally, educational, community, and professional theatre exist for different reasons. What are they? How do they meet their goals?
2. What is the value of creative dramatics?
3. What are the various types of professional theatres? How does each operate?
4. Why is it difficult for the theatre artist to find work on Broadway?

SUPPLEMENTARY READING

BOOKS

Brockett, Oscar. *Perspectives on Contemporary Theatre*. Baton Rouge: Louisiana State University Press, 1971.
Goldberg, Moses. *Children's Theatre: A Philosophy and a Method*. Englewood Cliffs, N.J.: Prentice-Hall, Inc., 1974.

Lesnick, Henry. *Guerilla Street Theatre*. New York: Avon Books, 1973.

Novick, Julius. *Beyond Broadway*. New York: Hill and Wang, Inc., 1968.

Price, Julia. *The Off-Broadway Theatre*. Metuchen, N.J.: Scarecrow Press, Inc., 1962.

Ziegler, Joseph. *Regional Theatre: The Revolutionary Stage*. New York: Da Capo Press, 1973.

CHAPTER 11
The Business End

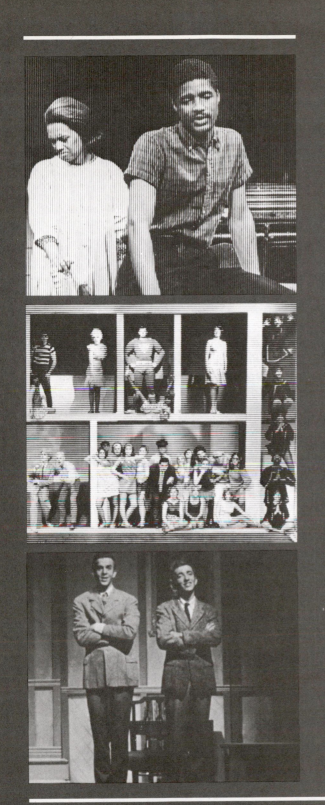

Before a play can be planned or presented, arrangements must be made for securing a theatre space, for promoting the show, for paying expenses, and when required, for paying salaries. The producer and business manager are as important to a production as any other person. The producer can be an individual or a group. The manner of financing and the way of handling business arrangements depend on the type of theatre.

Producing Educational and Community Theatre

In educational theatre the school itself or a department of the school is the producer. Often in elementary and high schools one person is in charge of all the arrangements—the artistic production as well as the business end. The same person is director, producer, manager, and often technical director. The money may be advanced by the school or by an organization in the school. If a class or drama club provides the money, the organization keeps the profit or retains it for future productions.

In college the expense of producing plays comes out of the departmental budget. The director and technical director often work on a production as part of their teaching load. Larger schools have a designer, a costumer, and other technicians on the staff. Many other duties of production are handled by graduate students, who may have assistantships in technical theatre, in publicity, in box office, or in house management. The people who work under them are volunteers and change from production to production. The major expenses in college theatre, other than salaries, consist of paying for materials and scripts. The physical theatre belongs to the college, so it does not cost anything for rental.

The community theatre organization too is the producer of its own shows, although the setup is somewhat different from educational theatre. Most often a board of trustees governs the practical aspects of planning a season and is responsible for approving expenditures. There usually are a house manager, a groundskeeper, and committee chairman who serve for a year at a time. The community theatre may or may not have its own building. If it does not, it is up to the board or its representative to secure a lease for rehearsal and production space. The theatre rarely is subsidized as in a school, which receives its support from the overall budget. The community theater must make enough money for maintenance and the purchase of new equipment as well as for each production.

In both university and community theatre a season of plays is planned in advance. Most often in community theatre the board, or a reading committee appointed by the board, has the final approval in the choice of plays. Occasionally, directors are given plays they do not like,

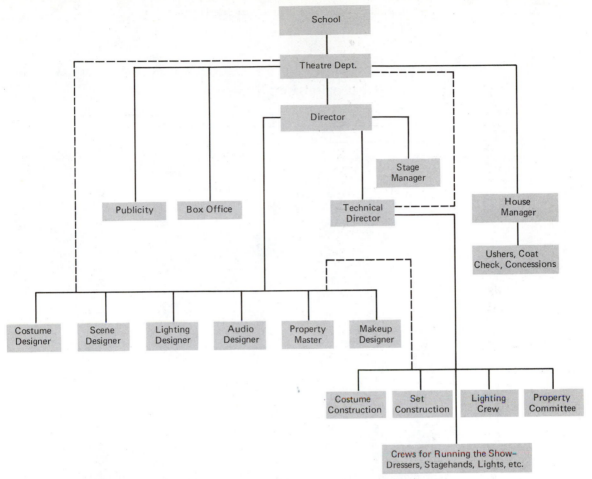

Educational theatre generally follows an organizational pattern similar to that shown in this chart.

but that is not the usual case. A full-time director can recommend and discuss a season with the board. Individual directors may turn in a list of several choices and usually will be allowed to direct a play on the list. Of course, in each theatre the policies vary.

In educational theatre the director also has some choice of what to direct, and in some schools the choice is entirely the director's. The department chairman or a theatre committee has the final say in planning a season at the college level. Usually, the chairman and the directors meet and plan the season together.

The important consideration for educational theatre is to plan a balanced season, whereas community theatre's major concern is selecting plays that draw well. For both groups it is important not to burden any

Community Theatre–Administrative Organization Chart

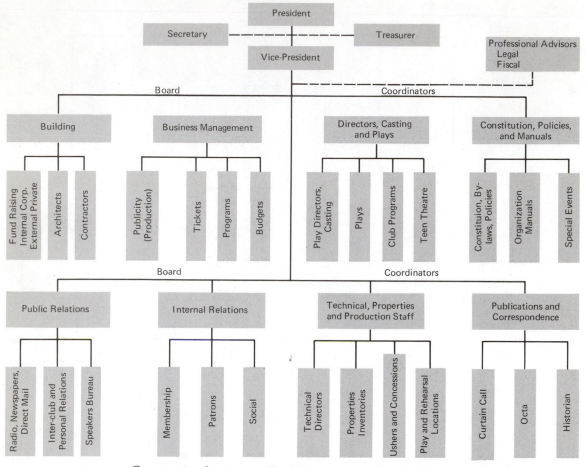

Community theatre usually follows an organizational pattern close to the one illustrated above.

technical area in play after play. For instance, it would be unwise to plan two elaborately costumed shows consecutively. In college the costumer is responsible for teaching, and in community theatre the costumer probably has another job.

Producing Professional Theatre

Professional theatre's goal is to make a profit for the investors. In summer stock resident companies and repertory companies the investors may be the organization itself. Sometimes there are outside investors, but they provide money for the organization and not usually for a specific production.

For Broadway and off-Broadway shows the entire procedure is different. Basically, a producer finds a play to present, hires people, makes all the financial arrangements, and rents rehearsal space and a theatre. "A play cannot be produced on Broadway unless its producers think it is likely to run for a year. Plays of 'mere promise' are excluded; the theatre is a place where promises are not kept."[1]

The full-time producer usually maintains an office, solicits the submission of scripts, often through literary agents, and has a permanent business staff. The producer may provide all the money, or more likely will seek backers, known as "angels." These people then form a corporation, usually just for the duration of a production. The producer, whether investing or not, receives up to half the profits.

Before any investment is made by backers or any preparations for production are completed, the producer takes an option on a play. An option is a contract with the playwright whereby the writer is paid a certain amount to give the producer exclusive rights for a limited time to produce the play. If the script is not produced within the time limit specified in the contract, the rights revert to the writer, who may seek another producer. Often producers do take options on plays that they never present for one reason or another.

If a play is accepted for production and arrangements are made, the producer reserves the right to make suggestions and changes. The same right extends to the backers. A producer may take an option on a script only if the writer agrees to changes beforehand. Often rewrites continue until opening night. A "play doctor" sometimes is called to change the script if the playwright cannot please the producer.

The Producer's Duties

Producer Cheryl Crawford describes her work this way:

Sometimes I think a producer is a person who is absolutely unable to do anything else, who has a strong interest in all the arts but the talent for none of them and enough business sense to know that sometimes you must dare to go to the edge of disaster to achieve what you desire. A producer is definitely a gambler. For the education of a theatre producer, the sky is the limit, which is what makes the profession so endlessly exciting, even though you never learn all it would be helpful to know. Since the joy is to bring a script and a physical production together, literature, poetry, plot construction, music (both classical and popular), architecture, painting, color,

[1]Eric Bentley, *The Theatre of Commitment and Other Essays on Drama in Our Society* (New York: Atheneum, 1967), p. 7. Reprinted by permission of the author.

A poster from a Broadway production. *(Photo by J. Vincent Fitzpatrick)*

form, the ability to read blueprints of sets, history, economics, psychology (normal and abnormal), psychiatry, and even anthropology—to help us understand the audience—all are involved. Everything human and inhuman is grist. And all-important is the ability to extract money from investors. This is the least attractive part of being a producer, at least for me.[2]

---

[2]Cheryl Crawford, *One Naked Individual: My Fifty Years in the Theatre* (Indianapolis: The Bobbs-Merrill Company, Inc., 1977), p. 1.

Producers in New York have extra work. First, unless they are providing all the money themselves, they must interest backers. They interest them by sending out material about the play. At times they arrange private readings for those who express interest. A second duty is to provide a proposed budget, including all the areas of production from the business staff to the theatre artists.

Next the producer hires a director, leases a theatre, and has the ultimate responsibility for publicity and sale of tickets. The producer negotiates contracts with the actors, designers, and technicians. The producer also is responsible for making arrangements for any out-of-town tryouts.

More and more producers are running the play in preview in the theatre where it will be presented. It may run for several days or several weeks before the actual opening, by which time they hope all the kinks have been ironed out. There may be little difference between the preview and the run of the show, but during the preview the critics do not review the production, and tickets are available at a reduced rate. Occasionally, a play will be tried out on college campuses, with the school picking up the tab.

Opening night is tense for a producer. After all the work, will the play succeed? Crawford describes the failures:

> There are two basic ways of falling on your face. You can make a downright error and reject a play that then becomes a hit. That hurts. A subtler pain, perhaps more insidious over the years, comes from what I call an abortion: when you and a project "miss" after you have expended precious time and money on it. I've had my fair share of both errors and abortions.[3]

Although producers have no direct working arrangements with the artistic end of a play in rehearsal, they approve any alterations that are made, because these changes will affect the show's audience-drawing potential. The producer's final responsibility is deciding when to end a show's run, whether it is after a day, a month, or several years.

If a production continues beyond opening night, it is up to the producer to meet all operating expenses and finally to begin splitting the profits among the investors. If the reviews are bad, the producer is the one who posts the closing notice, ending all arrangements.

> A genuinely intelligent producer will sit back at the end of an exhausting and possibly unprofitable season, assess what he has done "wrong" and what he has "guessed right" about, analyze his competitors' obvious gaffes and inexplicable lucky strikes, and try to sniff out the winds that are apt to prevail in another eight months. He goes through this little intellectual exercise for two reasons: if his vision of the theatrical future is correct, if he *knows* what he is doing when he buys his next script, he will become rich enough to pay his

[3]Crawford, p. 203.

This program cover for the Little Theatre of Tuscarawas County was designed by Larry Badgley.

THE LITTLE THEATRE
of Tuscarawas County
presents

THURBER
CARNIVAL

OCTOBER 22, 23, 28, 29, 30
NOVEMBER 4, 5, 6

taxes; he is also eager, all popular superstition to the contrary, to place himself in the esthetic vanguard, to prod the theatre along a bit in its eternal quest for perfection.[4]

Other Staff Members

Besides the producer and the theatrical artists there are many others involved in presenting a play. In New York theatre there are a general manager and a company manager. The house manager supervises a host of people, including ushers, doormen, and cleaners. The business staff also is extensive, with various secretaries, accountants, an attorney, and a press agent.

Although community and educational theatres generally do not

[4]Walter Kerr, *The Theater in Spite of Itself* (New York: Simon and Schuster, 1963), p. 15.

have so extensive a staff as does professional theatre, there still are many members. The house manager usually is responsible for all front-of-the-house matters. This work includes seeing that the theatre and the grounds are in proper order, arranging for ushers and ticket takers, sometimes arranging for the printing and delivery of programs, handling the checking of coats, and often being in charge of the concession stand.

Publicity managers also have many duties. The most important, of course, is to sell tickets. Second, they are responsible for projecting a good image of the theatre and for increasing public awareness of its existence and program. Last, they are responsible for publicizing each show. Although they have several others working with them, publicity managers have the final responsibility for all press releases for radio, television, and public appearances. The publicity manager works directly with the box office personnel, because both are responsible for ticket sales.

The box office supervisor or theatre manager provides the public with tickets. This person is responsible for advance sales, group sales, and sales during the play's run. Box officer supervisors must order tickets, place them in racks by row and night, and make sure that the box office is staffed. They make daily cash reports and a report at the end of each production. If they handle the box office for the season, they also prepare a yearly report.

Only after all the arrangements are complete, both front-of-the-house and backstage, can a show go on.

QUESTIONS FOR DISCUSSION

1. What are the responsibilities of a producer?
2. How are shows financed and produced in educational, community, and professional theatre?
3. What work on the business end falls to people other than the producer?

SUPPLEMENTARY READING

BOOKS

Crawford, Cheryl. *One Naked Individual: My Fifty Years in the Theatre.* Indianapolis: The Bobbs-Merrill Company, Inc., 1977.

Farber, Donald C. *From Option to Opening (A Guide for the Off-Broadway Producer).* New York: Drama Book Specialists Publishers, 1968.

Langley, Stephen. *Theatre Management in America.* New York: Drama Book Specialists/Publishers, 1974.

Plummer, Gail. *The Business of Show Business.* New York: Harper & Row, Publishers, 1961.

Selected Bibliography

The American Theatre Planning Board, Inc. *Theatre Check List: A Guide to the Planning and Construction of Proscenium and Open Stage Theatres.* Middletown, Conn.: Wesleyan University Press, 1969.

Archer, William. *Play-Making: A Manual of Craftsmanship.* New York: Dodd, Mead & Company, 1928.

Artaud, Antonin. *The Theatre and Its Double.* Translated by Mary Richards. New York: Grove Press, 1958.

Baker, George Pierce. *Dramatic Technique.* Boston: Houghton Mifflin Company, 1919.

Benedetti, Robert L. *The Actor at Work.* Rev. ed. Englewood Cliffs, N.J.: Prentice-Hall, Inc., 1976.

Bentley, Eric. *The Life of the Drama.* New York: Atheneum, 1964.

——————. *In Search of Theatre.* New York: Alfred A. Knopf, Inc., 1953.

——————. *The Theatre of Commitment and Other Essays.* New York: Atheneum, 1967.

——————. *The Theory of the Modern Stage: An Introduction to Theatre and Drama.* Baltimore: Penguin Books, Inc., 1968.

Bieber, Margarete. *The History of the Greek and Roman Theater.* 2nd ed. Princeton, N.J.: Princeton University Press, 1961.

Boleslavsky, Richard. *Acting: The First Six Lessons.* New York: Theatre Arts Books, 1933.

Boyle, Walden P. *Central and Flexible Staging.* Berkeley: University of California Press, 1956.

Brockett, Oscar G. *History of the Theatre.* Boston: Allyn and Bacon, Inc., 1968.

——————. *Perspectives on Contemporary Theatre.* Baton Rouge: Louisiana State University Press, 1971.

——————. *The Theatre: An Introduction.* 4th ed. New York: Holt, Rinehart and Winston, 1979.

Burdick, Elizabeth, et al, eds. *Contemporary Scene Design U.S.A.* New York: International Theatre Institute of the U.S., Inc., 1974.

Burris-Meyer, Harold, and Cole, Edward C. *Theatres and Auditoriums.* 2nd ed. New York: Reinhold Publishing Corporation, 1964.

Burton, Hal. *Great Acting.* New York: Bonanza Books, 1967.

Busfield, Roger M., Jr. *The Playwright's Art.* New York: Harper & Brothers, 1958.

Cassady, Marshall, and Cassady, Pat. *An Introduction to Theatre and Drama.* Skokie, Ill.: National Textbook Company, 1975.

Chaikin, Joseph. *The Presence of the Actor.* New York: Atheneum, 1972.

Chekhov, Michael. *To the Actor on the Technique of Acting.* New York: Harper & Row, Publishers, 1953.

Cheney, Sheldon. *The Theatre: Three Thousand Years of Drama, Acting and Stagecraft.* Rev. ed. New York: Longmans, Green & Co., Inc., 1972.

Clark, Barrett H., ed. *European Theories of the Drama.* Newly revised by Henry Popkin. New York: Crown Publishers, Inc., 1965.

Clurman, Harold. *The Fervent Years: The Story of the Group Theatre in the Thirties.* New York: Alfred A. Knopf, Inc., 1945.

——————. *On Directing.* New York: The Macmillan Co., 1972.

Cogswell, Margaret, ed. *The Ideal Theatre: Eight Concepts.* New York: The American Federation of Arts, 1962.

Cohen, Robert, and Harrop, John. *Creative Play Direction.* Englewood Cliffs, N.J.: Prentice-Hall, Inc., 1974.

Cole, Toby, and Chinoy, Helen K., eds. *Actors on Acting: The Theories, Techniques, and Practices of the Great Actors of All Times as Told in Their Own Words.* New York: Crown Publishers, Inc., 1949.

_____. *Directors on Directing.* Rev. ed. Indianapolis: The Bobbs-Merrill Company, Inc., 1963.

Cole, Toby, ed. *Playwrights on Playwriting: The Meaning and Making of Modern Drama from Ibsen to Ionesco.* New York: Hill and Wang, Inc., 1961.

Collier, Gaylan Jane. *Assignments in Acting.* New York: Harper & Row, Publishers, 1966.

Corrigan, Robert W., and Rosenberg, James. *The Context and Craft of Drama.* San Francisco: Chandler Publishing Co., 1964.

Corrigan, Robert W., ed. *Theatre in the Twentieth Century.* New York: Grove Press, Inc., 1963.

Crawford, Cheryl. *One Naked Individual: My Fifty Years in the Theatre.* Indianapolis: The Bobbs-Merrill Co., Inc., 1977.

Dean, Alexander. *Fundamentals of Play Directing.* Revised by Lawrence Carra. 3rd ed. New York: Holt, Rinehart and Winston, 1974.

Dietrich, John E. *Play Direction.* Englewood Cliffs, N.J.: Prentice-Hall, Inc., 1953.

Driver, Tom F. *Romantic Quest and Modern Theory: History of the Modern Theatre.* New York: Delta Books, published by Dell Publishing Co., Inc., 1970.

Duerr, Edwin. *The Length and Depth of Acting.* New York: Holt, Rinehart and Winston, 1962.

Egri, Lajos. *The Art of Dramatic Writing.* New York: Simon & Schuster, 1946.

Engel, Lehman. *The American Musical Theatre.* New York: The Macmillan Co., 1975.

Ervine, St. John. *How to Write a Play.* New York: the Macmillan Co., 1928.

Esslin, Martin. *The Theatre of the Absurd.* Rev. ed. Garden City, N.Y.: Anchor Books, 1969.

Farber, Donald C. *From Option to Opening: A Guide for the Off-Broadway Producer.* New York: Drama Book Specialists/Publishers, 1968.

Fergusson, Francis. *The Idea of a Theater.* Princeton, N.J.: Princeton University Press, 1949.

Fowlie, Wallace. *Dionysus in Paris: A Guide to Contemporary French Theatre.* New York: Meridian, 1960.

Fuller, Edmund. *A Pageant of the Theatre.* New rev. ed. New York: Thomas Y. Crowell Co., 1965.

Gassner, John. *Directions in Modern Theatre and Drama.* New York: Holt, Rinehart and Winston, 1965.

_____. *Producing the Play.* 2nd ed. New York: Holt, Rinehart and Winston, 1953.

Gillette, A. S. *Stage Scenery: Its Construction and Rigging.* New York: Harper & Row, Publishers, 1959.

Goldberg, Moses. *Children's Theatre: A Philosophy and a Method.* Englewood Cliffs, N.J.: Prentice-Hall, Inc., 1974.

Grenbanier, Bernard. *Playwriting.* New York: Thomas Y. Crowell Co., 1961.

Grotowski, Jerzy. *Towards a Poor Theatre.* New York: Simon & Schuster, 1969.

Guicharnaud, Jacques. *Modern French Theatre from Giraudoux to Beckett.* New Haven, Conn.: Yale University Press, 1961.

Hartnoll, Phyllis, ed. *The Oxford Companion to the Theatre.* 3rd ed. New York: Oxford University Press, 1967.

Heffner, Hubert. *The Nature of Drama.* Boston: Houghton Mifflin Company, 1959.

Hewitt, Barnard. *Theatre U.S.A.: 1665 to 1957.* New York: McGraw-Hill Book Company, Inc., 1959.

Hodge, Francis. *Play Directing: Analysis, Communication and Style.* Englewood Cliffs, N.J.: Prentice Hall, Inc., 1971.

Howard, Louise, and Criswell, Jeron. *How Your Play Can Crash Broadway.* New York: Howard and Criswell, 1939.

Hughes, Glenn. *The Penthouse Theatre.* New York: Samuel French, 1942.

Jacobsen, Josephine, and Mueller, William R. *Ionesco and Genet: Playwrights of Silence.* New York: Hill and Wang, 1968.

Jones, Margo. *Theatre-in-the-Round.* New York: Holt, Rinehart and Winston, 1951.

Jones, Robert Edmund. *The Dramatic Imagination.* New York: Meredith Publishing Company, 1941.

Kernan, Alvin B. *The Modern American Theatre.* Englewood Cliffs, N.J.: Prentice Hall, Inc., 1967.

Kerr, Walter. *How Not to Write a Play.* New York: Simon & Schuster, 1955.

_____. *The Theatre in Spite of Itself.* New York: Simon and Schuster, 1963.

Klein, Maxine. *Time, Space and Designs for Actors.* Boston: Houghton Mifflin Company, 1975.

Langley, Stephen. *Theatre Management in America.* New York: Drama Book Specialists/Publishers, 1974.

Langner, Laurence. *The Play's the Thing.* New York: G. P. Putnam's Sons, 1960.

Larson, Orville K., ed. *Scene Design for Stage and Screen. Readings on the Aesthetics and Methodology of Scene Design for Drama, Opera, Musical Comedy, Ballet, Motion Pictures, Television and Arena Theatre.* East Lansing: Michigan State University Press, 1961.

Laufe, Abe. *Broadway's Greatest Musicals.* Revised ed. New York; Funk and Wagnalls, 1977.

Lawson, John Howard. *Theory and Technique of Playwriting.* New York: Hill and Wang, Inc., 1960.

Lesnick, Henry. *Guerilla Street Theatre.* New York: Avon Books, 1973.

Lewis, Allan. *American Plays and Playwrights of the Contemporary Theatre.* New York: Crown Publishers, Inc., 1965.

——————. *The Contemporary Theatre.* New York: Crown Publishers, Inc., 1962.

Macgowan, Kenneth, and Melnitz, William. *The Living Stage: A History of World Theatre.* Englewood Cliffs, N.J.: Prentice-Hall, Inc., 1955.

Marshall, Norman. *The Producer and the Play.* 2nd ed. London: Macdonald & Co. (Publishers), Ltd., 1962.

McCrindle, Joseph F., ed. *Behind the Scenes: Theatre and Film Reviews from the Transatlantic Review.* New York: Holt, Rinehart and Winston, 1971.

McGaw, Charles J. *Acting Is Believing.* 3rd ed. New York: Holt, Rinehart and Winston, 1975.

Nagler, A. M. *A Source Book in Theatrical History.* New York: Dover Publications, Inc., 1952.

Nicoll, Allardyce. *The Development of the Theatre.* 5th ed. New York: Harcourt, Brace & World, Inc., 1966.

Novick, Julius. *Beyond Broadway.* New York: Hill and Wang, Inc., 1968.

Oenslager, Donald. *Scenery Then and Now.* New York: W. W. Norton & Company, 1936.

Parker, W. Oren, and Smith, Harvey K. *Scene Design and Stage Lighting.* New York: Holt, Rinehart and Winston, 1963.

Plummer, Gail. *The Business of Show Business.* New York: Harper & Row, Publishers, 1961.

Price, Julia. *The Off-Broadway Theatre.* Metuchen, N.J.: Scarecrow Press, Inc., 1962.

Rahill, Frank. *The World of Melodrama.* University Park, Pa.: The Pennsylvania State University Press, 1967.

Redgrave, Michael. *The Actor's Ways and Means.* New York: Theatre Arts Books, 1953.

Roberts, Vera Mowry. *On Stage: A History of Theatre.* New York: Harper & Row, Publishers, 1962.

Rockwood, Jerome. *The Craftsmen of Dionysus: An Approach to Acting.* Glenview, Ill.: Scott, Foresman and Company, 1966.

Rowe, Kenneth Thorpe. *Write That Play.* New York: Funk & Wagnalls Co., 1939.

Rowell, Kenneth. *Stage Design.* New York: Van Nostrand Reinhold Co., 1969.

Saint-Denis, Michel. *Theatre: The Rediscovery of Style.* New York: Theatre Arts Books, 1960.

Schechner, Richard. *Environmental Theater.* New York: Hawthorn Books, Inc., 1973.

Selden, Samuel, and Sellman, Hunton D. *Stage Scenery and Lighting.* 3rd ed. New York: Appleton-Century-Crofts, Inc., 1959.

Shroyer, Frederick B., and Gardeman, Louis G. *Types of Drama.* Glenview, Ill.: Scott, Foresman and Company., 1970.

Sievers, W. David, Stiver, Harry E., and Kahan, Stanley. *Directing for the Theatre.* 3rd ed. Dubuque, Iowa: William C. Brown Company, Publishers, 1974.

Smiley, Sam. *Playwriting: The Structure of Action.* Englewood Cliffs, N.J.: Prentice-Hall, Inc., 1971.

Southern, Richard. *The Seven Ages of the Theatre.* New York: Hill and Wang, 1961.

Stanislavski, Constantin. *An Actor Prepares.* Translated by Elizabeth Reynolds Hapgood. New York: Theatre Arts Books, 1936.

Tidwroth, Simon. *Theatres: An Architectural and Cultural History.* New York: Praeger Publishers, 1973.

Warnock, Robert. *Representative Modern Plays: Ibsen to Tennessee Williams.* Glenview, Ill.: Scott, Foresman and Company, 1964.

Wellworth, George. *The Theater of Protest and Par-*

adox: Developments in the Avant-Garde Drama. 2nd ed. New York: New York University Press, 1971.

Willet, John, ed. *Brecht on Theatre.* New York: Hill and Wang, Inc., 1964.

Williams, Tennessee. *Where I Live: Selected Essays.* New York: New Directions, 1978.

Ziegler, Joseph. *Regional Theatre: The Revolutionary Stage.* New York: Da Capa Press, 1973.

Glossary

Absurdism or Theatre of the Absurd a movement of the fifties and sixties in which playwrights dramatized the absurdity and futility of human existence. Generally, absurdist drama is nonsensical and repetitive.

Aesthetic distance the detachment that allows us to appreciate the beauty of a work of art.

Antagonist opposes the protagonist; the antagonist can be a person or persons, society, a force such as a flood or a storm, or a conflicting tendency within the protagonist.

Apron or Forestage the area of a proscenium stage that extends in front of the grand drape.

Arena stage the type of stage in which the audience surrounds the playing area.

Aside a speech delivered directly to the audience by a character in a play; supposedly, the other characters on stage are unable to hear what is said.

Asymmetrical balance making mass, shape, and color differ from one side of the stage to the other, but keeping the total weight or mass the same so that there is a feeling of balance.

Automatism visual or verbal gag that is repeated many times.

Backdrop theatrical canvas painted and hung with weights at the bottom; usually backdrops stretch across the stage.

Battens rods to which drops (or other scenery) are attached to be raised and lowered in a proscenium stage.

Blocking the planned movement or business in a play; the stage directions for the actor.

Body language the emotions, attitudes, and states of physical being we communicate through body movement and position.

Box set a setting that generally represents an indoor location and is constructed of flats.

Burlesque a type of low comedy that relies on beatings, accidents, and vulgarity for its humor.

Business physical action taken by the actor.

264

Catharsis   the purge of emotions; the release of emotional tension.

Character comedy   a play whose humor directly involves the actions and eccentricities of the central character.

Character inconsistency   comedy that results from a trait that does not seem to fit with a character's personality.

Character makeup   makeup that makes an actor appear different from normal.

Circular structure   a type of organization in which the action of a play shows no real progression from one point to another but ends as it began.

Climax   the high point of the plot; the moment when an irrevocable action occurs that determines the outcome of the play.

Comedy of manners   a play that deals with the foibles or amoral characteristics of the upper class.

Conflict   opposition; antagonist and protagonist engaged in a struggle to triumph over one another.

Constructivism   including in the setting only those elements that are necessary to the action of a play.

Counterweight system   a system of ropes and pulleys used to fly scenery in a proscenium theatre.

Cue   the final line or action that signals that it is time for an actor to begin the next action or speech.

Derision   making fun of people or institutions for the purpose of social reform.

Dialogue   the conversation between or among characters in a play; the lines or speeches of the characters in a play.

Drama   all written plays, regardless of their genre or form.

Dramatic action   everything that occurs in a play and advances it toward a conclusion; the motivation and purpose of a play; the physical, spiritual, psychological, and emotional elements that hold a play together.

Dramatic time   the amount of time represented by a play; an hour onstage may represent any amount of time, although more time usually is represented as having passed than the actual two hours or so it takes to present a play.

Ellipsoidal reflector   a type of spotlight that has a framing device and is quite controllable. It allows no spill of light from one area to another.

Emotional memory   remembering how one felt in a particular set of circumstances and then relating those emotions to similar circumstances in a play.

Empathy emotionally relating to or identifying with a character, a theme, or a situation in a play.

Ensemble concept the willingness of actors to subordinate themselves to the production as a whole.

Episodic structure a series of loosely related events that make up a play.

Exaggeration humor through overstatement and intensification.

Exposition any background information necessary to the understanding of a play; it may be presented through dialogue, setting, and properties.

Expressionism a style that presents the inner reality of the major character; the audience witnesses the workings of the character's mind.

External approach concerned with the technique of acting, or what outward signs of emotion can be used to portray that emotion.

Falling action or Denouement the part of a story play that occurs after the climax. It shows the results of the climax.

Flashback a theatrical convention in which the audience, through the eyes of a character in a play, is able to see scenes from the past before the time in which the play exists.

Flat a frame constructed of one-by-three boards, covered with canvas, painted, and used most often for interior or exterior walls of a building in a stage setting.

Floodlights nonfocusable lighting instruments used for general illumination.

Floor plan a drawing of the setting as seen from above.

Fly space the area behind the top of the arch and above the floor of the stage.

Formalism using the physical appearance of the stage rather than a designed setting; using only what is absolutely necessary. For example, ladders instead of houses in *Our Town*.

Found space or Environmental theatre any available space, not a formal theatre structure, adapted to a theatrical production.

Fourth wall the imaginary wall that exists between the actors in a representational play and the audience; through this wall the audience sees the action of the play.

Fresnel a type of spotlight that provides a circle or oval of light with a softened edge.

General lighting lighting that provides visibility on the whole stage.

Given circumstances the background information provided about a character or the play as a whole. Actors take the given circumstances as a beginning in establishing a character.

Grand drape   the heavy, front curtain in a proscenium theatre.

Hand props   articles that are handled or carried by the actors.

Happenings   a type of unstructured theatre presentation, generally involving the audience, in which there was little planning; the purpose was to break down the separation of life and art.

High comedy   humor through verbal wit that appeals to the intellect.

Immediacy   the quality of a work of art that makes it important or relevant to the time in which it is presented to the public.

Impressionism   a style in which the designer and director determine what they wish to stress most and apply this element to the setting; the style deals with the design exclusive of the script.

Improvisation or Improvisational theatre   building a scene or a play on the spur of the moment with little pre-planning and no script.

Inciting incident   the point of a play at which the initial balance is upset and the plot begins to build.

Incongruity   humor through showing differing or opposing elements together, such as tennis shoes with a formal gown.

Internal approach   seeking within oneself the emotions and experiences to portray a character in a play.

Low comedy   humor that relies on physical actions.

Mimetic instinct   the human need or desire to imitate; through the mimetic instinct we acquire much of our learning.

Monologue   a long speech delivered by a character in a play, either to the audience or to other characters.

Motivation   the reason for taking any action; why the protagonist in a play attempts to reach a certain goal.

Naturalism   a theatrical style which attempts to duplicate life, or in effect, transfer actual life to the stage.

Neoclassicism   a style popular during the Italian Renaissance, with a strict five-act format and a completely unified production.

Pace   the overall rate of speed in handling lines and business.

Plot   the progression of a story from the point of attack through the climax and denouement.

Point of attack   the place in a story where the writer decides to begin the action.

Presentational style   a broad category of theatrical style which is audience centered; the actors, director, and designer make open acknowledgement of the audience.

Properties   articles that can be moved or carried in the course of a play. Set properties include such objects as curtains and paintings; hand props include anything that the actors use or carry.

Proscenium or Proscenium arch   a picture-frame stage; the framing device that isolates the stage area and provides the focal point for the action. The audience views the action through an imaginary fourth wall.

Protagonist   the major character in a play; generally, the protagonist tries to reach a certain goal and is opposed by the antagonist.

Raked stage   a stage that slopes upward from front to back.

Realism   a style that attempts to present life as it is, but selectively; not all details are presented but only those that are essential for the audience's understanding of the play and for the establishment of the mood.

Representational style   a broad category of style that is stage centered; the actors make no acknowledgement of the audience, but try to duplicate life.

Rising action   the building or intensification of the struggle between the protagonist and the antagonist.

Ritual   a repeated pattern of behavior, which may have its basis in religion, pageantry, or individual behavior. It originally meant a controlled sequence of action to achieve a supernatural goal. Now it also refers to a type of play structure in which a pattern of action is repeated.

Role playing   changing one's ways of behaving in different situations; modifying behavior to fit the situation.

Romantic comedy   a comedy whose humor lies in the complications the hero and heroine face in their love for each other.

Romanticism   a style characterized by freedom, gracefulness, and a belief in humankind's basic good.

Rhythm   the flow of the lines; the speed with which the actors pick up cues.

Satire   gentle mockery for the purpose of reform.

Schematics   outlines of the head with the face divided into planes or areas, showing the color or type of makeup to apply to each area.

Scrims   semitransparent cloths usually serving as backdrops; when lighted from the rear they look semitransparent; when lighted from the front they look opaque.

Selective visibility   providing focus through lighting.

Set dressing   articles such as draperies or paintings that are attached to the walls of the set.

Set props   articles that stand within the setting, including furniture, trees or bushes, and rocks.

Setting   the environment or physical background for a play; the visual symbol of a play.

Situation comedy   a comedy whose humor derives from placing the central characters in a comedy in unusual situations.

Soliloquy   a theatrical convention in which a character thinks aloud, revealing innermost thoughts.

Specific lighting   lighting for special effects, such as to suggest sunlight or to set the mood.

Spine or Super-objective   the major goal of a character in a play.

Spotlights   focusable lighting instruments customarily used for specific illumination.

Stock characters   character types in which a certain trait or traits, such as miserliness, are highly exaggerated.

Story play   a play that has a plot and builds in intensity from an inciting incident to a turning point and climax.

Straight makeup   makeup that accentuates an actor's natural features.

Striplight   a troughlike lighting instrument with lights a few inches apart, covered with lenses in the primary colors.

Surprise   humor through the unexpected.

Symbol   one thing that stands for another. In the theatre the setting and lights, for instance, represent a background or environment for the action, while the actors symbolize the characters in the play.

Symbolism   a style that presents life in terms of allegory; it depicts subjective or internal reality, determined by the playwright.

Symmetrical balance   giving either side of a setting exactly the same elements in the same relationship to each other.

Teasers   short curtains that are used to mask the lighting instruments and fly space in a proscenium theatre.

Theatricalism   a treatment of a play in which audience members are constantly reminded that they are in a theatre; the fourth wall is broken down and the audience uses its imagination in the matter of setting.

Thematic structure   the organization of a play unified around a particular idea or theme.

Thrust stage   a stage that juts into the seating area, the audience sits on three sides.

Timing the use of pauses in delivering lines.

Tormentors curtains hung at either side of the stage to mask the backstage area.

Turning point the moment in a plot when the action can go no further without something irrevocable happening.

Unity a harmony in the way all the elements of a play combine.

Universality the trait of having meaning for everyone in all places and times.

Upstaging actors' drawing attention to themselves to the detriment of the production.

Wagon stage a platform on castors that can be wheeled on and off the stage.

Well-made play in current theatre refers to a play with a plot; historically, a play that presented a particular social problem for which the playwright offered a solution.

Wings Flats that stand independently and are placed a short distance apart from the front to the back of a stage; also the areas to the right and left of the playing area in a proscenium theatre

Appendix: Overview of Theatre History

Greece and Rome   800 B.C.–100 B.C.

800 B.C.–600 B.C.	Dances and dithyrambs in honor of Dionysus
600 B.C.–400 B.C.	Four festivals held each year in honor of Dionysus
ca. 535 B.C.	Thespis, the first actor, won the first play contest
525 B.C.–456 B.C.	Aeschylus wrote *Orestian Trilogy*, etc.
496 B.C.–406 B.C.	Sophocles wrote *Oedipus Rex*, etc.
480 B.C.–406 B.C.	Euripidus wrote *Medea*, etc.
ca. 448 B.C.–380 B.C.	Aristophanes wrote *The Clouds*, etc.
404 B.C.–336 B.C.	Era of Middle Comedy
400 B.C.–200 B.C.	Play production continued until the second century
ca. 364 B.C.	Etruscan drama introduced into Rome; Roman drama lasted until sixth century A.D.
ca. 343 B.C.–ca. 291 B.C.	Menander, writer of New Comedy
ca. 330 B.C.	Aristotle wrote *The Poetics*
325 B.C.	Theatre of Dionysus completed; other theatres built through the first century
ca. 270 B.C.–204 B.C.	Livius Andronicus, first important Roman dramatist
254 B.C.–184 B.C.	Plautus wrote *The Menaechmi*, etc.
ca. 185 B.C.–159 B.C.	Terence wrote *The Eunuch*, etc.
ca. 65 B.C.	Horace wrote *Ars Poetica*
15 B.C.	Vitruvius wrote *De Architectura*

Middle Ages   900 A.D.–1500 A.D.

	Various forms of secular drama including the folk play, the farce, and the interlude, were presented throughout the Middle Ages
925 B.C.–1215 A.D.	Elements of drama were a part of the church service; tropes from 925 B.C.–1066 A.D.; liturgical drama in Latin and vernacular to 1215 A.D.
ca. 1100 A.D.–ca. 1300 A.D.	Trobadours performed

Middle Ages   900 A.D.–1500 A.D. *(continued)*

ca. 1140 A.D.	*Drama of Adam*, possibly the first play written in French
1200 A.D.	Mystery play cycle began
ca. 1200 A.D.	Religious plays began to be performed out-of doors
1210 A.D.	Pope Innocent III outlawed performance of plays in church proper
13th century A.D.	Secular drama began in France
ca. 1375 A.D.	*Second Shepherd's Play*
1400 A.D.–1550 A.D.	Morality plays, e.g., *Everyman*, presented; later became secularized
1402 A.D.	Confrérie de la Passion established by Charles II; given theatrical monopoly in Paris in 1518 A.D.
1429 A.D.	Twelve plays of Plautus rediscovered
1464 A.D.	*Pierre Pathelin* presented, one of many French farces.
1469 A.D.–1529 A.D.	Juan del Encina, called the father of Spanish drama
1470 A.D.	Horace's *Art of Poetry* published
1473 A.D.–1554 A.D.	Serlio divided scenery into three categories
1484 A.D.	Vitruvius' *De Architectura* published
1494 A.D.–1576 A.D.	Hans Sachs wrote Shrovetide dramas
ca. 1497 A.D.–ca. 1580 A.D.	John Heywood wrote farces
1498 A.D.	Aristotle's *Poetics* published
1518 A.D.	Greek and Roman plays published
1513 A.D.–1520 A.D.	Machiavelli wrote *La Mandragola*

Italian and Spanish Renaissance   1500–1700

1474–1533	Lodovico Ariosto wrote *La Cassaria*, etc.
1500–1600	*Intermezzi* popular
1510–1565	Lope de Rueda, Spain's first important popular playwright
1515	Gian Giorgio Trissino's *Sofonisba*, first Italian tragedy patterned on Greek drama
1545	Sebastiano Serlio published *Architettura*, detailing scene design and special effects
1547–1616	Miguel de Cervantes, wrote *Don Quixote*
1548	Hotel de Burgogne built in Paris for performance of serious plays
1550–	*Comedia dell' arte* popular into the eighteenth century
1562–1635	Lope de Vega of Spain wrote more than 1800 plays
1574–1654	Nicola Sabbatini, wrote *Manual for Constructing Theatrical Scenes and Machines*
1579	Corral de la Cruz, first permanent theatre in Spain
1580–1680	Spain's Golden Age of Literature, *El Siglo de Oro*

Italian and Spanish Renaissance   1500–1700 *(continued)*

1600–1681	Pedro Calderón de la Barca, wrote *auto sacramentales*, a form of religious drama
1608–1678	Giacomo Torelli, perfected the chariot and pole system of scenery

English and French Renaissance   1500–1700

1506–1556	Nicholas Udall, wrote *Ralph Roister Doister*, ca. 1533
1552	*Gammer Gurton's Needle* written
1554–1606	John Lyly wrote comedies
1558–1594	Thomas Kyd, wrote *The Spanish Tragedy*, ca. 1587
1561	Sackville and Norton wrote *Gorboduc*, first English tragedy
1564–1593	Christopher Marlow, wrote *Dr. Faustus*, etc.
1564–1616	William Shakespeare
ca. 1570–ca. 1632	Thomas Dekker, wrote *Shoemaker's Holiday*, etc.
ca. 1572–ca. 1632	Alexandre Hardy, first professional French playwright
1572	Acting first recognized as a lawful profession in England
1572–1637	Ben Jonson, wrote *Volpone*, etc.
1573–1652	Inigo Jones designed court masques
1574	Master of Revels began censoring English plays
1576	The Theatre build by James Burbage
1576	Blackfriars, London's first private theatre, built
1579–1625	Francis Beaumont (1584–1616) and John Fletcher (1579–1625), collaborated on *The Maid's Tragedy*, etc.
1580–1639	John Ford, wrote *'Tis a Pity She's a Whore*
1599	Globe Theatre built
1606–1684	Pierre Corneille, wrote *The Cid*, etc.
1622–1673	Molière, wrote *The Miser*, etc.
1628–1679	Comediens du Roi at Hotel de Burgogne
1631–1700	John Dryden, wrote *All for Love* (1677), etc.
ca. 1635–1710	Thomas Betterton, English actor
1638	Neoclassicism established in France
1639–1699	Jean Racine, wrote *Phaedra* (1677), etc.
1642	English Parliament closed theatres and banned theatrical performances
1650–1687	Nell Gwynn, English actress
1656	*Siege of Rhodes* presented
1660	English theatres reopened
1660–1700	Heroic tragedy and comedy of manners flourished
1670–1729	William Congreve, wrote *The Way of the World* (1700)

English and French Renaissance   1500–1700 *(continued)*

1680	*Comédie Française,* the first national theatre company, established in France
1698	Jeremy Collier wrote an attack on immorality of the English stage

Eighteenth Century

1657–1787	The Bibiena family dominated scene design throughout Europe
1671–1757	Autobiography of Colley Cibber provided much information about the English theatre
1672–1729	Richard Steele, wrote sentimental comedy, e.g., *The Conscious Lovers* (1722)
1678–1707	George Farquhar, wrote *The Beaux Stratagem* (1707), etc.
ca. 1682–1761	John Rich, perfected the pantomime, England's most popular form of play
1685–1732	John Gay, wrote *The Beggar's Opera* (1728)
1693–1739	George Lillo, wrote domestic tragedies, e.g., *The London Merchant* (1731)
1694–1778	Voltaire, wrote French neoclassic tragedies, e.g., *Zaire* (1732)
1697–1766	Carolina Neuber (1697–1760) and Johann Gottsched (1700–1766), bought about reforms in the German theatre
1699–1797	Charles Macklin, realistic English actor
1707–1793	Carlo Goldoni of Italy wrote comedies, e.g., *The Fan*
1713–1784	Denis Diderot of France advocated reforms in drama and staging to make them realistic; wrote *The Father of a Family,* a bourgeois drama
1721–1802	Roger Kemble, English actor, whose nine children also acted
1729–1781	Gotthold Lessing, wrote *Hamburg Dramaturgy,* first important German dramatic criticism; also wrote *Minna von Barnhelm,* to become Germany's first important playwright
1730–1774	Oliver Goldsmith, through *She Stoops to Conquer,* tried to reestablish ''humorous'' comedy rather than continuing with sentimental comedy
1732	Covent Garden opened
1732–1799	Beaumarchais, wrote *The Barber of Seville* (1775), etc.
1737	Licensing Act in England; plays censored through Lord Chamberlain's office
1740–1812	Phillipe Jacques de Loutherbourg, increased use of realism in stage design; reproduced actual sites
1751–1816	Richard Brinsley Sheridan, wrote *School for Scandal* (1777), etc.

Eighteenth Century *(continued)*

1752	Lewis Hallam (1714–1756) brought an English acting company to North America, where it was firmly established by 1780
1759–1805	Friedrich Schiller, wrote *The Robbers* (1782), a romantic drama
1767–1787	Storm and Stress movement in Germany
ca. 1790	Realistic scenery and costumes coming more into use

Nineteenth Century

1749–1832	Johann Wolfgang Goethe, wrote *Faust, Part I* (1808), etc.
1761–1819	Kotzebue, German playwright, influenced rise of melodrama
1763–1826	Francois Joseph Talma, French actor
1766–1839	William Dunlap, wrote *History of the American Theatre* (1832)
1773–1844	Pixérécourt, French playwright, formalized melodrama
1784–1862	James Sheridan Knowles, wrote *Virginius*, etc.
1787–1833	Edmund Kean, English romantic actor
1800–1850	Romantic movement flourished
1802–1885	Victor Hugo set forth aims of French romanticism in *Preface to Cromwell* (1827); his *Hernani* (1830) was the height of romanticism
1803–1870	Alexandre Dumas *pere* wrote romantic plays, e.g., *Henry III and His Court*
1806–1872	Edwin Forrest, American actor
1809–1852	Nikolai Gogol, wrote *The Inspector General* (1836), etc.
1813–1863	Friedrich Hebbel, wrote *Maria Magdalena* (1844), etc.
1813–1883	Richard Wagner, sought fusion of all the arts
1820	Gas lighting was coming into use
1824–1895	Alexandre Dumas *fils* dramatized *Camille* (1852); wrote about social problems
1826–1914	Saxe-Meiningen, usually considered the first modern director
1828–1906	Henrik Ibsen, Norway's most important playwright; wrote in a variety of styles
1829–1916	Tommaso Salvini, Italian actor
1830–1904	Fanny Janauschek, Czech actress
1830	August Comte's (1798–1857) theory of positivism influenced move toward realism
1832	The box set was introduced into England by Madame Vestris and continued to gain in popularity.
1833–1893	Edwin Booth, American actor

Nineteenth Century *(continued)*

1838–1905	Sir Henry Irving, first English actor to be knighted; also a theatre manager who worked toward realism
1840–1902	Emile Zola advanced move to naturalism; wrote *Thérèse Raquin* (1873)
1844–1909	Helena Modjeska, Polish actress
1845–1923	Sarah Bernhardt, French actress
1836–1911	William S. Gilbert (1836–1911) and Arthur Sullivan (1842–1900), collaborated on operettas, e.g., *H.M.S. Pinafore* (1878), etc.
1849–1912	August Strindberg, wrote *The Father* (1887), etc.
1851–1929	Henry Arthur Jones, wrote *Michael and His Lost Angel* (1896), etc.
1852	George Aiken's dramatization of *Uncle Tom's Cabin* became the most successful melodrama of the century
1855–1934	Arthur Wing Pinero, wrote *The Second Mrs. Tanqueray* (1893), etc.
ca. 1855	Romanticism began to wane around mid-century, and was replaced by realism
1854–1900	Oscar Wilde, wrote *The Importance of Being Earnest* (1895), etc.
1858–1924	Eleonora Duse, Italian actress
1859	Darwin's *The Origin of Species* influenced the move toward realism
1860–1904	Anton Chekhov, wrote *The Sea Gull* (1896), etc.
1862–1946	Gerhardt Hauptmann, wrote *The Weavers* (1892), etc.
ca. 1875	Naturalism flourished during the last quarter of the century
ca. 1880	Symbolism developed
1887	Theatre Libre founded in Paris by André Antoine
1889	*Freie Bühne* founded in Germany by Otto Brahm
1898	Moscow Art Theatre founded by Stanislavsky and Nemirovich-Danchenko

Twentieth Century

1856–1950	George Bernard Shaw, wrote *Saint Joan* (1923), etc.
1862–1932	Adolphe Appia, scene designer and lighting theorist
1863–1938	Constantin Stanislavsky, developed "The System" of acting
1867–1933	John Galsworthy, wrote *The Silver Box* (1906), etc.
1867–1936	Luigi Pirandello, wrote *Six Characters in Search of an Author* (1921), etc.
1868–1936	Maxim Gorky, wrote *The Lower Depths* (1902), etc.
1871–1909	John Millington Synge, wrote *Riders to the Sea* (1904), etc.
1872–1966	Edward Gordon Craig, scene design theorist
1873–1943	Max Reinhardt, director of German theatre
1878–1945	Georg Kaiser, wrote *From Morn till Midnight* (1916), etc.

Twentieth Century *(continued)*

1879–1949	Jacques Copeau, French producer
1882–1944	Jean Giraudoux, wrote *Amphitryon 38* (1929), etc.
1883–1922	Yevgeny Vakhtanyov, Russian director
1884–1964	Sean O'Casey, wrote *Juno and the Paycock* (1924), etc.
1887–1954	Robert Edmund Jones, designer
1888–1967	Lee Simonson, designer
1888–1965	T. S. Eliot, wrote *Murder in the Cathedral* (1935), etc.
1888–1953	Eugene O'Neill, wrote in a variety of styles
1890–1938	Karel Čapek, Czech, wrote *R.U.R.* (1921), etc.
1893–1939	Ernest Toller, German, wrote *Man and the Masses* (1921), etc.
1896–1948	Antonin Artaud, theatre theorist
1895–1979	Oscar Hammerstein (1895–1960) and Richard Rogers (1902–1979), collaborated on *Oklahoma* (1943), etc.
1897–1975	Thornton Wilder, wrote *Our Town* (1938), etc.
1898–1956	Berthold Brecht, developed concept of Epic Theatre; wrote *Mother Courage* (1937), etc.
1900–	Frederick Lowe, collaborated with Alan Lerner (1918–) on *My Fair Lady* (1956), etc.
1900–1950	Realism was the foremost theatrical style
1900–1971	Tyrone Guthrie, English director
1901–1976	Jo Mielziner, designer
1904–	Sir John Gielgud, English actor
1905–1980	Jean-Paul Sartre, wrote *No Exit* (1944), etc.
1906–1963	Clifford Odets, wrote *Waiting for Lefty* (1935), etc.
1906–	Samuel Beckett, wrote *Waiting for Godot* (1953), etc.
1907–	Sir Lawrence Olivier, English actor
1910–	Jean-Louis Barrault, French actor-director
1910–	Jean Anouilh, wrote *The Lark* (1953), etc.
1910	Expressionism developed as a theatrical style
1910–	Jean Genet, wrote *The Blacks* (1959), etc.
1911–	Max Frisch, wrote *Biedermann and the Firebugs* (1958), etc.
1912–1971	Jean Vilar, French director
1912–	Eugène Ionesco, wrote *The Bald Soprano* (1949), etc.
1913–1973	William Inge, wrote *Picnic* (1953), etc.
1913–1960	Albert Camus, wrote *Caligula* (1945), etc.
1914–	Tennessee Williams, wrote *The Glass Menagerie* (1945), etc.
1915–	Arthur Miller, wrote *Death of a Salesman* (1949), etc.
1916–	Peter Weiss, wrote *Marat/Sade* (1964), etc.
1918–	Theatre Guild founded
1920–	Joseph Svoboda, Czech director
1921–	Friedrich Duerrenmatt, wrote *The Physicists* (1962), etc.
1921–	Joseph Papp, American producer and founder of the New York Shakespeare Festival
1924–	Marlon Brando, American actor

Twentieth Century *(continued)*

1925–	Peter Brook, English director
1927–	Neil Simon, wrote *California Suite* (1976), etc.
1928–	Edward Albee, wrote *Who's Afraid of Virginia Woolf?* (1962), etc.
1929–	John Osborne, wrote *Look Back in Anger* (1950), etc.
1930–	Harold Pinter, wrote *No Man's Land* (1975), etc.
1930–1965	Lorraine Hansberry, wrote *A Raisin in the Sun* (1959), etc.
1931–1941	The Group Theatre
1933–	David Storey, wrote *The Changing Room* (1971), etc.
1933–	Jerzy Grotowski, founded Polish Laboratory Theatre
1934–	LeRoi Jones, wrote *Slave Ship* (1967), etc.
1935–	Ed Bullins, wrote *The Taking of Miss Janie* (1975), etc.
1936–	Jean-Claude van Itallie, wrote *The Serpent: A Ceremony* (1969) etc.
1942–	Peter Handke, wrote *They Are Dying Out* (1974), etc.
1945	Theatre Workshop founded in England by Joan Littlewood
1947	Actors Studio founded by Robert Lewis, Elia Kazan, and Cheryl Crawford
1949–1963	The Living Theatre of Judith Malina and Julian Beck
ca. 1950	Trend toward off-off Broadway productions began
1951	Circle-in-the-Square founded
ca. 1950	Absurdism popular into the 1960s
ca. 1955	Trend toward Resident Theatres began
1961	Cafe La Mama founded by Ellen Stewart
1963	The National Theatre founded in England
1963	The Open Theatre founded by Joseph Chaikin and Peter Feldman
ca. 1965	Guerilla theatre active in the 1960s
ca. 1965	Happenings popular in the 1960s
1968	The Performance Group founded by Richard Schechner
ca. 1970	Trend toward visual imagery

Index

Page numbers in italic type indicate illustrations.